Soviet
Military
Policy

A HISTORICAL ANALYSIS

Raymond L. Garthoff

FREDERICK A. PRAEGER, *Publishers*
New York • Washington

Books That Matter

Published in the United States of America in 1966
by Frederick A. Praeger, Inc., Publishers
111 Fourth Avenue, New York, N.Y. 10003

This book is Number 170 in the series
Praeger Publications in Russian History and World Communism

Printed in the United States of America

To VERA

Preface

Communism has always been associated with the violence inherent in sociopolitical revolution. The establishment of Communist rule in Russia added the dimension of state relations to the "class conflict" and posed the question of war between states of the two clashing "systems."

A great deal has happened since the Bolshevik Revolution, and many elements in the situation have changed. The primary purpose of this study is to analyze the relationships of war, peace, and revolution in Soviet policy. In order to do this, it is necessary to consider continuities and discontinuities in Russian policy from the pre-Revolutionary period; changes in the role of Marxism-Leninism in operative Soviet foreign policy; changes in "world Communism"; and, most broadly, changes in the world. Thus, while the main focus of the book is on Soviet attitudes and actions, differing positions taken now by other Communist parties and states—especially Communist China —are also considered.

The term "military policy" extends the field of our concern well beyond use of arms in war. It is not my purpose to up-date and extend earlier analyses of Soviet military doctrine and Soviet strategy in the nuclear age. But in a broader frame of reference, military power enters into Soviet society, ideology, internal and foreign policy, and policy-making, in many ways. And these are all evolving aspects of Soviet Communism. This study examines various relevancies of military power to Communism in the past, present, and future.

Several chapters of this book have appeared earlier as articles or chapters* (though most of them were written with this ultimate

* The author wishes to thank the Yale University Press for permission to use Chapter 1, an earlier version of which appeared in *Russian Foreign Policy: Essays in Historical Perspective* (1962); Harvard University Press for Chapter 2, an earlier version of which appeared in *The Transformation of Russian Society Since 1861* (1961); Ohio State University Press for Chapter 3, part of which earlier appeared in *Total War and Cold War* (1962); Princeton University Press for Chapter 12, an earlier version of which appeared in *Communism and Revolution* (1964). Chapter 4 draws on two articles that appeared in *World Politics* (1951) and *Problems of Communism* (1953); Chapter 7 appeared earlier in *East Europe* (1965); the second part of Chapter 8 in *Problems of Communism* (1957); an earlier version of Chapter 9 in the *Annals of the American Academy for Political and Social Science* (1963); and part of Chapter 11 in *Foreign Affairs* (1962).

study in mind), but all have been either revised or freshly written especially to make this volume complete and up to date, in response to the need for a comprehensive interpretation of the role of military power in Soviet internal and foreign policy.

I have personally found it rewarding to coordinate historical, political, sociological, strategic, and "Kremlinological" approaches. Consequently, this study draws upon all in examining both Soviet and world Communist theory and practice on questions involving the roles of military power.

I want to thank all who have indirectly helped to inspire this work. I also wish to express my deep thanks to Phyllis Pesce for her able and patient typing of the manuscript.

RAYMOND L. GARTHOFF

Washington, D.C.
November 1, 1965

Contents

I

The Military in Modern Russia

1. Military Influences and Instruments in Russian Policy, 1860–1965

Among the factors affecting the uses of military power in foreign policy, three are fundamental: (1) the basic international aims and world view of the national leaders, (2) the prevailing political, military, and geostrategic environment of the world at large and of any state in particular, and (3) the conceptions of the role of military interests in national policy-making and of military means and measures in national policy. Of these three factors, the first is perhaps the most significant and also the most amenable to wide variance with broad political changes. The environmental factors are subject to important changes as the distribution of power shifts in the world, and as technology alters the form, scale, and even the meaning of war. The more specific questions of military considerations and instrumentalities are least likely to change drastically. Following an analysis of the historical development of military considerations in Russian foreign policies over the past century, the elements of continuity and change will be summed up in terms of these three basic aspects.

In the nineteenth and early twentieth centuries, Russia fully accepted the contemporary European-centered national-state system based on a balance of power as the fulcrum of international politics. In no essential respect was Czarist foreign policy distinguished from the policies of the other powers. Russia sought to increase its voice in the system, to play the game of alliances to advance its aims while preserving mutual deterrence from general war, to industrialize and modernize the homeland, improving its strength. It joined the colonial race, but in the American or Continental pattern of expanding into unclaimed or nominally held adjoining regions rather than by reaching far abroad. Finally, it sought to extend its political influence among the weaker states of the Balkans, Middle East, and Far East.

Russia recognized its strengths and weaknesses in the general world balance of power (in contrast to its failure in evaluating basic internal

3

weaknesses), though it did not always assess specific relationships correctly. Despite serious logistical shortcomings that showed up in all the major wars in which it engaged during the period, Russia did not have any critical military inferiority—or superiority. National policy reflected a continuing concern over naval and maritime limitations, which proved acute both in the Crimean and Russo-Japanese wars, but such strategic considerations cannot be said to have dominated foreign policy.

War was seen, as it was elsewhere, as a normal diplomatic recourse; it was a background consideration weighting all diplomatic dealings. The two occasions of war against a major power in the last half century of Imperial Russia (Japan in 1904 and Germany in 1914) represented respectively the prelude and the finale to absolute catastrophe. But these and the more successful Turkish and Balkan wars were part of the game of politics. And, until the grand exception of 1914, a full century of post-Napoleonic wars were all "limited wars."

The consideration given to military factors and the participation of military leaders in policy-making were roughly comparable to those in other states; variations reflected primarily differing circumstances and the personalities involved. Although lacking a strongly developed and consistent attitude toward preventive war—such as evolved in Imperial Germany during this period—Russian military leaders often stressed "military necessity" and favored military solutions when more important political considerations outweighed, or should have outweighed, them. The cardinal example, of course, was the insistence of General Sukhomlinov (Minister of War) and General Yanushkevich (Chief of the General Staff) on the military necessity of general mobilization in late July, 1914—even at the cost of precipitating war.[1] No matter that Sazonov, Izvolsky, and Grand Duke Nikolai Nikolayevich favored war; it was the argument of military necessity that persuaded Czar Nicholas. Though no other case can match this one in its historical consequences, other examples abound. For instance, General Yanushkevich argued convincingly that Romania's entry into the war was so important a military advantage that political concessions should be made to secure it; actually, the diplomatic move was successful but the promised military gain was rapidly converted into a burdensome military liability, lengthening the front and tying down large numbers of Russian troops.[2]

Perhaps the stress on military alliances was due as much to political sponsorship as to the influence of military leaders. But there is no denying the importance of military factors in the whole nineteenth-century balance-of-power alliance system and the Russian belief that following the weakening of the Russian alliance with Germany as Austro-German ties grew, it was necessary to turn to an alliance with France and later with England. It may be useful to recall that the strengthening of the political bond with France in the 1890's and 1900's was largely due to the growth in technical military ties, for military men in both countries apparently wanted, above all, a stable and rational basis for military planning. And when the "logical" time came, this bond may have influenced all sides in the decisions leading to war; certainly it served to ignite the chain reaction that exploded into World War I.

A rather different case exemplified the internal political impact of domestic measures undertaken for military ends. In 1916, Nicholas was led to decree an unprecedented conscription of the Central Asian peoples for service behind the battle lines. The result was a costly half-year military effort to subdue rebellion caused by strong opposition to the decree and, moreover, a final gain of only half of the quarter million conscripts originally expected.[3]

Military representations did not, of course, always lead to error—or to war. At the time of the Balkan crisis of 1909, Russian military weakness, attested to by military leaders, was instrumental in leading to Russian diplomatic capitulation to Austria.[4] But more often, the military leaders were either bellicose (as in the Balkans in 1912–13, when Kokovtsov had to curb General Sukhomlinov's desire to intervene),[5] or myopic in seeking apparent military advantages, when pursuing them incurred greater political, and even military, disadvantages (as in urging Romania's entry into World War I or in pressing the policy of expansion in southern Manchuria and Korea which led to the Russo-Japanese War). Finally, as we shall see, local military commanders often pursued their own policies to the detriment of Russian diplomatic aims.

Military weaknesses did contribute to two dramatic political initiatives. One was the sale of Alaska and the Aleutians to the United States in 1867, a decision reached as a direct result of Russian weakness vis-à-vis England. The initial proposals were made soon after the Crimean War, and in 1860, Rear Admiral Popov wrote a memorandum stating that the Navy had no objection to the proposed sale.[6] Thus, rather than risk English (or American) seizure of Alaska in the course of renewed conflict, the Russians preferred to strengthen the multilateral balance of power in the North Pacific by increasing the stake of the United States in the region.

The other remarkable innovation was the Czar's appeal to the powers in 1898 for an international conference on disarmament, on grounds of both moral principles and the financial and economic burdens of the arms race. Neither the first Hague Conference in 1899, attended by twenty-six states, nor its successor in 1907 accomplished much beyond agreement on some rules of warfare. Nonetheless, the Hague conferences were the first in what has since become a major series of illustrious if generally ineffective negotiations. The motives behind the initial Russian proposal are still somewhat obscure, but the idea probably originated with Witte, after Foreign Minister Muravyev had raised the problem of the great cost of meeting an Austrian artillery build-up while Russia was already engaged in a major infantry modernization program.[7] General Kuropatkin, Minister of War, strongly objected. But Czar Nicholas favored the idea, especially its high moral ideals. Incidentally, the alignment of views in the Russian Government in 1898 foreshadowed clearly the usual if not invariable pattern of later decades: the budgetary authority proposed arms cuts, the foreign office agreed and made the plan, the head of state warmly approved, and the military leaders strongly opposed.

The last half century of Imperial Russian rule saw military instrumentalities used in a variety of ways to extend or support the boundaries of the state. The most notable and direct use was in the waging of wars of colonial conquest in Central Asia in the 1860's and 1880's. By 1860, the uncivilized and underpopulated nomadic steppes of Kazakhstan had been pacified and were being colonized, but pressure on the khanates of Khiva, Kokand, and Bukhara soon led to open warfare. In 1864, the Russians launched a successful campaign against Kokand, and Gorchakov dispatched a note to the powers, justifying Russian expansion into the area to ensure the security of the borders and to extend civilization. This was accepted. Gorchakov also assured them that the Russian objective had been reached at Chimkent. However, unknown to St. Petersburg and without authorization, General Cherniayev had at that time already attacked Tashkent (unsuccessfully), which, in turn, led the British to suspect these assurances.[8] In 1865, Tashkent fell, and in 1868, Bukhara. In 1871, Captain (later the famous general) Skobelev, reportedly used the occasion of a courier visit to Krasnovodsk to make up an alleged order to attack Khiva, which was discovered to be his fabrication only after considerable preparations had actually been made and shortly before the campaign was to be launched.[9] Finally, and most seriously, in 1885, Russian troops decisively defeated the Afghan Army at the border—in violation of orders from St. Petersburg.[10]

In all these cases the British saw Russian deceit, where in fact there was simply lack of control from St. Petersburg. After the resolution of the last Anglo-Russian crisis in 1885, the tension subsided; by 1890, the Russians had filled the "vacuum" areas of Central Asia, and turned their attention elsewhere. The whole period saw a national policy of expansion in the area, but the local commanders often caused political tensions by their overeager and sometimes insubordinate aggressiveness. Although the Czar and Government usually accepted the fruits of conquest, their approval for advancing was given only by small steps, as each new border required further measures to ensure its tranquillity.

The year 1860 marked the end of the march of the Russian flag across Siberia, with the Treaty of Peking establishing the borders of Russia and China in the Far East, along the Amur and Ussuri rivers. It did not, however, mark the end of Russian interest in expansion, or even in the use of military means, in the still vaguely controlled Chinese borderlands of Manchuria, Korea, Mongolia, Tuva, and Sinkiang.

In the year the first assault was made on Tashkent (1864), a native uprising in the Chinese province of Sinkiang expelled the Chinese authorities and left a troubled situation. The Russians, who had earlier reached agreements with the Chinese on the frontiers in this area as well as in the Far East, occupied the Ili Valley and Kuldzha in 1871 with a force that eventually numbered nearly 100,000 men. At first, China refused to cede a large area to Russia, but in 1881 signed a treaty ceding a portion of it. The Russians then withdrew their troops. Later, during "maneuvers" in 1911, Russian troops again crossed into Sinkiang in the Altai Mountains of the north (Dzhungaria), and in 1912 moved again into the Kuldzha area, although Sazonov overruled proposals for a reoccupation of the whole Ili district.[11]

With the Chinese revolution against the Manchu Dynasty in 1911, the Mongols of Outer Mongolia broke away from Chinese rule. Russian arms and troops were, with prompting, requested and forthwith sent, and within a year a virtual Russian protectorate had been established over the new "independent" Mongolia. Russian influence was considerable in neighboring Tuva (Uriankhai) to the northwest of Mongolia, but despite the urgings of military and mercantile interests, the Council of Ministers decided in 1911 not to annex Tuva. However, in 1914, Russia did establish a protectorate, and in 1916, troops were brought in. On the eastern side of Mongolia, the Russians were interested in annexing the Barga area of northern Manchuria, and secretly gave military assistance to rebels there.[12]

The relative importance of these areas to the Russians on the eve of World War I was evident in a February, 1914, memorandum of Durnovo, former Minister of the Interior, urging a reorientation toward Germany on the ground that Russia's territorial objectives were in areas of friction not with Germany but with England. His list of Russian objectives was: Persia, the Pamirs, Kuldzha, Kashgaria, Dzhungaria, Mongolia, and Uriankhai—all but Persia in the Sino-Russian borderlands. The means of expansion were largely military and economic; a constant restraining influence, however, was consideration of diplomatic repercussions.[13]

The chief, or at least the most fateful, area of expanding Russian interests was in Manchuria. Here Russia was faced not only with a weak China but also with Japan, and in the decade after 1895 the conflict between them deepened. On the Russian side, three lines of policy contended: the path of economic expansion, the road of general expansion by any means, and military consolidation. The first was championed by Witte, who sought to avoid such complicating measures as the acquisition of Port Arthur in 1898. The second was the policy of an imperialistic group led by Privy Councillor Bezobrazov, Admirals Abaza and Alekseyev, and others. Plehve, Minister of the Interior, also favored this approach, but for other reasons. It was this group's influence on Russian policy from 1900 to 1904, more than anything else, that led to the disastrous war with Japan. Finally, the third policy was that favored by the military leadership in St. Petersburg; it was based on the simple theory that if the frontier could be straightened out and reduced in length by the permanent occupation of northern Manchuria, the garrisons along the border could be reduced and the rail lines to the Far East efficiently laid and placed under full Russian control. This objective, even though strategically "defensive," could not be achieved by peaceful economic penetration, so the strength of these military considerations was thrown behind the line of direct expansion.[14]

Military means were not the primary ones even for the expansionist group, although a few may have desired war. (Plehve, for instance, is reported by Witte to have said to War Minister Kuropatkin: "We need a small victorious war to stem the tide of revolution.")[15] Russian officers were sent to Korea to train the Korean Army in 1897, but under a Russo-Japanese agreement were withdrawn the following year. Port Arthur was built up as a strong naval base. In 1900, the Russians had used the occasion of the Boxer Rebellion to occupy all the main centers of Manchuria with some 50,000 troops; although these troops were to have been withdrawn by 1903, they were not.[16]

When the Japanese sounded the Russians out for a compromise of interests in 1901, Russian military and naval influences worked against any concessions in Korea. The Japanese, bolstered by an alliance with Great Britain, felt able to resort to war a few years later when renewed friction erupted on the Russo-Korean border.[17]

The Russo-Japanese War finally came, bringing defeat, and the Russians were compelled to settle for a restriction of their influence to only the northern part of Manchuria. Only once again, in 1911, did the question of possible Russian military expansion into China proper and Manchuria arise; Sazonov and Kokovtsov successfully defeated this idea, even though a Russian ultimatum was ignored by the Chinese and an opportunity for intervention was at hand.[18]

In the Middle East, taking advantage of the 1907 agreement with Great Britain on spheres of influence in Persia, the Russians sent troops into the country in 1911, during a diplomatic dispute with Tehran.[19] Russia also gained influence there by providing commissioned and noncommissioned officers for the Persian Army (the "Persian Cossack Brigade") in the late nineteenth and early twentieth centuries.

Turkey and the Balkans were the other major theaters of Russian diplomatic and military interest. Resorting to war in 1877 led to a successful campaign against Turkey, though its benefits were limited by the other powers. In the ensuing political intrigues and local wars in the Balkans, the Russians did not themselves engage in military action. Efforts to infiltrate by providing military advisers (to Serbia in 1876, and to Bulgaria from 1881 to 1885) ended unsuccessfully, owing in part to thoroughly inadequate control over the advisers.[20]

This recapitulation of the use of military means to expand influence or control reflects the generally reluctant attitude of St. Petersburg, balanced by occasional pro-war sentiment of local officials, particularly military (in the Balkans, 1876–77, in Central Asia in the 1860's and 1880's, and in the Far East from 1900 to 1905 and again in 1911–12). Military force was also used to suppress the Polish rebellion in 1863 and the disturbances in Central Asia in 1916. But, in general, military power was the instrument of choice only in the colonial conquest of the backward areas of Central Asia.

Although the Great War in 1914 was engendered by the alliance system, once begun, it was regarded by the Russians (as well as by the other powers) as a means of gaining certain limited expansionist objectives: in the case of Russia, the Straits and Constantinople (promised by the Allies in a secret treaty in 1915), Tuva and northwestern Sinkiang, and perhaps northern Iran. But such was not to be, and instead the war marked the end of the Russian, as well as the German, Austrian, and Turkish empires, and the end of an era.

Bolshevism was as revolutionary in international as in internal politics. Indeed, the Bolshevik leaders refused for some time to distinguish between the two. Their outlook excluded acceptance of the state system and the international balance of power, and they regarded themselves as the vanguard of a world-wide movement historically destined to sweep away the whole existing system. War was a phenomenon bred by the old capitalist state system. Revolution was the means for overthrowing the old order. The Bolsheviks were dedicated in their belief in a particular pattern of history.

Although their objectives were universal, the new leaders soon found themselves forced to operate in terms of the constraints of a national framework. The chief immediate aim was survival of the revolutionary base in Russia, requiring virtually all energies to be concentrated for the first few years on winning the civil war and repelling foreign intervention. The first major foreign political act of the new order, the peace talks at Brest-Litovsk in early 1918, reflected uncertainty in dealing with the unanticipated situation of international relations of Communists with capitalists. "No war, no peace" was, if eloquent, also preposterous; and very soon the leaders came to recognize the need for temporizing, for a compromise during a short time before the revolution swept Europe.

The Bolsheviks had always equated principles of conduct with expediency in a given "relation of forces," and at the time of Brest-Litovsk they had thus debated—and discarded as inexpedient—the alternative of "revolutionary war," the first of a series of reformulations of the relationship between "war" and the advance of Communism.[21] Force was one of the weapons of the class struggle, but internal revolution was preferred to external liberation. And revolution was expected imminently in a number of countries.

As the new regime in Russia, the Bolsheviks renounced all of Imperial Russia's economic, political, and military rights (and obligations) abroad—in Turkey, Persia, Afghanistan, Sinkiang, Tuva, Manchuria, and China. Moreover, Poland, Finland, Estonia, Latvia, Lithuania, the Ukraine, Georgia, Armenia, and Azerbaidzhan were all "permitted" to opt for independence. This was a shrewd propaganda move, in recognition of the practical impossibility of extending Bolshevik control further at that time; it was also a reflection of the fact that "national" independence was viewed as largely irrelevant since the revolution would sweep aside all such artificial trappings of the old order.

Russia had nonetheless become the "base" of the revolution, and although it was the international working-class movement in the various countries that was regarded as the main force for change, the Bolshevik leaders wanted to provide such military aid as was possible to this end. In Finland, Latvia, Estonia, the Ukraine, and the Trans-caucasus, this effort in 1918 and 1919 was scarcely distinguishable from the Civil War. The year 1919 marked a turning point, from near-defeat to near-victory for the Reds in Russia, and from near-victory to defeat for the Reds in Europe. The Spartacist revolt in northern Germany, the erstwhile successful establishment of a Soviet republic in Bavaria, the temporary rise of a Bolshevik Hungary, and sympathy strikes in France and England showed widespread, if in-sufficient, revolutionary force. Aid to the Spartacists was simply im-possible. However, at least in the case of the revolution in Hungary, we know that the Commander in Chief of the Red Army in Moscow ordered the appropriate field command to curtail other operations and move toward Hungary in order to establish "direct, intimate contact with the Soviet armies of Hungary."[22] A serious adverse turn in the events of the civil war at home forced this move to be canceled, and by the time intervention would have been possible, the Red rule in Hungary had been decisively defeated.

Gradually, the Bolshevik leaders came to understand that the world revolution was not going to come so soon as they had believed and that they needed peace to consolidate their control and build strength in Russia. As early as October, 1919, when the White Army in the Baltic was finally defeated and forced from Russia, it was de-cided (at Lenin's insistence, over Trotsky's protests) not to advance in pursuit into Estonia.[23] The watershed of decision, however, was the failure of the invasion of Poland in 1920. Again, following the defeat of the Poles in the Ukraine, a split decision was made, this time to advance into Poland. In this instance, even Trotsky opposed the ad-vance. Lenin later admitted the error of this move, for the Polish people were "not ready" and revolution could not be exported; after-ward, he told Trotsky that Soviet troops should never again be used directly to aid a revolution abroad.[24]

Military force was used in 1921 to establish Communist rule in Georgia (which, unlike Armenia and Azerbaidzhan, had not fallen to internal Bolshevik revolutionaries). Even there, Georgian Reds were used in the initial operations.[25] Also in 1921, the Red Army set up in Outer Mongolia the first satellite Communist regime. Though the occasion was provided by pursuit of the remnants of anti-Bolshevik Russian forces, the "Mongolian People's Government" was first established (on Russian soil) and requested Soviet military assistance.[26] Probably under a similar arrangement, Soviet troops also occupied what became the "People's Republic of Tannu Tuva" that same year. Military advisers and arms were provided to establish local armies. In both cases, the Russian protectorate of 1912–17 was thus reestablished by military occupation under Red auspices only a few years later. Similarly, in Persia, only two years after the magnanimous relinquishment of Imperial Russian rights, the Red Army occupied Enzeli and Astara and aided a local rebellion in 1920 to establish the "Soviet Republic of Gilan." This "republic" was provided with arms, military advisers, and even Red Army insignia. However, dissension within the Gilan government between the Communists and their fellow-travelers prevented an advance on Tehran and induced Moscow to agree in 1921 to a treaty with Iran under which the Red Army withdrew. The "republic" was thereupon quickly suppressed by the Iranian Army.[27]

Having consolidated rule in the Caucasus and having withdrawn from Iran, in 1921 the Bolshevik leaders acceded to the requests of the Turkish rebels under Kemal for military aid. Arms, money, and military advisers were sent. Trotsky had favored more direct military assistance, and Stalin was among those who opposed it.[28] No attempt was made to subvert the new Turkish movement, which soon established its rule. These were new tactics more effective than rash revolutionary enthusiasm.

The Soviet need for a longer breathing spell became more and more evident, and in 1921, the necessity of using military force to suppress the major mutiny at Kronstadt and the rebellion in Tambov Province underlined the urgency and depth of this problem. But in addition to the domestic considerations that led to the New Economic Policy, a revised view of the world also caused the Bolsheviks by 1922–23 to settle down to a period of "temporary coexistence" with the capitalist states and with the world nation-state system. Internally, this was accompanied by the establishment of the multinational Union of Soviet Socialist Republics. Externally, the U.S.S.R. sought diplomatic recognition and began to conduct conventional diplomatic activities. The Soviet leaders aimed particularly at playing upon "contradictions" among the capitalist states, simultaneously using the subversive instrument of the Comintern. The Russians recognized the border states, and sought international recognition for the U.S.S.R. The Treaty of Rapallo with Germany in 1922 marked a breakthrough from diplomatic isolation.

The new situation called for the U.S.S.R. to avoid war while consolidating its internal power and building up its strength. The geostrategic relation of forces compelled a defensive military orientation; the Red Army was reduced from over five million to about half a million men and was organized on a peacetime basis as a regular national army. Gone were the "international detachments" formed at the time of the first regiments of the Red Army.[29] Ended were the proposals, like that of Tukhachevsky, for a "General Staff" and troops for the Comintern.[30] In 1922, Moscow was host to a disarmament conference of the East European countries, precursor to later, much more grandiose Soviet efforts in that field.

The most significant military development related to Soviet foreign policy in the post-civil-war years was the remarkable mutual assistance in military preparation which developed with Germany as early as 1919. By 1922, a series of concrete joint military activities had clandestinely got under way. The association was based on post-Versailles Germany's desire for secret miiltary training away from the surveillance of the victorious Allies, and on the weakness of Russian military technology. With German assistance, production of tanks, aircraft, and munitions (and attempts to produce poison gas) was organized in Russia for the benefit of both armies, and a number of German military training establishments were created in Russia, while some Russian officers studied in Berlin.[31]

Meanwhile, Soviet leaders (through the Comintern) had been making subversive preparations in Germany, including the clandestine dispatch of several hundred Red Army officers as advisers to the German Communists. By 1923, there was an ill-coordinated Communist uprising which was speedily suppressed by the Reichswehr—then receiving artillery munitions from Russia under the secret military aid agreements.[32] This dramatized a glaring contradiction in Soviet policy, and the utter failure of this, the third Communist revolt in Germany, marked the last Soviet attempt to stir up a revolution in the West. World revolution was still a dream; the U.S.S.R. was a fact.

As the years went on, Soviet leaders increasingly directed their energies to internal matters. The struggle for the successor to Lenin, and Stalin's later efforts not merely to dispose of rivals but also to subdue the Party to his autocratic rule, made its imprint on foreign policy. Moreover, the building of "socialism in one country" marked an indefinite extension of the original compromise with the outside world and reflected primary interest in the Soviet state. The avowed aims of the original revolutionary leaders continued despite the liquidation of the men themselves, and this ideological factor remained paramount so far as the international outlook of the Soviet state was concerned. The aims were unchanged, but the means became increasingly important. And as occasions arose calling for sacrifice either by the Soviet state or by the forces of the revolution abroad, Moscow's decision invariably—and as time went on, even automatically—favored the Soviet state.

It became an axiom of Soviet policy that war should be avoided as long as possible. The existence of the single socialist state in a "capitalist encirclement" was considered precarious. Survival as well as advance required diplomatic efforts to exploit divisions in the hostile capitalist world. Soviet policy was therefore basically defensive, as any provocative move in the prevailing relation of forces of the 1920's and 1930's would be "adventuristic." In this context, disarmament propaganda was begun as early as the Moscow conference of East European states in 1922, and by 1928 the Soviet Union championed complete disarmament in the League of Nations. The Soviet interest in disarmament was purely tactical, but it was serious. Military force was not overtly used from 1921 until a sharp alteration of the political scene had by 1939 made more aggressive military action on the western periphery both feasible and seemingly necessary to improve the Soviet posture for defense.

Stalin outlined Soviet foreign policy in a speech to the Central Committee of the Communist Party in 1925 (not made public until 1947). In that speech, he noted that it was the Soviet aim to avoid war, and—if war should come—"to enter last. And we must enter in order to throw the decisive weight onto the scales, the weight which can tip the scales."[33] This policy eventually led to the diplomatic juggling in 1939, ending with the alliance with Nazi Germany. Until June 22, 1941, this tactic seems to have paid off. Meanwhile, the Russians found their only opportunity in almost two decades for direct territorial advance by tightening up their strategic defenses in the western borderlands in the face of German expansion. Of Finland, the Baltic states, Byelorussia (Poland), and Bessarabia and Bukovina, overt war was waged only in Finland, where a political miscalculation precipitated a war the Soviets had not desired. However, military power was indirectly employed in all these cases: as a weapon of diplomatic pressure and then as an instrument of infiltration in the agreements for stationing troops in the Baltic states; for successful, direct diplomatic blackmail on Romania; and for occupation of eastern Poland after its defeat by the Germans.

For almost two decades, military instruments had occupied a very subordinate place in Soviet foreign policy, and military force was not overtly employed. However, its indirect use had been significant in several areas. One was the eastern borderlands. Mongolia and Tannu Tuva were, of course, protectorates remaining from the revolutionary (with interruption, from the prerevolutionary) period. China itself, again Sinkiang, and Afghanistan all became objects of attempted military infiltration. During its civil war of the late 1930's, Spain became another area. And on the Manchurian borders, Russia twice in the late 1930's resorted to arms in local clashes with the Japanese.

China was the most important case. Soviet leaders were quite successful in establishing an intimate relationship with the revolutionary Kuomintang in China in the early 1920's. Sun Yat-sen sent his chief of staff, General Chiang Kai-shek, to Moscow in 1923 to arrange for military assistance. The Russians agreed, but their chief aid—other than financial—was a bevy of military advisers under Borodin and General Galen (later better known as Marshal of the Soviet Union Blücher). Russian military and other advisers played a considerable role; for example, in the key 1926 Northern Campaign a senior Russian military adviser accompanied each of the ten corps, and assisted in the headquarters planning. The advisers were influential in creating a system of political officers and political indoctrination, and in establishing the Whampoa Military Academy, although Sun reportedly did bar them from the General Staff itself. By 1926 and 1927, due partly to the activities of the Russian advisers in supporting Communists in the Kuomintang and partly to the ambitions of the Nationalists, Chiang conducted two successive *coups d'état* against the leftists. Defeated, the Soviets withdrew their advisers.[34]

Parallel but separate Soviet military aid was given, with large-scale dispatching of Russian military advisers, to two Chinese war lords in the north, Generals Feng Yu-hsiang and Kuo Sun-lin. This venture also ended in failure for the Soviets. The only known case of a Chinese request for Soviet troops was made through Karakhan by General Kuo in 1925, but Moscow decided against this course as too risky. In 1929, in connection with General Feng's attack on the Chinese Nationalists in Manchuria, Soviet Russian and Mongolian troops did actually enter China to secure the Chinese Eastern Railway, but they were soon withdrawn.[35]

The use of Soviet military advisers to press a policy of subversion of the Nationalist Kuomintang, rather than to build a separate Chinese Communist movement, was the subject of deep division within the Soviet leadership. Stalin was responsible for the course actually followed, but Trotsky and the others who opposed it were unable to use its failure against Stalin effectively. Nonetheless, Stalin later took the lesson into account in his general policy, as did the Chinese Communists themselves in their struggle. Later, from 1937 to 1941, the Russians again gave military aid to the Chinese Nationalists to prevent Japanese domination of China.

A new opportunity to use military assistance and influence, without attempting to subvert the associate, arose meanwhile in Sinkiang in the 1930's. In 1931, the Russians signed a secret agreement with the virtually independent provincial governor, Chin Shu-jen, which included a secret provision for military assistance. The same arrangement was reaffirmed with his successor, General Sheng Shih-ts'ai, who ruled Sinkiang from 1933 to 1943. The Russians were first asked for direct military assistance against other Chinese war lords in 1934, and they forthwith provided two brigades of NKVD troops and combat air support to General Sheng. Again, in 1937, Sheng turned to the Russians for aid, and again troops and air cover were sent. One Soviet regiment remained at Hami in eastern Sinkiang, in Chinese uniforms, for six years. During this period, arms and uniforms were also provided for a Sinkiang army of 10,000 men, a Soviet military aircraft assembly factory was built at Urumchi (as an "agricultural implements manufacturing plant"), and several hundred Soviet fliers were secretly trained at an aviation training school at Kuldzha in 1938–39. Many of the 885 aircraft supplied to the Chinese Nationalists in the 1937–41 period were, in fact, assembled at the Urumchi plant, and many of the 200 Russian volunteer airmen who briefly served in China at that time had trained at Kuldzha. During this period, the Russians also gained considerably from economic exploitation of the area.

By 1942, General Sheng anticipated defeat for the Russians, so he made a sudden shift of allegiance to his nominal government at Chungking. He demanded withdrawal of all Soviet troops and advisers and, by 1943, after hard negotiation, a purge, and a local show of force, the Russians complied. Another page in the history of Russian infiltration of Sinkiang was turned.[36] However, as soon as they could again direct their attention to Sinkiang, the Russians moved to restore their position. In late 1943 and early 1944, local Kazakhs, and later other people of eastern Sinkiang, rose in revolt. Soviet and Mongolian support was extended, including direct military assistance, and by late 1944 the rebels established an "East Turkestan Republic" in the Ili-Kuldzha-Altai regions. The Russians did not interfere in rebel actions against Chinese Communist forces or Chinese Nationalists. An uneasy truce was finally made in 1945, arranged through the "mediation" of the Soviet consul general in Urumchi.[37] The outcome remained in doubt.

About the time the Russians first used troops in Sinkiang, in 1934, an internal reverse suffered by the pro-Soviet Emir Amanullah of Afghanistan caused the Soviet regime to decide to dispatch two divisions to his aid. However, Amanullah was defeated before the Soviet troops reached Afghanistan, and Moscow swiftly counter-manded the orders, so that no overt Soviet military intervention actually occurred.[38] Both the initial decision and the decision to reverse it illustrate the importance Soviet leaders assigned to an advantageous political situation as a necessary precondition to direct intervention.

The Spanish Civil War of 1936–39 was especially complicated by the intervention of Germany and Italy on the side of the rebels. The Russians used this intervention to facilitate their decision to aid the left-wing Spanish Government. Aside from economic and finan-cial aid, the Russians clandestinely supported the International Bri-gade, which they contrived to control so as to use it to gain control of the whole Loyalist side, as well as to mobilize "anti-Fascists" every-where. No Russians were permitted to enter the Brigade—only West-ern Communists. However, the Russians did send the Loyalists about 2,000 Red Army advisers and specialists, who tested new weapons and tactics, advised, and observed. (They were for a time under General Berzin, for many years head of Military Intelligence.)[39] The Russians succeeded in their infiltration, subversion, and propaganda—but the Loyalists lost the war.

A different circumstance surrounded the border battles of the Rus-sians with the Japanese on the Manchurian frontiers. Following uneasiness over border incidents in 1935 and 1937, two local wars flared up in 1938 and 1939, as the Japanese tested Soviet reactions. In the first, the battle of Lake Khasan (Changkufeng) on the Soviet-Korean border in July-August, 1938, two Soviet divisions were com-mitted to hold two hills in disputed territory. The second campaign was more extensive. In the region of Khalkin-gol (Nomonhan), fight-ing on a large scale began over Japanese-Manchukuoan incursions into Outer Mongolia, where Soviet troops were then stationed. From May to September, a series of clashes grew until more than 50,000 men were engaged, and several hundred aircraft on both sides were destroyed. Again, the *status quo ante* was re-established.[40] While offensive uses of military power were cautious, defensive use was less restrained.

The Red Army used its two-decade respite to modernize and to grow. From 1923 until 1937, it remained at a nearly constant personnel strength, rising from about 560,000 to about 590,000 (plus a territorial national guard force of about 250,000). Only then did the Russians begin to build the size of their standing forces, to about 4,200,000 by June, 1941.[41] Throughout this period, however, armored, airborne, and air forces were developed, and from 1938 to 1941 a major naval building program was begun. The development of the Red Army was assisted by the extensive military cooperation with Germany. This mutual aid continued from the early 1920's until 1933 and, on a smaller scale, even into the early years of the Nazi regime, until Hitler finally severed the connection in 1934–35.[42] Later, under the Soviet- German Pact of August, 1939, limited military cooperation was resumed until 1941—particularly in the sphere of naval affairs.[43] When war came, the Soviet armed forces were at peak strength, though not really prepared. Paradoxically, one reason was that the Red Army was too heavily concentrated in the forward areas occupied in 1939, and had not yet effected a proper shift from its old abandoned frontier defense line to the new borders.[44]

Military leaders played little part in Soviet policy-making during this period. Any potential increase in their role was thwarted by the Great Purge, which struck the military heavily, in 1937–38. During the war itself, while the officer corps was permitted to assume unprecedented authority in purely military matters, any tendency to extend this authority to over-all matters of national strategy was suppressed.

The war that began in 1941 was the long-expected trial by fire. Later, the defeat of the enemy was seen as due to the strength of the Soviet system, the prewar concentration on power-building economic policies, the defensive foreign policy of coexistence, and skillful exploitation of contradictions in the divided capitalist world. The first three and a half years of the "Great Fatherland War of the Soviet Union" were required to check the invader's advance and expel him from the U.S.S.R. By and large, the conduct of the war during this period did not offer opportunities for additional foreign political uses. The new alliance with the Western Allies did, however, raise the possibility of gains apart from the immediate mutual benefits of the struggle with the common foe, and Stalin never lost sight of them.

The later stages of the war opened a new era of expansion in the wake of the successful Soviet counteroffensive against Germany. For example, the Russians created Polish and Czech liberation armies, over which they had much influence, to accompany the Red Army into those countries. This helped pave the way for later Communist seizure of power. In the case of Poland, they even created a puppet "government" in Lublin while the war was still in progress in that country. A particularly brutal illustration of the Soviet-calculated political use of their wartime military advance was the intentional inactivity of General Chuikov's army just across the river while the beleaguered Polish Home Army was being slaughtered in Warsaw by the Germans. This conveniently erased the most vigorous part of the non-Communist underground in Poland. The Soviet leaders also subordinated purely military considerations, such as calculation of casualties, to the political objectives of liberating Berlin, Vienna, and Prague before the Western Allies—less aware of the great political significance this would have in the world—did. Thus, by the end of the war in Europe, the Russians had completed their great defensive effort with a counteroffensive of sufficient strength to carry them into Central Europe, opening up new potentialities for expansion.

For the Russians, the final curtain call was their last-minute entry into the war against Japan. Having been promised most of their objectives by the Western Allies at Yalta as reward for assistance against the Japanese, the Russians denounced their nonaggression treaty and then, while it was still in effect, attacked in August, 1945. They would in any case have stepped in to share in the fruits of victory, but Stalin was able to minimize the blame for his violation of the nonaggression treaty by requesting, and getting, a letter from President Truman asking the U.S.S.R. to enter the war.[45] The Russians were, of course, aware of the imminence of Japanese defeat, since the unwary Japanese had turned to the U.S.S.R. as intermediary for peace feelers to the United States. Soviet propaganda and historiography since the war have claimed that the main role in the defeat of Japan was played by the brief Soviet campaign against the Kwantung Army in Manchuria and Northern Korea.

With the end of World War II, a new era opened.

The Soviet Union emerged from the war temporarily weakened, but with two great assets. Its defensive position was much strengthened by the total defeat of the two great powers on the east and on the west, which gave the Soviet Union opportunities to determine the destiny of a series of neighboring states. But because of its relative weakness in 1945, the U.S.S.R. could exploit these opportunities only just short of risking a new clash with the Western powers. In February, 1946, Stalin called for a new internal drive to build Soviet strength,[46] once again subordinating the full efforts of the nation to building the international power of the state.

The outcome of the war permitted a consolidation of the gains of 1939–40 in Eastern Europe, with a territorial extension in Finland and Poland, and, in addition, the acquisition of half of East Prussia and the cession of the Carpatho-Ukraine by the new Czechoslovak Government. In the Far East, by agreement with their erstwhile Western allies, the Russians regained all that Imperial Russia had ever held there: the Kuril Islands and southern Sakhalin, confirmation of Outer Mongolia as independent of China (and tacitly as a Russian dependency), and a renewed lease on the Chinese Eastern Railway and on Port Arthur in Manchuria. Even before the war ended, the U.S.S.R. had annexed Tannu Tuva in a move that did not even come to the attention of the rest of the world until two years later, in 1946.[47] Thus it regained its irredenta and certain Imperial holdings abroad, and bolstered its strategic frontiers.

The Red Army's occupation of the major part of Eastern and Central Europe offered still greater opportunities—though not for incorporation into the U.S.S.R. Soviet military occupation was the key to the gradual Communist take-over in Poland, Hungary, Romania, and Bulgaria during 1946 and 1947, and of the later formation of a puppet regime in East Germany. Soviet military might also played a role in the Communist *coup d'état* in Czechoslovakia in 1948, although Soviet occupation there had ended in 1945. In all these countries, the Russians used their dominant military and political power as the background for subversion and seizure of power by internal maneuver and *coup d'état*. Yugoslavia was only briefly and in part entered by Soviet troops, and the dominant element in establishing Communist rule there was the independent wartime Communist partisan force of Tito. The Albanian Communists also gained power by internal struggle. In Manchuria and Inner Mongolia, the relatively brief presence of the Soviet and Outer Mongolian military assisted indigenous Communist armed forces but did not establish a Communist regime. Indeed, the Soviet sacking of Manchuria implied that Communist rule was not soon expected. The Chinese Communists gained power only after several years of civil war, undertaken against Stalin's advice.[48] Only in North Korea was a puppet regime later set up.

Occupation was not invariably used to aid or extend Communist rule. In Austria, the occupation was not used to subvert the neutral government, evidently because this was considered too risky; the Russians did not want to jeopardize their stake in the four-power administration of Vienna; moreover, the necessary potential for subversion did not exist. In Finland, the Russians did not even occupy the country. A *coup d'état* on the Czech model failed, largely because the key Communist who had been installed as Minister of the Interior proved to be a more loyal Finn than Communist. Notwithstanding uncontested Soviet military power in the area, and the fact that Finland was a former Axis power, the Russians were too cautious to intervene with force. In Iran, an effort was made (as in 1920) to create an independent state in the Soviet-occupied area in the northwest of the country, but when (under strong Western pressure, directly and in the new United Nations) the Soviet Army belatedly withdrew in March, 1946, the puppet regime there collapsed.

In the areas beyond the shadow of Soviet military might, efforts to extend Soviet power were few, cautious, and, invariably, failures. Subversion was not attempted anywhere in Western Europe, despite an unprecedented temporary position of Communist influence, and even participation, in several governments. Only in Greece was a subversive military campaign waged. Soviet demands to take part in the occupation regime in Japan, and thus to get a foothold in that country, were rebuffed by the United States. Similarly, the Russians were unable to establish themselves in the Mediterranean and Africa, despite efforts to obtain a trusteeship over one or more of the former Italian colonies, and strong indirect pressures on Turkey concerning both the Straits and the once-Russian-ruled provinces of Kars and Ardahan in the Transcaucasus.

The immediate postwar period provided one other—now familiar— opportunity for indirect military penetration: Sinkiang. The inconclusive armistice of 1945 between the Soviet-supported "East Turkestan Republic" and the Chinese Nationalist provincial authorities was followed by further Soviet infiltration of the rebels and, in September, 1946, by direct intervention of Soviet and Mongolian troops, which occupied the Kuldzha-Ili and Altai regions. The rebel Kazakhs and Muslims had been further divided by active Soviet infiltration, and a majority turned against the Russians in a new rebellion in 1947. In this combat, about one third of the Soviet-equipped and Soviet-paid local Kazakhs changed sides and joined the new anti-Soviet forces. At about this time, the Soviet consul general in Urumchi approached the Chinese Nationalist viceroy, General T'ao Shih-yueh, and urged him to declare the independence of Sinkiang, promising that the U.S.S.R. would not only recognize but protect

it by stopping the Chinese Communists from advancing into Sinkiang. After the failure of this effort, time ran out on Soviet infiltration, and Soviet troops were withdrawn from all but certain border areas. In 1949, the Chinese Communists easily secured control of the province and wiped out the local Soviet-trained Kuldzha troops. An "air accident" that same year killed most of the formerly Soviet-sponsored Kuldzha (formerly the East Turkestan Republic) leaders while they were en route to Peking.[49] Later, in a nationwide purge of "local nationalists" in 1958, the Ili Kazakh area suffered proportionately more than any other region; the next year, a decision to use the Cyrillic alphabet for their language was reversed.[50] In 1962, in the wake of civil unrest and alleged Soviet exploitation of it, the last Soviet consulates (at Urumchi and Kuldzha) were closed by the Chinese, who also sought to seal the border after some 60,000 Kazakhs fled to the U.S.S.R.[51] Thus ended the century-long series of attempts to extend Russian control into Sinkiang north of the Tien Shan range.

The general line of postwar Soviet foreign policy was determined by the rough division of the world as seen by Stalin and as expressed in the concept of "the two camps." With the emergence of a number of Communist regimes, a "system of socialist states" arose. This development of a "socialist camp" counterpoised against the capitalist or "imperialist camp" was heralded as an important change in "the relation of forces in the world arena." The concept of the two camps was partly ideological but chiefly political. It represented, first of all, the framework for consolidation of postwar gains, and only secondarily, a vehicle for expansion elsewhere. By sharply dividing the world and counting as part of the other camp all who were not under Moscow's hegemony, it severely hampered expansion of influence in other parts of the world. Even when challenged internally by the defection of Yugoslavia, the Communist Bloc did not resort to military force to overthrow the leadership of the Yugoslav Party and Government. Offensively, beyond the Bloc's borders, pressure was exerted in the Berlin blockade in 1949–50, but stopped short of military involvement. Only in Korea, in 1950, did the Russians believe they had an opportunity to use military force to advance their control. The country was divided; the United States had not only withdrawn its forces but official statements were read to mean that the United States would not use military power to defend South Korea. Finally, the move was made by proxy and did not directly involve the Soviet Union. The unexpected American response was met by extending proxy to Chinese "volunteers" rather than by committing the Soviet Union to the fray. The final result was a stalemate (as in Berlin) in which the Communists failed to achieve their initial expansionist objectives and had to settle for the *status quo ante*. Both the Berlin blockade and the Korean War marked attempts to deal with anomalous situations spawned by the war, or, to put it in terms of offensive aim, marked the final postwar attempts to reach for tempting local objectives.

Before the new era, which opened in 1953, considerable changes had occurred in the Soviet military instrument. In 1946, the "Workers' and Peasants' Red Army" was renamed the "Soviet Army," a change reflecting the long-maturing and significant evolution of that body from the early revolutionary army of the civil war to a national army and arm of the state. This change was one of many that cumulatively marked a shift of political structure. As in other sectors of Soviet society, the postwar tasks of the armed forces were concentrated on the build-up of the power of the Soviet state, and of the Communist Bloc, for the long run. Thus in the immediate postwar period, massive Western demobilization was soon followed by a Soviet reduction from over 11 million men to under 3 million by 1948. (Later, during the Korean War period and Western remobilization, the total rose to nearly 6 million by the mid-1950's.)[52] Efforts were concentrated on modernizing the armed forces as a whole, on providing a token long-range air force armed with nuclear weapons, and on developing advanced weapons systems for the future. Military doctrine continued virtually unchanged, and in 1953 was simply an elaboration and canonization of Soviet military doctrine of 1945. But the slowly developing military thinking was not incongruous with the virtually unchanged and single-minded role of the military instrument in Soviet policy: for defense in the unlikely case that an enemy should attack, and to garrison and maintain the new Soviet empire. The only overt use of military power had been the rather conservative one of remaining where they had advanced to during the war, while political means were employed in most, though not all, situations to acquire this occupied territory. Nonetheless, the Soviet armed forces were developing into an instrument with other potentialities, which would later be recognized and exploited as Soviet political strategy reawakened.

The current era of Soviet foreign policy has been distinguished by important changes in outlook, objectives, and vitality which have arisen from three significant developments: the death of Stalin and of the Stalinist system; the implications of nuclear-missile weapons

for world politics, including an end of the former strategic inferiority
of the U.S.S.R. in the world balance of power; and the decline of
colonialism and the rise of neutralism and pacifism in the world.

The Soviet leaders have continued to display a Marxist-Leninist
outlook and a conviction that the entire world will ultimately turn
to Communism. In terms of hopes, as well as expectations, the Soviet
leaders' aims continue to be revolutionary. Actual Soviet policy, however, has now been keyed primarily to the real power situation of the
U.S.S.R., to ideologically sanctioned calculations of risk in any initiative, and to preoccupation with preserving and advancing the Soviet
system in the U.S.S.R. The Russians have seen many new opportunities for the world-wide advance of Communism by political, economic, and subversive means, particularly in the disintegration of the
old colonial system. But while the new military strategic situation in
the world has greatly enhanced their security, it has not favored
offensive use of Soviet military power. Nuclear war has not been
regarded as a feasible instrument of policy because the uncertain risks
and the certain costs have become too great. Inasmuch as the ideology was never based on reliance on war as the chief means of
achieving the triumph of Communism, there has been no clash
between expectation and expediency. Even so, the Russians have
since 1956 revised Leninist doctrine by solemnly rejecting the inevitability of war. Since 1960, they have also rejected the strong implication of postwar Stalinist discourse, which would be that since
World War I brought the birth of the first socialist state, and World
War II a series of socialist states, a third world war would be the
logical eventual path to the complete extension of socialism throughout the world. Thus the old relationship between war and the revolution has been reviewed and significantly revised to accord with the
power realities of the age.[53]*

Soviet strategy has shifted from Stalin's forced-pace defensive
build-up at home, postwar consolidation of gains, and probing to
extend and buttress the outer walls of the socialist bloc. During the
late 1950's, this policy was superseded by offensive coexistence, with
conflict waged by all appropriate measures short of war, including the
calculated use of threats based on increased Soviet military power.
Nuclear war was relegated to the desperate, defensive last resort
should there be no alternative, but military instruments remained
important means of offensive infiltration and pressure. Their chief
role has been to counter and neutralize Western use of nuclear power

* See Chapters 10 through 12.

to prevent Communist gains. Thus military stalemate has been regarded by the Russians as facilitating the world revolution by preventing the imperialists from using military force to halt the historical movement of political and social revolutionary forces.

Military demonstrations and disclosures have become an effective means of serving Soviet policy. Achievements in space and missile technology in particular have had an enormous political effect in the world, exceeding their contribution to military capability, significant as that is. Being "first" in prestige-laden fields such as space exploration has been cultivated (with unintended assistance in the West) as one of the signs that Communism is the wave of the future. Less spectacularly, military parades (including display of missiles), naval courtesy visits, aviation records, and a host of other lesser reminders of the large and modern Soviet military force have served to re-emphasize the continuing capability for conventional as well as nuclear warfare.

Since 1955, military aid and assistance to non-Communist countries has become a potent tool of Soviet policy. The Middle East was first, and has been the chief target area for such aid (Egypt, Syria, Iraq, Yemen, Afghanistan). Gradually, however, almost all areas of the world have been penetrated—for example, Indonesia, Algeria, Somalia, and Cuba. By the end of the first decade of military-assistance programs in 1964, over $3 billion worth of military aid had been given. In Indonesia alone, military aid totaled about $1 billion. These programs not only create a certain dependency—for replacement parts, ammunition, standardization of arms, and the like—but also exert a subversive influence through Soviet and satellite advisers in these countries and by training their local representatives in the U.S.S.R. In some cases, this has abetted or stimulated local violence or guerrilla warfare. But often, such arrangements have had broader political impact on Soviet relations with these and other countries, and in turn on the relations of such countries with the West. Even within the Communist camp, such aid has been used not only to strengthen the bloc, but, sometimes, as with Communist China (until such aid was virtually cut off in 1960) to limit in certain important ways the military forces and thus the policies of these allies, which might not otherwise be amenable to Soviet suasion.*

Also since 1955, disarmament has become an increasingly important "military" instrumentality of Soviet foreign policy. While the chief

* See Chapters 7 and 9.

role of this issue has certainly been its political-propaganda effect in the world, it has limited direct relation to military aspects of Soviet policy as well. As of this writing, agreements have been reached on nonmilitarization of Antarctica; on a ban on nuclear-weapons testing in the atmosphere, space, and under water; and on endorsements of a U.N. resolution banning the placing of weapons of mass destruction in outer space. The Russians have shown interest in arrangements that would hamper the West in developing or deploying its nuclear power, and that would reduce the chances of war by miscalculation. Unilateral Soviet arms reductions undertaken for other reasons (as in 1955 and 1960) are also expected to make a modest contribution to Soviet foreign policy objectives, and in some special cases have been so designed. In particular, the withdrawals from Austria, the leased base at Porkkala in Finland, and Port Arthur in China—all in 1955—permitted the U.S.S.R. to claim credit for having no foreign bases (except garrisons within the Communist bloc under the Warsaw Pact).

Direct employment of military force has been used only when Soviet policy was pressed *in extremis* and there was no alternative for preserving a threatened position already held. The suppression of the East German revolt of June, 1953, and the Hungarian Revolution of October, 1956, were the only cases of resort to military force. In the case of Poland in October, 1956, the Russians preferred to accept a setback rather than use naked military might; their second intervention, in Hungary, against the Nagy Government, was made only after Hungary had passed the extreme point of attempted withdrawal from the Warsaw Pact and the imminent surrender of power by the Communist Party.*

The current period of Soviet foreign policy has been marked by limited, indirect, political exploitation of increasing military power. A new peak of defense and deterrent strength has not only offered greater security but has also tended to neutralize the opponent's possible resort to military power to check Communist gains through nonmilitary means. Though the Chinese Communists disagree with the Soviet avoidance of direct limited military actions, there are no signs of significant strategy disputes among Soviet leaders. The military leaders have not favored making changes to accord with some of the logical implications of this policy (as reflected in force reductions and in reorganization), but there are no indications that they would favor a more radically belligerent policy.†

* See Chapter 8.
† See Chapter 3.

Soviet foreign political aims and methods as they have developed in recent decades will probably not change so long as the prevailing geostrategic and political "relation of forces" continues.

Russian foreign policy over the past century affords an excellent opportunity for analysis of military instruments and considerations in foreign policy since the country has exhibited such wide swings in the conceptions of the leaders and in national aims, and the times have led to such great political and military shifts in the balance of world power.

The element of fundamental change—and it is not less than that—is in the difference of outlook and objective. Czarist Russia, for all of its virtues and faults, was in harmony with the world political order. While the international political structure itself showed instabilities, it was at least based on a constant general framework, marked by the satiability of its members at varying degrees short of the sun. Today, the Russians reject, oppose, and confront the world political order. The revolutionary drive of Bolshevism has subsided—and may yet alter in its nature—as the Soviet state continues its coexistence with the rest of the world; but so far, the Soviet outlook has not accepted reconciliation with the world. War, however, has not been seen as the motivating force of historical change—least of all in the nuclear age—even though Soviet territorial expansion has been based on the limited use of military force. Indeed, despite the perverse political perspectives of Marxism-Leninism, the ideology militates against preoccupation with war or reliance on military means to achieve its unlimited aims.

The main element of continuity lies in the form, and often the targets, of particular military instrumentalities. The reappearance of familiar politico-military methods is due largely to basically unchanged geographic and other local environmental factors. An example is the continuing Russian expansionist designs in the unsettled Far Eastern and eastern Central Asian borderlands, which has persisted under Czarist and Communist regimes, and despite the existence of "fraternal" socialist systems of the U.S.S.R. and Communist China. Prominent among the choice of means has been the preference for limited wars with limited objectives, though the reasons have varied greatly.

Over the past decade, the military technological factor has made an impact the full significance of which we still may not recognize. In the 1960's, as in the 1920's, the Soviets favor coexistence, rivalry in economic development, and disarmament—though for different reasons. Thirty to forty years ago, the Russians were moved by a paramount defensive concern to favor these nonmilitary instruments; now these methods are seen as the *only* favorable ones for advance.

Personalities and shifts in internal political mechanisms and forces, including the role of military leaders, are always important, and sometimes critically so. But such factors usually channel or trigger the release of more basic forces.

Military considerations are an important factor in foreign policy decisions about other instruments of action, often in indirect, unintended, or unrealized ways. "Military necessity" may be a mirage sought by frail political judgment, as in the "necessity" to mobilize in July, 1914. "Military requirements" are, by definition, absolute needs, but in fact, they are almost always desiderata rather than necessities. Presumed military advantage can often be more concretely expressed than the no-less-real political disadvantages, and may therefore unduly weight foreign policy decisions. For example, taking Port Arthur in 1898 seemed advantageous, but it set in train events culminating in the disastrous war with Japan in 1904–5. The military advantages of acquiring strategic Finnish territory in 1939 scarcely outweighed the bad political effects of the venture, and may have encouraged Hitler to underestimate Soviet military strength. Military alliances have a special attraction that sometimes obscures the fact that they are often attainable only at great political cost (in terms of lost maneuver, excitement of the opponent's fears, stimulation of counterefforts, even disruptions in the internal solidarity of the allied country). For example, the Franco-Russian alliance of the 1890's eventually turned German war planning into other, deep channels, to Russia's detriment. The military profession certainly requires special skills and yields special insights into means of waging war, but it cannot be regarded as competent in deciding basic questions of foreign policy, such as war and peace, or in defining the appropriate objectives and limits of war, which remains always a political act whether or not it is so recognized.

Only history will tell whether the elements of continuity or those of change in Czarist and Soviet foreign policy are the greater. In general, the differences are chiefly in policy aims, while continuities prevail in diplomacy and in the employment of means, including military ones. And although ultimate ends are important, the means have increasingly become more important and perhaps dominant.

2. The Military as a Sociopolitical Force in Russia, 1861–1965

Russian society over the past century has mirrored both change and continuity. Some aspects of Russian life and society would have proceeded very much along the lines that they followed whether or not the Revolution had occurred; certain others were given direction or were stimulated by the course of political developments. The evolution of the military as a social group and as a political force in Russian society reflects elements of both historical continuity and change.

At present, as in the late nineteenth century, a technological revolution is affecting military affairs. Now, as then, a new *type* of professional officer is coming into being. And, now, as then, a new military class is being born in Russia. But the differences, too, are significant. Then, military professionalism contributed to the *breakdown* of a traditional, established social and political order; now, the military professional is part of a broad *build-up* of a new class society. And, although now, as then, the military is largely apolitical, it is so for different reasons, against a different political trend in other classes of society.

The half century preceding World War I was marked by important changes in the composition both of the Russian officer corps and of the enlisted ranks. The Crimean War, and later the Russian-Turkish and Russian-Japanese wars, exposed severe shortcomings in the personnel of the Russian Army, as well as in the system of supply and the level of weaponry.

From 1861 to 1881, War Minister Dmitri Milyutin (brother of the great reformer Nikolai Milyutin) instituted a series of reforms that were of great significance for the Army in its subsequent social evolution.[1] In 1861, the term of service for the enlisted man was reduced from twenty-five to sixteen years. It was followed in 1874 by an unbonding of these virtual serf-soldiers, and compulsory universal military service was introduced. The term of active duty was again reduced, to a period varying from a half year for the university-educated to six years for those without complete primary education. In the 1860's and 1870's, the soldiers' training was broadened so that many who had not had sufficient schooling could learn to read and write. Generous exemptions were granted for "only sons" and other breadwinners. Finally, conditions of service and discipline became less harsh, and corporal punishment was abolished. Equality of all classes before the law was established, and higher military standards were achieved as well.

Equally great changes were made in the system of selecting and preparing officers. From the 1860's on, officers were required to have experience as regimental commanders before becoming eligible for general's rank. In the mid-1860's, Milyutin converted most of the military schools into *gymnasia*, and established certain higher *junker* schools for technical specialties.

After Milyutin's departure, in the 1880's, caste distinctions in the officer corps were revived, with encouragement from the government. Officers were exempt from the laws prohibiting duels. The military *gymnasia* were changed into "Cadet Corps" schools. And the 1885 Manifesto creating the Bank of the Nobility expressed the wish that "the Russian nobles preserve a dominant place in the military leadership."[2] However, the basic line of development of the new officer corps was not affected.

From 1861 to 1914, the officer corps developed from what had been a segment of the nobility who served part-time, to a group of professionally and technically qualified men drawn from all classes. This change reflected the general social change taking place as a by-product of growing industrialization, urbanization, educational progress, and other factors. But it was also a response to the definite need for a modern army. As war and armaments became more technologically advanced, it was necessary to have officers with corresponding technical qualifications. In the war years 1812–13, some 14 per cent of the military budget had been spent on military ordnance and technology; in 1904–5, this share had risen to 25 per cent; and in 1914–15, it jumped to 60 per cent. The jump was also notable in absolute terms—from 80 million gold rubles in 1812–13 to 12 billion gold rubles in 1914–15.[3]

Measures taken to overcome the technical backwardness revealed in the wars affected some branches more than others—the navy, engineers, and artillery more than the infantry and cavalry. The advancement of technically qualified officers, regardless of their birth, was opposed by many traditionalist line officers, but necessarily it continued. Especially in the navy, the line officers corps preserved an aristocratic character by reluctantly admitting the growth of a separate corps of naval engineers and technical officers, most of whom were not from the nobility. The men of this corps, products of special naval engineering and shipbuilding schools, were for a long time denied naval rank—they became colonels or generals, never captains or admirals—and when they were finally given epaulettes, the shoulder boards were narrower. Incidentally, discriminatory rank remains in today's Soviet Navy, though it was long ago discarded by such other modern navies as once used it.

What about the nontechnical officers corps? The Guards, navy officers of the line, and much of the cavalry determinedly maintained their aristocratic character and composition. The Guards officers were drawn from certain select preparatory Cadet Corps schools which, traditionally, were restricted to the nobility and associated with specific Guards regiments. Even there, only about 60 per cent of the Guards officers were of the hereditary nobility; another 28 per cent were sons of "personal nobles"—that is, individuals granted non-hereditary status in the nobility; all officers were granted "personal" nobility, and many of the cadets in that category were the sons of officers.[4] Not until 1913 were *all* schools opened to *all* qualified applicants.

In the army as a whole, though, changes occurred more rapidly. In a typical military school in Moscow during the late 1860's, 81 per cent of the men were of the hereditary nobility, and 9 per cent sons of personal nobles; by the late 1870's, some 45 per cent were of the nobility, 33 per cent were sons of personal nobles, 13 per cent were of bourgeois origin, and 11 per cent were from the clergy. By the late 1880's, only 12 per cent were nobles, 57 per cent were personal nobles, 16 per cent were from the bourgeoisie, and 5 per cent were from the peasantry. Finally, by the beginning of World War I, 9 per cent were nobles, 28 per cent were personal nobles, 28 per cent were bourgeoisie, and 19 per cent were peasants.[5] In fact, by 1912, even in the Academy of the General Staff only 48 per cent were hereditary nobles.[6] General Alekseyev, last Commander in Chief under the Czar, was not born of the nobility. General Denikin, Alekseyev's successor as Commander in Chief of the White Army, was the grandson of a serf. Both were graduates of ordinary *junker* military schools open to all. The officer corps of the Russian Army continued to be composed of "nobles" because Russian law provided that on reaching officer status, any man automatically acquired "personal" nobility. And those reaching the rank of colonel were granted "hereditary" nobility.

The nineteenth and twentieth centuries saw the decline of pre-Napoleonic professional armies and the rise of large citizen armies. Although the illiterate Russian soldier of the 1850's, who had been handed over by his master for twenty-five years' service, was unquestionably "professional," the soldier of a few decades later was better adapted to the professional requirements of contemporary warfare. This was especially true of the officer corps. In the early and mid-nineteenth century, military service had been a part-time duty levied on all nobles in Russia. Many of the aristocracy served only a few years of active duty and then retired to full-time social life. For officers, the average length of duty rose from ten years under Nicholas I to eighteen years in the early 1900's.

In the long run, the professionalization of the officer corps from 1861 to 1914 would have created a new stratum of society. Initially, however, the caste of military aristocracy disintegrated into a heterogenous compound. Moreover, the emerging group tended to become increasingly isolated from the rest of society.

Nationality, too, was a complicating factor. During much of the nineteenth century, a "see-saw" controversy existed over discipline and military doctrine, involving the ethnic Great Russians versus the Baltic-German nobility. The 1885 Manifesto favored the preservation of "a dominant place in the military leadership" by "the *Russian* nobles," but the army had come to include a large number of officers and generals from the various nationalities of Russia (including the Baltic Germans). At the turn of the century, by contrast, the Guards had about 90 per cent Russian officers—the balance being chiefly Baltic Germans and men from princely Georgian families.[7]

Before the Revolution, most of the officers were stanchly conservative, and, of course, loyal, but essentially apolitical. The echoes of the Decembrists were faint by the latter part of the nineteenth century, because the intelligentsia and the officer class were no longer intimate—another effect of the growing isolation of the military class from the rest of society. True, the social mores and traditions of service to the Czar were reinforced by military discipline that inhibited active political interest. Moreover, the training of the officer, though by no means inferior, was simply not a liberal education. While the social composition of the officer corps became more varied, the regular officers continued to be drawn from the military school systems, which were set apart from the ardently political and frequently radical universities.

The apolitical stand of the officer corps was underscored when, after the proclamation of the Provisional Government, there were no attempts at a royalist counterrevolution. The Kornilov affair, the sole apparent exception, was inspired more by misunderstanding and a fear of the rise of Bolshevism; it was not the spearhead of a monarchist movement.* Former Imperial Army and Guards officers have frankly acknowledged their pre-Revolutionary political ignorance, which reflected simple lack of *interest* in political affairs.

In the crisis of 1905, many officers were politically indecisive, and in the face of the army's widespread but passive opposition to dispelling the rebels, the Guards proved the regime's most reliable support. To correct the political immaturity of the officers, courses in political science and current political events were instituted in the military schools in 1907.[8] Three years later, however, these courses were abandoned, for they proved too provocative.

During World War I, the officer corps underwent further rapid change. The heavy losses of the first year, especially among the Guards, seriously diluted both the officer corps and the regular troops. The 50,000 regular officers, plus 35,000 reserves who were added upon mobilization in 1914, totaled less than the number of officer casualties in 1914–16 alone.[9] The casualties did include many of the new wartime officers, but the depletion of the regular prewar cadre officer corps was tremendous. It was necessary, therefore, to commission several hundred thousand new officers during the war—generally men with very little military training except, perhaps, for noncommissioned service.[10]

By 1917, the officer corps was of a very different nature from what it had been in 1914. New officers were drawn from the peasant noncommissioned officer staff and from the young intelligentsia; both groups, for varying reasons, had been imbued with patriotism in the early years of the war, but by 1917 and 1918 they were not inclined to continue the war. The "Guards Regiments," which defected to the Revolution in 1917, were not the authentic Guards Regiments, whose remnants were at the front; they were the regimental training battalions in the capital, which had not been selected or trained in accord with traditional standards.

* In the late summer of 1917, differences arose between Prime Minister A. F. Kerensky of the Provisional Government and General L. G. Kornilov, Commander in Chief of the Army, over means of enforcing discipline in the army and the leftward trend of Petrograd Soviet. In September, General Kornilov ordered an army unit to march on Petrograd, dispose the Soviet, and, if necessary, depose Kerensky, too. Kornilov, however, did not attempt to restore the monarchy. The unit he sent refused to fire on other troops loyal to the Provisional Government; its commander, General Krymov, committed suicide; and General Kornilov was arrested.

The Imperial Russian officer corps underwent substantial changes both in social composition and attitude during the fifty years preceding World War I. Like Russian society as a whole, it was adjusting to the changed economic conditions of the country and of the world. The political evolution, however, failed to keep pace with the times.

The Bolshevik Revolution violently ruptured the development of the officer corps. During the Civil War, between 50,000 and 100,000 officers of the old army were taken into the new Red Army, and some 200,000 entered the White armies.[11] More than 10,000 civil servants of the Ministry of War were absorbed, as were the major part of the General Staff and military academies of the old army.[12] By August, 1920, the Red Army had taken in more than 48,000 former officers of the Imperial Army,[13] many of whom were wartime-promoted officers. In 1921, however, many of these officers were dismissed.[14]

Even more impressive than their numbers was their influence. A number of former career General Staff colonels and lieutenant colonels exerted considerable influence—men like S. S. Kamenev, Vatsetis, Shaposhnikov, Kork, Uborevich, Primakov, and Lebedev. The professional officers—some representing the new prewar technical experts, others, the career military drawn from the nobility—were not as influential politically as the new breed of military chiefs from the Bolshevik Party (Frunze, Podvoisky, Voroshilov) or from the Revolution itself (Budënny, Blücher). The revolutionaries and guerrilla fighters often were more hostile to the military science and modern weapons specialists than the old line officers had been thirty years earlier. Thus, for a decade or more following the Civil War, a conflict raged between the "proletarians" and the "military specialists."

Beginning about 1931, the professionalization of the army was renewed in earnest. The old officers continued to dominate military thinking, even though by this time they were only a small minority of the total officer strength.[15] In 1929, a survey of military writers showed that over 80 per cent were former Imperial Army officers, one-third of them former colonels or generals. And of the hundred authors of the 1929 *Field Regulations*, seventy-nine had been officers in the old Army.[16]

The turning point came in 1931, when Mikhail Tukhachevsky—nobleman, ex-lieutenant of the Guards, future marshal of the Red Army—rose to *de facto* control of the Army. The Red Army moved toward modernization, and the officer corps toward a distinctive place in Soviet society.

From the Revolution on, the Bolshevik Party was hard pressed to

ensure the control and assimilation of the new officers. As late as
1924, only 32 per cent of the officers were affiliated with the Communist Party; by 1928, an estimated 65 per cent were members.[17]
But in 1928, only 32 per cent of the influential military writers were
Party members.[18] Moreover, although Party membership increased,
the data on social (class) origins show that the Red Army continued
to depend on "alien" elements. In 1923, the officer corps was composed of 13.6 per cent workers, 52.7 per cent peasants, and 33.7 per
cent "others." By 1927, the comparable figures were 22.4 per cent
workers, 56 per cent peasants, and only 21.6 per cent "others." As
late as 1926, "higher officers" (generals) were 7.3 per cent workers,
31.2 per cent peasants, and 61.5 per cent "others." Similarly, "senior
officers" were 44.7 per cent from the "other" classes, and even "mid-
dle-rank officers" were 20.6 per cent in this category.[19] And in the
Zhukovsky Air Academy in 1922, only 40 per cent were "workers and
peasants" and 35 per cent Party members; but in 1927, though over
77 per cent were Party members, still only 50 per cent were workers
and peasants.[20]

The Soviet regime did not rely upon increased Party membership
among the officers to provide Party control. "Military commissars"
were introduced in 1918 to control the "military specialists," as former
Imperial Army officers were termed. The institution of political
officers has of course continued ever since.

The stabilization of the new officer corps came about during Marshal Tukhachevsky's rise, from 1931 to 1937. As in the latter part of
the nineteenth century, the plan was to establish a professional group
of specialists in the military art and in military technology. But this
generated certain social aspects that were not in keeping with the
official ideology. The new officer class wanted a return to traditional
and hierarchical personal ranks, insignia, and privileges, and the
opportunity to give these advantages to their sons. Beginning with
the mid-1930's, some of these demands were met. In 1935, ranks
were restored, except for general officer grades, which were not given
until 1940; moreover, the creation of the rank of marshal was an
"imperial" addition that had not been found even in the pre-Revolutionary army. New salary scales not only favored the military, but
also reflected the growing gap between officers and enlisted men, and
between junior and senior officers. Hundreds of special stores, theaters, and clubs were established for military officers and their families. In 1937, as if in "exchange" for the execution of Marshal
Tukhachevsky and his associates, the Red Army officer corps was
presented with the most ultramodern rest sanatorium, at Sochi.

The class of officers just emerging was given lessons in French, in polo, in dancing, and in the social graces. Many of the newly "cultured" Civil War heroes divorced their too-proletarian wives and married young women with more appropriate social *savoir-faire*. It again became necessary, as before the Revolution, for junior officers to have their commanding officers' approval before they could marry.

Count Ignatyev, the Imperial Army Attaché in Paris before the Revolution, returned to the Soviet Union in the 1930's and became a consultant on precisely such matters of cultural form. Thus, in custom and deportment, as well as in military art and tactics, "specialists" from the old regime were found indispensable.

As a new military tradition—and class—was evolving, the political development of Stalin's dictatorship burst into the Great Purge. The purges wiped almost clean the slate of senior officers in the Red Army. Three of the five marshals, 13 of the 15 army commanders, 57 of the 85 corps commanders, and 110 of the 195 division commanders were purged.[21] About half of the officer corps members were adversely affected. But this severe jolt to the new military class contributed, in the long run, to the emergence of a more homogenous group. Those hardest hit by the Purge were the Old Bolsheviks, who took to military affairs in the Civil War, and the former Imperial officers. The Purge was instrumental, then, in the advancement of the new officers. The rapidity with which some rose was astonishing; for example, Rychagov, a senior lieutenant in 1937, had become a lieutenant general three years later, and by 1941, when he was 35, Commander in Chief of the Air Forces.

The proportion of Party members continued to grow, though irregularly, for the purges hit Party members heavily, and led to an increase in non-Party officers both in 1934 and in 1937–38. In the armed forces as a whole, Party membership in 1939 was what it had been in 1931, about 50 per cent, some 10 per cent below its high point of nearly 60 per cent in 1933.[22]

During this period before the war, the army finally became entirely a regular army, and the last of the territorial troops were integrated by 1939.[23] Many of the new officers had become competent specialists in the mechanized and technical branches—the air forces, armored forces, and others. A professional military leadership was being developed to meet the new military technology.

World War II, like the Purge, decimated the ranks of the prewar professional officer class—but also contributed to raising its standing.

Under the impact of the preliminary campaigns in Poland and Finland, generals' ranks were restored, and firm discipline was established in 1940. Saluting was now required, including even that of noncommissioned officers by privates. The political officer (military commissar) had been again raised to a coequal position in 1937, but after 1940 (except for a year in 1941–42) he was again nominally subordinate to the commanding officer. In 1942, the *pogony*, the once-hated golden epaulettes, returned to adorn the new military elite. Guards units were formed, and given extra pay and privileges. Finally, the officers were granted the opportunity to cultivate a "hereditary" line by sending their sons to new exclusive cadet schools, established in 1943. These schools, like the new Orders for valor and achievement, were named for distinguished Imperial military heroes—the Suvorov and Nakhimov (naval) schools. Young boys are accepted at the age of eight or nine, so that they grow up in an atmosphere of military caste.

The Soviet officer today is the only military representative of a modern world power to sport epaulettes and velvet lapels, leather boots, and a dress dirk at his side. Marshals (several grades), generals, field grade officers, and junior officers are carefully separated, and each has separate messes and recreational facilities. A field grade officer and a company grade officer are not social equals. Personal orderlies are assigned to field grade, as well as to general, officers.

A strong sense of social solidarity pervades the military. In present-day Russia, to an extent greater than in any other major power, garrison life still exists. It, too, accentuates the solidarity among fellow officers. Class inbreeding is not uncommon, and although this may not be a typical example, it may be relevant to note that Marshal Zhukov's daughters are married to the officer son of Marshal Vasilevsky and to the nephew of Marshal Voroshilov. It is clear from accounts of Soviet career officers that the regular professional officers and their families tend to be drawn to one another. Ever since the early 1930's, they usually draw the line short of association with the political officers—and almost always avoid the secret police counter-intelligence officers in the armed forces.

Opportunities to observe and talk with Soviet officers make it clear that they—and their wives—are quite content with their security and their relatively high standard of living. Young officers and enlisted men, too, do not show the skeptical criticism of the regime so widespread among students. The pride of young air force lieutenants in their sharp uniforms, the superior air of smartly elegant colonels at Sochi, the deference shown a general entering a Moscow hotel—all, though not unique, are signs of the pronounced class structure in the Soviet Army.[24]

How does the emergence of a privileged military caste affect the social structure at large? The military tend to associate with their fellows more than do the other privileged groups—artists, writers, scientists, and managers. There may be more interclass contact among some other groups, but all Soviet society is moving toward a pyramid of increased class stratification. The evolution of a separate military caste within the privileged social stratum does not contradict the broader trend.

The recent development of a military caste is thus different from the growth of a new military class in the late nineteenth century, for then it was at the cost of contributing to the disintegration of long-established, rigidly stratified classes based on birth. However, the new trend does widen the gulf between officers and enlisted men.

In many ways, present-day social status has much in common with the older period, owing both to circumstances and to conscious efforts to revive past tradition. The political effect of this sociological phenomenon, however, is quite different.

As it developed into a distinct social class, the military could not fail to become, to some degree, a political entity. As an institution, it could not fail to be affected by the shifting political weight of other institutions. And particularly in the post-Stalin period, important changes in the political balance of Soviet institutions have greatly altered and increased the potential political role of the military.

The death of Stalin was a key development. *All* other Soviet institutions automatically became more important as the institution of the all-powerful autocrat disappeared. In the ensuing political readjustment, first the secret police and later the governmental and managerial bureaucracies were weakened. While the Communist Party machine gained most in political power, the military—almost by default—also rose in stature. As a consequence of the unavoidable involvement of the military in issues weighted with strategic decisions, but also contested between factions of Party rivals, the senior military chiefs came to play a significant political role. There is no evidence that the military were driven by political ambition. Rather, the nature of the issues forced their political involvement. Marshal Zhukov was removed after he became a political figure and sought to pursue certain policies. Although some of these policies directly concerned the professional military class, Zhukov's fall from power did not keep the military from their institutional involvement or basically reduce their status. It did, however, mark an abrupt decline in the active representation of the military in national policy-making.*

The military has shown no inclination toward political opposition, nor has it displayed much positive political interest. The Party's constant harping on increased political indoctrination, and the intensity of the reaction to Party Presidium member Zhukov's desire to ensure that such nonsense didn't interfere with raising the professional qualifications of the military bear eloquent witness to the awareness of the Soviet leaders of the essentially apolitical posture of the military as a whole. True, some 90 per cent of the officers are affiliated with the Party, but the Soviet leaders realize that Party membership is ordinarily more a formality than a reflection of zeal.

Today, as in the latter half of the nineteenth century, technological revolution deeply affects the military. In the mid-twentieth-century technological reorientation of the army, just as in the last century, new specialists are needed—now men conversant with the military application of nuclear energy, rocket power, and space flight.[25] The social upheaval caused by the introduction of such men is much less severe now than eighty years ago, owing both to the different pattern of society and to the tendency to train career military men in these specialties. There is a strong tendency to advance scientific and technological fields through research done in military institutions. In turn, this cultivates an apolitical attitude, for many of the military's new scientific-technical men do not even deign to join the Communist Party. Presumably, all unit commanders and staff officers of major's or higher rank must be Party members, but some technical specialists have even become generals without joining the Party. Despite the intensive political indoctrination in the armed forces, and the advantage to career, the percentage of officers who are Party members (86 per cent) did not rise between 1952 and 1958; by 1961, it had reached 90 per cent, and it remained at that level in 1965.[26]

The renewed professional concentration on military technical development accompanies a rejuvenated approach to questions of military science and the military art. The renaissance in both fields is largely a product of the post-Stalin era.[27] Like the parallel trend under Marshal Tukhachevsky three decades earlier, military professionalization continues regardless of the political fate of its most prominent innovators, such as Marshal Zhukov.

What does this mean for the future? In another decade or two, a new generation of officers will have risen, men who have a new out-

* The changing role of the military in Soviet politics is discussed in more detail in Chapter 3.

look. Gone will be the marshals who, like Konev and Timoshenko, earned their spurs in the Civil War; the horse-drawn *tachanka* sporting a heavy machine gun will be as foreign as the bow and arrow. The outlook of the new men will almost surely be less, rather than more, political—unless, of course, in the meantime the political structure has been rent asunder.

The military has acquired social status, material rewards, and prestige; it has neither sought nor been given commensurate political power. Doubtless, the Zhukov affair has inhibited the military from seeking a more active political role; nonetheless, the military as professionals have continued to become embroiled in political issues.*

Two key aspects of change and continuity in the role of the military as a social force during the last century are highlighted in view of their fundamental significance: *social status and stratification*, the privileged place of the military in society and the social structure; and *political prestige and power*, the apparent and actual extent to which the military share in national decision-making.

The social status of a given group does not always reflect its role in society. But such status is usually related to either past or present functional importance—or, at the least, to the image of the functional importance. Russian society in the latter part of the nineteenth century was gradually and reluctantly adapting to new conditions of life. The Russian nobility, unlike, for example, the English aristocracy at a parallel stage of development, did not adjust to the new economic system by merging with the class of mercantile and industrial entrepreneurs. In the army, in the Petrine period, feudal primacy of rank and command based solely on aristocratic hierarchy was ended. The reforms of Milyutin in the 1860's and 1870's established a basis for merging various classes with the military-career segment of the nobility. So the military aristocracy, unlike the Russian autocracy and nobility as a whole, *did* come to terms with the changing needs of the times. By 1914, the evolution of a new military class was well advanced, and though there was friction, it was overcome. The result was that the new military class, with its heterogeneous origin, rose to the social sphere of the hereditary nobility.

This viable solution to the problem of social adjustment was accompanied by a political accommodation. Although the military class maintained a good relationship with the regime, the basic relationship between the regime and society as a whole was decaying. After the

* See Chapter 3.

abdication of the Czar, the military served the new Provisional Government without question. And later, a surprising proportion voluntarily served the radical Bolshevik regime. A fundamentally apolitical attitude enabled the military to encompass the patriotic shifts from Russian czar to Soviet commissar. In fact, the stretch was sometimes more easily bridged than that between strong liberal opposition to the old regime and acceptance of the new Bolshevik autocracy. In a positive way, the superprofessionalism of the military had a certain influence on the new regime. This was foreseen by the Old Bolshevik Mekhonoshin, who, in evaluating the inherited bureaucracy of the Ministry of War, told Lenin: "This machine cannot be remodeled. It is more likely to change us than be changed by us."[28]

The new Workers' and Peasants' Red Army was no more a continuation of the old Imperialist Army than the new regime was of the old one. The early social egalitarianism of the society was mirrored in the army. But the army has also kept in step with the new, and in some respects, even more highly stratified, social structure that has evolved in the Soviet state. The present social standing of the military in the Soviet Union—with its material rewards, hierarchical system, and prestige—is unsurpassed among contemporary world powers.

The political role of any social class is an integral and important part of its being. It is neither logically inherent nor historically established that the social function of any class and its importance to society should determine its political power. Armies and police forces, as the armed guardians of society, have a unique potential for influencing political decision. But their actual political power depends upon the structure and stability of society as a whole, and the accepted locus of decision-making.

The Soviet Army today, like the Russian Army of fifty and more years ago, is essentially apolitical. Nonetheless, its potential political role, in the light of changes in the internal political balance over the years since Stalin's death, is peculiarly great. That the ruling Party machine is aware of this high potential is evident from the preemptive ouster of Marshal Zhukov, the first spokesman for the military to have been admitted (if but briefly) to policy-making councils.

The privileged military caste in mid-twentieth-century Russia is one component of an increasingly stratified society. Whether it and all the other new privileged classes will indefinitely be content to permit a single artificial and parasitic class, the career Communist Party machine, to hold a monopoly of political power remains a question for the historian of the future.

3. The Marshals and the
Communist Party, 1945-65

Civil-military relations in the United States and Western Europe can be discussed in considerable detail. By using official records, interviews, and personal observation, historians, journalists, civilians, and military personnel contribute to the bulk of information. In the Soviet Union, however, such records are not generally available. For example, focal issues such as annual budget debates and appeals to public or legislative opinion either are nonexistent or assume very different forms in the U.S.S.R. Aspects of personal or *factional* maneuvers are never complete or accurate in every detail; but the *institutional* relationships are more fully documented.

As the "Great Fatherland War" drew to a close in 1945, a new period in Soviet policy opened. It was not, however, the shining new era that many in the Soviet Union had been anticipating. To stave off the popular dissatisfaction a renewed conflict would induce—this time with the allies of yesterday as the foes of tomorrow—Stalin permitted a brief respite. In the early months after the war, homage was paid the new heroes whose names had been associated with the great victories of the people and their Army. From May through September, 1945, there were newspaper accounts of awards, promotions, and honors for the marshals and officers of the Red Army. For himself, Stalin created the rank of Generalissimo, and Beria was made a Marshal of the Soviet Union. But it was Marshal Georgy K. Zhukov to whom the crowd turned in victory celebration. Unfortunately, there is very little reliable information on the role played by the military leaders during this brief period. The temporary wartime political and military high commands, the State Defense Committee (GKO) and the military headquarters staff (*Stavka*) of the Supreme Command, were abolished soon after hostilities ended. Marshal Zhukov remained in Berlin; at home, Stalin retained his post as People's Commissar of War.

Military leaders were referred to, and appeared, less frequently.

More was heard of the role of the Party and of Generalissimo Stalin. In January, 1946, the leading marshals were included in the lists of nominations for the first postwar elections to the Supreme Soviet,[1] but within a year, a number of these same marshals were in disgrace or had been banished, and some were even in prison.

Stalin's Supreme Soviet "election" speech on February 9, 1946,[2] marked a massive shift of line. It launched the Soviet people again into socialist construction for the greater power of the state, and the Soviet state onto a path of belligerence and isolationism. About that time, the organs of government were renamed to correspond to the emphasis on the state. The "peoples' commissariats" became "ministries," and the "Workers' and Peasants' Red Army" became the "Soviet Army." On March 21, 1946, Decree No. 629 established the structure of the High Command in a newly unified Ministry of Defense. Stalin remained as Minister in order to groom his former First Deputy, Party stalwart, General of the Army Nikolai A. Bulganin, as his successor. Marshal Aleksandr M. Vasilevsky remained as Chief of the General Staff, and Marshal Zhukov was brought back from Berlin to serve as Commander in Chief of the Ground Forces. Admiral of the Fleet Nikolai G. Kuznetsov was retained as Commander in Chief of the Navy; Chief Marshal of Aviation Aleksandr A. Novikov was removed and replaced by Marshal of Aviation Konstantin A. Vershinin; General of the Army Andrei V. Khrulev remained as Chief of the Rear Services, and the sixth of the deputy ministers. On the whole, then, the wartime military leadership was retained, though the Air Force command was shaken up and several leading air marshals disappeared. Also, Politburo member Bulganin assumed a senior and more prominent "military" position.

A few months later, Zhukov was replaced by Marshal Ivan S. Konev and sent to command the distant and unimportant Odessa Military District. In March, 1947, Stalin stepped down and was succeeded as Minister of Defense by Bulganin, who became a Marshal of the Soviet Union. (With the sole exception of Sokolovsky, who had replaced Zhukov in Berlin in 1946, there were no other promotions to the rank of Marshal of the Soviet Union between 1945 and 1955.) Also in 1947, there was a more widespread purge of wartime military leaders. Chief Marshal of Aviation Aleksandr Ye. Golovanov, wartime chief of the heavy-bomber force, and several other senior airmen were removed. Admiral Kuznetsov, Chief of the Navy since 1939, was court-martialed for allegedly imparting to the Western Allies more than had been necessary during the period of the wartime alliance. He was demoted two ranks and removed as chief.[3] In the same year, the Council of Ministers approved "Theses on the Political Organs of the Armed Forces of the U.S.S.R.," which increased the importance of these control bodies within the military establishment.[4] Finally, a new State Secrets Act in June, 1947, made it very difficult for military men to speak freely on those rare occasions when they expressed themselves in public.[5] Within two years after the war, the marshals had lost their wartime legacy of power and popularity. The Soviet military men were gradually being removed from positions of potential political temptation; meanwhile, publications—from children's history primers to General Staff treatises—no longer mentioned the wartime services of the military leaders. Military doctrine, as well as military history, was set in an impersonal mold.[6]

Two years passed before the military leadership began to emerge from this mold. In March, 1949, Marshal Vasilevsky replaced Bulganin as Minister of Defense; several months later, Colonel General of Aviation Pavel F. Zhigarev replaced Vershinin as Commander in Chief of the Air Forces; in February, 1950, a separate Ministry of the Navy was established, and in mid-1951 Kuznetsov was again made its chief, though still not with his wartime rank. In 1950 and 1951, Marshal Zhukov was permitted two brief public appearances, which, after an absence of five years, served to remind the world of his existence.[7] Evidently, Stalin had decided to resuscitate a competent military leadership. One manifestation of the increased desire for an efficient military machine was a secret decree in the fall of 1951 re-emphasizing the policy of unified command.[8] Although political officers were retained as deputy commanders, their subordination to the commanders in professional military matters was more clearly defined. At the time of the Nineteenth Party Congress in October, 1952, an unprecedented number of senior professional officers were made members of the Central Committee of the Party. Vasilevsky, Sokolovsky, Konev, and Kuznetsov became members; and twenty-six other professional marshals, generals, and admirals (including Zhukov) were given candidate status.[9]

A final development of the Stalin period was the revelation, on January 13, 1953, of the so-called "doctors' plot."[10] The announcement of the Kremlin doctors' alleged murder plot was worded like a veiled indictment of the secret police, and touched off a vigilance campaign that promised to develop into a major purge. Significantly, the alleged objects of the plot were all military men: Marshal Vasilevsky, the Minister of War; Marshal Konev, still believed to be a Deputy Minister and Inspector General; Marshal Leonid A. Govorov, Deputy Minister; General of the Army S. M. Shtemenko, Deputy

Minister and Chief of the General Staff; and Admiral A. V. Levchenko, Deputy Minister of the Navy. Even the two alleged victims—Zhdanov and Shcherbakov (who died in 1948 and 1945, respectively)—had been wartime generals, although primarily they were leading political figures. Were the military pointedly being told that they would benefit by acquiescing in the coming purge of the Party and the Police? Was the military leadership itself divided? Conspicuously absent were Marshal Zhukov, now secretly returned to be Deputy Minister and Inspector General; Marshal Sokolovsky, who appeared in February as Chief of the General Staff; and Admiral Kuznetsov, Minister of the Navy. With all these questions still unanswered, the purge died with the purger.

Another important problem of the postwar Stalin years was the effect of the Kremlin's factional intrigues on the military leaders. It is beyond the scope of this book to analyze the political maneuvering among Stalin's associates as it affected individual military leaders. But it is clear even from incomplete data that there was a vast and complex arena of such action. If we cannot trace all the detail, we can sketch much of the outline. Moreover, many of the vague outlines become clearer in the post-Stalin period.

The entrance of the military into the factional drama was caused by the new postwar relationship between political and military leaders. A few marshals had already been rated as high on the Party rolls as many of the political leaders, but the war produced new, and sometimes deep, relations based on personal acquaintance. Friendships and cliques evolved within the senior officers corps; in some cases, whole groups developed ties—or antipathies—to a political figure with whom they had served in the field or dealt in the capital. Although there was, of course, a shifting of senior commanders, two main categories developed: the Army Group and Army commanders at the front, and the *Stavka* or Supreme Headquarters planners in Moscow. The chief *Stavka* strategists, however, not only planned in Moscow; they were also sent to the field to assume temporary over-all command for major operations. Let us take the example of Stalingrad—probably the most important generally as well as in its long-run effect on personal relationships. (This example also illustrates differences that arose between the political leaders on the State Defense Committee [GKO] in Moscow and those serving in the field as political advisers to the Army Groups.) As we shall see, this historical case is relevant to current alignments.

In the field, the Army Group (Front) most directly involved in the defense of Stalingrad (now Volgograd) was the Stalingrad Front, under Colonel General Yerëmenko. Among the Army commanders in his force were Lieutenant Generals Chuikov, Malinovsky, and Moskalenko. Major General Biryuzov was Chief of Staff of the Second Guards Army under Malinovsky, and Major General Krylov was Chief of Staff of the Sixty-second Army under Chuikov. Among the other generals active in the Stalingrad operations were Rokossovsky, Batov, Bagramyan, Golikov, and Popov. The senior political adviser and member of the Military Council of the Front was Lieutenant General N. S. Khrushchev.

As the Battle of Stalingrad reached a climax and the crucial counteroffensive phase drew near, Stalin sent down not only the plans for the operation but also an echelon of senior commanders and advisers to carry it out. General of the Army Zhukov, Deputy Supreme Commander, and Colonel General Vasilevsky, Deputy Chief of the General Staff, were given over-all command. Colonel General of Aviation Novikov was placed over all air forces, and Colonel General of Artillery Voronov was later put in charge of eliminating the encirclement. Georgy Malenkov was dispatched as the State Defense Committee's representative to oversee the whole operation. Not unnaturally, some resentment was felt by most of the senior field commanders there. When Zhukov, Vasilevsky, Novikov, and Voronov were promoted to the rank of marshal for their services at Stalingrad, none of the field commanders was similarly promoted to that rank.

During the next two years, the generals who had formed the core of the field command at Stalingrad assumed command in the four Ukrainian Fronts of the armies that swept across the southern part of Central Europe. The *Stavka* marshals frequently assumed command of the various northern Byelorussian and Baltic Fronts. Thus, a rivalry that arose in the Stalingrad campaign was perpetuated. Moreover, it so happened that a disproportionate number of the commanders and the political figures whose wartime service was centered in the Ukraine were themselves, by birth or political career, associated with that region.

During the postwar Stalin period, some of the "Southern" political and military leaders, including Khrushchev, returned to the Ukraine. The military district command in Kiev was first under Chuikov, and later under Grechko; Popov was in the Crimea. Moskalenko served with Khrushchev from 1945 to 1949 and, like Khrushchev, went to Moscow in 1949. Many other generals from this clique saw service in Siberia; Malinovsky commanded the Maritime District; Krylov, the adjacent Far Eastern Military District; Zakharov and Yerëmenko, the East and West Siberian Military Districts. As we have observed,

Zhukov was for many years in a distant and minor command. But the core of Stalin's senior military command consisted of the *Stavka–* GKO leaders on whom he had learned to rely during the war years: Bulganin, Vasilevsky, Kuznetsov, Antonov, and Shtemenko. Even the field commanders and staff officers who were in favor—Konev and Govorov, Sokolovsky and Malinin—were men who were not part of the Southern clique.

Under Stalin's dictatorship, the military had been reduced to administrators of the military bureaucracy. To avoid the creation of the kinds of cliques or subdomains he had to allow during the war, Stalin juggled senior military personnel. From 1946 to 1953, they were not only cut off from politics but were even denied initiative within their own realm of competence. Though some mystery surrounds the doctors' plot on the eve of Stalin's death, with its involvement of certain military leaders, and though there may have been other political controversies in the preceding five years that affected military men, on the whole, civil-military relations in the postwar Stalin period offer little of historical significance.

With the death of Stalin the autocrat, all other major Soviet institutions automatically increased in importance.[11] Within a week, the Ministry of War under Marshal Vasilevsky and the Ministry of the Navy under Admiral Kuznetsov were combined in a new Ministry of Defense under Nikolai Bulganin. Marshal Zhukov joined Vasilevsky and Kuznetsov as First Deputy Ministers in the new establishment. But the primary reason for the armed forces' increased authority can be found in the shifts in power, and in the new relationships of other Soviet institutions.

The first major step was drastic: the purge of Beria in July, 1953, followed by downgrading the secret police. There have been rumors that Marshals Zhukov and Konev personally played a role in Beria's arrest.[12] Whether or not the rumors are well-founded, the fact is that the military did acquire new stature after the decline of the police. The same Plenum of the Central Committee that sanctioned Beria's arrest named Zhukov to Beria's vacated seat on the Central Committee. In the next three months, at least ten senior generals and admirals were promoted—the first in a series of belated promotions. Military men in disgrace were rehabilitated; Chief Marshal of Aviation Novikov, for example, was released from a labor camp. Finally, the influence of the political officers in the armed forces was gradually curbed. All this, however, did not necessarily mean a change in real political power. That such a change did occur between 1953 and 1955 was a consequence of the struggle for power between two political factions favoring divergent policies.

Malenkov, Stalin's successor as Prime Minister, sought to increase the power of the governmental and managerial institutions at the expense of the Party bureaucracy. He pursued a course aimed at increased investment in consumer-goods industries and agriculture. Khrushchev, Stalin's successor as Party Secretary, led the opposition to Malenkov's policies. Among the first indications of divergence from the Malenkov line were two discussions in a restricted General Staff journal in September and October, 1953, which emphasized the heavy-industry requirements for defense and gave only passing reference to the new consumer-goods policy.[13] By late 1954, Khrushchev and his associates had launched a campaign against Malenkov's policy and for a return to higher investment in heavy industry. The military press supported this campaign, and introduced the additional theme that heavy industry was required to raise the level of armaments.[14]

In 1953 and 1954, Malenkov reduced the announced military budget, and actual military spending fell still further. Late in 1954, as deliberations on the 1955 budget began, the conflict was intensified. Military men began to emphasize in public speeches the need for constant attention to military preparedness, while Malenkov and several of his associates, in March and again in November, 1954, pointedly and unprecedentedly did not do so.[15] These and several other issues were resolved by the January, 1955, Plenum of the Central Committee, which removed Malenkov from the premiership. The new budget, adopted at the same time, raised the military appropriation by twelve per cent and restored the larger investment in heavy industry. Another issue arose over Malenkov's practice of dipping into the state reserves (stockpiles) to accelerate the popular consumer program. This policy ended with his fall. "Reserves comprise our might and strengthen the defense capability of the country," Bulganin reassured the military in his debut as Prime Minister; "to increase the state reserve is . . . our most important task."[16]

With the triumph of Khrushchev and Bulganin over Malenkov, Marshal Zhukov became Minister of Defense. A month later, twelve generals and marshals were promoted, six to the highest rank, Marshal of the Soviet Union. Soon after, six more were promoted to General of the Army. Among those promoted in 1955 were several former close associates of Zhukov and of Konev, but also a conspicuously large number of members of the Southern clique, who may have been included at the instance of Khrushchev. Thus Moskalenko was promoted both in 1953 and 1955, becoming Marshal of the Soviet

Union in 1955; Grechko (who was not at Stalingrad, but who was a Ukrainian and a long-time close associate of Khrushchev) was also twice promoted; Chuikov, Yerëmenko, and Bagramyan became Marshals; and Krylov, Popov, M. Kazakov, and G. Zakharov were among the new Generals of the Army. Most of these generals, it should be noted, fully deserved promotion on the basis of their records.

By early 1955, at the close of the initial, or Malenkov, period of the struggle for the succession, the military seemed to have won its place in the new post-Stalin order. A new era in which there was a renaissance in military doctrine was flourishing as well.

The period from February, 1955, to October, 1957, may best be understood in terms of an alliance between Khrushchev and Zhukov, which lasted until Khrushchev concluded that Zhukov was becoming too powerful. It was not, of course, a question of equal or shared power; Khrushchev was always the more powerful. But it was an alliance of mutual convenience, born early in the post-Stalin period, in which each enjoyed the support of the other in consolidating his position. Khrushchev was building his personal power within the Party, and the power of the Party within the state; Zhukov was exercising his authority in developing Soviet military thought and training, and in building a modern military establishment. Ultimately, they clashed over the dividing line between the authority in the Party of the one and the authority within the military sphere of the other.

Khrushchev's rise was abetted by the maneuverings of various military and political men. History was rewritten to highlight Khrushchev's wartime role. Particularly during the first half of 1955, political figures whom the Party had sent to the front during the war were singled out for praise in order to divert attention from the wartime State Defense Committee in Moscow, whose key members had been Malenkov and Beria. Most often, the only living persons mentioned were Khrushchev and Bulganin. Of the senior marshals, however, only Konev—and on one occasion Chuikov and Bagramyan—participated in what was essentially a Party effort, suported by Colonel General A. V. Zheltov, chief of the main political administration. On the occasions when Konev and the political officers made their ingratiating statements, Marshals Zhukov, Vasilevsky, Sokolovsky, Biryuzov, and Admiral of the Fleet Kuznetsov studiously avoided referring to any living political figures.

Political articles—and the writings of some junior members of the

Southern clique—referred to Khrushchev's role at Stalingrad, but seldom after 1955 to Malenkov's presence there. Khrushchev's role as a wartime leader, however, was not really stressed until after Zhukov's fall from power. Similarly, following Khrushchev's ouster in October, 1964, the process of rewriting history restored him to a deservedly modest wartime role.

It is remarkable that through the late 1940's and the 1950's there were so few disagreements over strategy within the Soviet military establishment, and between it and the political leadership. Even the new doctrinal approaches in 1955, apparently caused no serious conflict. In 1955, however, a dispute developed over the value of a modern conventional ocean navy. Zhukov, supported by his Army associates, and Khrushchev decided to cut sharply investment in a conventional navy and Admiral of the Fleet Kuznetsov—who evidently objected—was replaced by Admiral Sergei Gorshkov (a Southerner, both in wartime and postwar service). Later, in 1956, there probably were disputes over operational control of long-range ballistic rockets and over future manned-bomber programs. Chief Marshal of Aviation Zhigarev was relieved and named Chief of the Civil Air Fleet, to conduct the development of modern jet transports built instead of bombers, while long-range missiles were organized under a separate command to be headed by Chief Marshal of Artillery M. I. Nedelin.

Within the Soviet military establishment, interservice rivalries may have existed—and may now exist—on a wider scale than observers in the West can divine. But, for several reasons, such rivalries cannot reach the scope and intensity of comparable rivalries in major Western countries. One reason is the historical tradition of the land-oriented, continental horizon of the Russian military and the dominance of the ground soldiers. A second is political—the severe limitations on the development of any point of view that has not already been sanctioned by the Party leadership. By its very nature, the Soviet political system does not encourage the belief that such thinking, even in private, is in the national interest. A third reason is sociological and psychological: the difficulty of developing new ideas without expressing, debating, and refining them, and the near-impossibility of getting some service minority to adopt unofficial ideas. Finally, the ideological-political foundation of Soviet military thought is based on a conviction of the need for and value of a balanced and varied military capability, which discourages interest in theories proclaiming the superiority and sufficiency of any particular service.

The Twentieth Congress of the CPSU in February, 1956, marked both the consolidation of past leadership and policies—in the military establishment, as well as in the Party—and the initiation of new ones. Marshal Zhukov was made a candidate member of the Presidium of the Party, the first professional officer ever granted such status. He, Konev, Sokolovsky, and Vasilevsky were retained as members of the Central Committee; Malinovsky and Moskalenko were added. Twelve other military leaders were made candidate members, a considerable decrease from the former representation. The complete absence of senior officers of the political administration was unprecedented, and shows their decline in importance under Zhukov's administration of the Ministry of Defense.

The selection of officers acceptable to Khrushchev had great political significance. In addition to raising Malinovsky and Moskalenko to membership (the latter had not previously been a candidate), the Committee gave candidate status to Bagramyan, Chuikov, and Yerëmenko—all from the Southern clique. Particularly in the cases of Moskalenko and Grechko, it was evident that Party Secretary Khrushchev was selecting factional adherents. Although Khrushchev showed some favor to the Southern clique, to other personal friends and supporters, and to Zhukov's personal rival Konev, the Khrushchev-Zhukov axis remained in force. In the course of his "secret" speech denouncing the cult of Stalin, Khrushchev praised the wartime commanders in general and Marshal Zhukov in particular, standing as Zhukov's loyal defender against Stalin's hints that Zhukov was not a good soldier. The military, gratified by the opportunity afforded by the deflated Stalin image, continued to revise military history and doctrine, and quietly went about rehabilitating military men whom Stalin had purged.

Both before and after the Party Congress, the authority of the professional commanders was largely free of political interference. In late 1955, the position of political officer at the company level was abolished. Senior officers were permitted to meet the compulsory political-education requirements by what was euphemistically termed "self-study." But the relationship between the Party organizations and the professional commanders needed clarification. Accordingly, in April, 1957, the Central Committee decreed *Instructions to the CPSU Organizations in the Soviet Army and Navy* to replace those issued ten years earlier.[17] This decree, and an accompanying order from the Minister of Defense, marked a compromise between Army and Party views on the division of authority. But the compromise did not settle the issue; various discussions still emphasized the restrictions placed on either the political organs or the officers.

The four lines of command—the professional military, the political administration, the Party organization, and the secret-police counter-intelligence—have always extended from the ministry itself into every battalion of the armed forces. But by 1957, the professional military had gained in influence relative to the others.

Suddenly, in June, 1957, Khrushchev's various opponents in the Party leadership joined in an effort to depose him. Malenkov, Molotov, and Kaganovich obtained a majority in the Presidium, but Khrushchev refused to accept their decision. He insisted upon carrying the matter to the Central Committee, which is always heavy with men of the Party machine and which, moreover, he had packed with his supporters at the Twentieth Party Congress. It was a critical time for Khrushchev, and although he was supported by many key Party officials, unquestionably it was of great, conceivably crucial, importance that he also had the full support of Marshal Zhukov and the military. Zhukov told the Central Committee Plenum that the Soviet armed forces would not "permit" anyone to "bid for power." Now elected to full membership in the Presidium, Zhukov subsequently spoke "on behalf of the armed forces" in pledging continued support to the Party leadership under Khrushchev.[18]

This was the apogee of the Khrushchev-Zhukov axis. Indeed, these two seemed to be the most powerful men in the Soviet Union. But could the newly successful Party chief permit Zhukov such a position? This time, Zhukov had extralegally pledged the Army's support to Khrushchev, but, on some future occasion, might he not attempt to range this power against him? Should Party Presidium member Zhukov be permitted to make charged political statements "on behalf of the armed forces"? One facet of the new situation from June to October, 1957, was Khrushchev's wariness of the Marshal's rising power and popularity. But two other facets also deeply affected the civil-military relationship.

We have noted the flux in internal power relationships following the death of Stalin. The professional Party apparatus under Khrushchev ultimately became dominant, but this was not so in 1953 or 1955, or indeed, until 1957. With the purge of Beria, the power of the police had been drastically reduced. The governmental and managerial bureaucracy had been greatly weakened by the two defeats of Malenkov and his associates, and by decentralization. Meanwhile, the Party leaders were divided. The military gained in relative importance from these changes, and under Zhukov, they acquired a substantial degree of autonomy. The whole trend of his administration was, while not anti-Party, non-Party. "Military science" itself was defined in terms stressing purely professional military competence. This clashed with Party policy, not because the military sought to usurp political prerogatives, but because it threatened to become a self-contained professional body within the state. Khrushchev and the Party could not accept this, since their whole aim was to revitalize the Party as the driving force in all activities of the state. It is precisely the growing tendency toward an autonomous, professional governmental and economic bureaucracy, a would-be independent intelligentsia, and a professionally autonomous military establishment, which the Party has considered a main internal concern.

Another aspect of the basic incompatability of the Khrushchev-Zhukov axis is worth considering. In words unlikely to reappear in the post-Zhukov era, a Soviet General Staff organ (circulated among selected Soviet officers) stated in 1955: "The missions of strategy are set by politics, but political leaders must know the potentialities of strategy, in order to set tasks before it skillfully at each concrete historical stage."[19] As Zhukov pressed for recognition of the principle that career officers should not be criticized in Party meetings or by political officers, he evidently began to assume that as the leading military strategist he could not be challenged on strategic judgments in the Presidium of the Party. Although the evidence is not conclusive, there are good reasons to believe that in the months from June to October, 1957, Zhukov spoke with authority not only on military strategy in the specific sense of doctrine and plans (over which there was no dispute), but also on strategic implications of other policies. In short, since military and political strategy must be integrated, Zhukov wanted to do some of the integrating. But so did Khrushchev, and the outcome is well known. Accordingly, since Zhukov's ouster, the military strategists have resumed the role of framing military strategy on the basis of policy handed down from the Presidium.

The removal of Marshal Zhukov was accomplished by a devious stratagem, though with no overt signs of difficulty. Zhukov was sent on a visit to Yugoslavia in October, 1957, and while he was in Belgrade a week-long extension of his trip, to include a visit to Albania, was announced. Thus Zhukov was kept out of Moscow for a three-week period while Khrushchev lined up Malinovsky and others in the military and political leadership for his removal. On October 26, Zhukov returned to Moscow and was met by a delegation of military and political leaders who informed him of his dismissal from the post of Defense Minister, a move immediately made public. Then, for several days the public was kept in the dark, while an extended discussion of the whole matter of military-political relations took place in the Central Committee. Finally, on November 2, it was announced that Zhukov had also been removed from the Presidium and the Central Committee; he was castigated for fostering a personal cult, and for attempting to "abolish the leadership and control of the Party" over the armed forces. The initial plan had been to shift Zhukov quietly to a post of no real authority, but when he fought the issue, there could be no compromise short of his capitulation, disgrace, and complete retirement.

It seemed likely that Marshal Konev would succeed Zhukov. Konev was the senior First Deputy, a rival of Zhukov's, and he had been ready to help Khrushchev with the rewriting of his wartime service. But Khrushchev selected Marshal Malinovsky, the third-ranking military man and the senior marshal of the Southern-Stalingrad clique. At the same time, Sokolovsky, Zhukov's Chief of Staff, who had been Chief of the General Staff of the armed forces ever since the late days of Stalin, continued in office. Initially, all of the deputy ministers were retained. Thus Khrushchev allayed any suspicion of a large-scale purge of the High Command. In a sense, he showed that he recognized the political importance of the military institution and that he did not intend to attack it. But Malinovsky was not given Presidium status, and the armed forces were again given a position below the national policy-making level. Now Khrushchev's was clearly the final voice in matters of national security—the one that Marshal Zhukov had begun to assert before his fall.

Marshal Malinovsky's former position as First Deputy Minister and Commander in Chief of the Ground Forces went to Khrushchev's old friend Marshal Grechko. In the year following Zhukov's ouster, nearly two thirds of the military-district and other key commands were shifted.[20] Most of these were routine transfers, but some close associates of Zhukov were removed. As a result of the shuffling of posts in the High Command, an interesting picture emerged: the Southern clique came to hold most of the key positions. Malinovsky, of course, was now Minister; Grechko headed the ground forces; Popov was deputy to Grechko; Yerëmenko had come to Moscow to head the Academy of the General Staff (the Soviet National War College, which until 1958 had been named for Voroshilov); Bagramyan had become Deputy Minister and Chief of the Rear Services for the whole military establishment; Golikov became head of the Political Administration; Moskalenko and Chuikov remained in their key command positions at Moscow and Kiev, and Krylov now joined them at the third center as commander of the Leningrad Military District. Admiral Gorshkov remained naval chief. But, as we have noted, Marshal Konev was still the senior First Deputy Minister for General Affairs and head of the Warsaw Pact Command, and Marshal Sokolovsky remained as First Deputy Minister and Chief of the General Staff of the Soviet Armed Forces.

In April, 1960, Marshals Sokolovsky and Konev, the two remaining holdovers from the Zhukov administration, were retired. They were the leading military men who had not publicly supported Khrushchev's announcement of January 14, 1960, to reduce the armed forces substantially and to alter its force structure. All of the key places in the Soviet Military High Command were now filled by members of the Southern clique. Marshal Grechko assumed Konev's post, Marshal M. Zakharov took Sokolovsky's place, and Marshal Chuikov moved up from Kiev to Grechko's old position, fourth in the hierarchy, as Commander in Chief of Ground Forces. In May, 1960, some 267 generals and 30 admirals were promoted. Later in 1960, upon the death of Chief Marshal of Artillery Nedelin, Moskalenko was named Chief of the Rocket Troops, and General Krylov assumed command of the key Moscow Military District. In April, 1962, Marshal S. Biryuzov replaced Moskalenko as Commander in Chief of the Strategic Rocket Forces; Marshal of Aviation V. Sudets replaced Biryuzov as Commander in Chief, Air Defense Forces; and Moskalenko replaced Chief Inspector Marshal Rokossovsky, who retired.

Disputes with Khrushchev over military policy continued, and in March, 1963, Marshal Zakharov was replaced as Chief of the General Staff by Marshal Biryuzov. Marshal Krylov succeeded Biryuzov as Commander in Chief of the Strategic Rocket Forces. In July, 1964, Marshal Chuikov was publicly named Chief of Civil Defense, but lost his other position as Commander in Chief of Ground Forces. Sometime in mid-1965, after the ouster of Khrushchev, Chuikov was restored to the Ground Forces command.

And what of the Stavka marshals? Zhukov, Vasilevsky, Sokolovsky, Kuznetsov, Novikov, and Voronov are now in retirement. (On the political side, former GKO members Beria, Malenkov, and Bulganin have left the stage.) Although various considerations enter into command appointments, the difference in the fates of these two major cliques is dramatic.

At the Twenty-second Party Congress in November, 1961, military representation on the Central Committee was substantially enlarged. The number of full voting members was increased from six to fourteen: Marshals Malinovsky, Grechko, Zakharov, Moskalenko, Chuikov, Biryuzov, Vershinin, Golikov, Bagramyan, Konev, Krylov, Admiral of the Fleet Gorshkov, General of the Army Yakubovsky, and Admiral Fokin. The number of candidate members was raised from twelve to seventeen. In all, 23 of the 31 had been members of the Southern clique.

The military leadership since 1960 has been more cohesive than in any other recent period, though there are personal and service differences that may give rise to differing attitudes. During Khrushchev's rule, all owed their status largely to his favor. But although the fortunes of individuals are of interest when they are as persistent and as politically relevant as they were in the case of Khrushchev's association with the Southern clique of marshals, the main question has always been institutional. Marshal Malinovsky is, after all, absorbed with military interests and charged with defining, advocating, and fulfilling military requirements. Actually, the institutional autonomy of the military establishment was not basically altered by Zhukov's fall. And, inevitably, it led to conflicts between Khrushchev and the marshals, and will almost certainly lead to differences between the marshals and Khrushchev's successors.

Since 1960, the significance of the World War II clique alignments has faded. Differences over policy among the military leaders, and between them and the political leaders, have become more important. Thus, months before Khrushchev's fall, Marshal Malinovsky went so far as to speak favorably of Marshal Zhukov's role in the Stalingrad campaign, and even indirectly to slight Khrushchev's role.

Inasmuch as one of the key charges against Zhukov had concerned his attempts to avoid Party-political interference in the military, the regime set out to restore Party control at all levels. In what may have seemed a paradoxical move, Colonel General Zheltov, the chief of the main political administration since 1953, was replaced a few months after Zhukov's ouster by a spit-and-polish professional officer —a Southerner from Stalingrad—Colonel General (later Marshal) Filip A. Golikov. In terms of what the regime has attempted to do, however, this move was readily understandable.

In the post-Zhukov era, considerable stress has been placed on creating a real relationship between professional and Party-political interests. This has been neither easy nor altogether successful. Soviet military newspapers have indicated a persistent failure to achieve real rapport between Party-political work and professional interests. But if the autonomous interests of the military career officers have not been dissolved, their further development has been arrested. The

Instructions of the Central Committee to Party organizations were revised late in 1958, and *Instructions* were also issued to Komsomol organs, to remove some of the ambiguous allowances made in the compromise effected in 1957. A new *Decree on Political Organs of the Armed Forces* was also issued in October, 1958.[21] In short, an effort has been and is still being made to interest professional commanders and staff officers in Party-political work, and to provide a better grounding in military affairs to political officers and Party units. A model, if not a goal, of interchangeability has been mentioned—and indeed was personified—by Golikov; and leading commanders at lower levels are being urged to assume the leadership of local Party units.[22] But creating, rather than merely promulgating, a higher degree of Party-political consciousness throughout the armed forces has been difficult. Golikov was later replaced by a one-time police and Party figure, "General" A. A. Yepishev, in May, 1962. And in 1963, new Party *Instructions* were issued, which have not had notable effect.

The higher levels of command have also been affected by the efforts to establish a closer rapport between the professional commanders and the political and Party organs. Soon after the fall of Zhukov, in April, 1958, a *Decree on Military Councils* resurrected the institution of the Military Council, with the senior officer of the political administration in each military district or Army Group serving as a member along with the two or three senior commanders. Similarly, a new tie has been cultivated between the military district and the corresponding regional republic or oblast-level Party organs. Both developments bring the officer corps more nearly parallel with the local governmental, agricultural, and managerial bureaucracies, and leave it less of an autonomous and self-contained system. In June, 1963, Committees of Party-State Control were also introduced into the armed forces.

The military leadership is called upon for counsel when certain major policy issues are discussed, before the final decision by the Presidium and its submission to the Central Committee of the Party. The military advise as technical specialists, but it is difficult to separate such advice from participation in making national strategy and foreign policy.

The most sensitive issue of the period since Zhukov's ouster was the Party and Government decision late in 1959 to reduce drastically the size of the armed forces. At that time, the drastic cut planned could be accomplished only by altering the structure of the forces. This program, announced by Khrushchev on January 14, 1960, had many purposes and implications. Those most affected by the decision were the military leaders—indeed the whole career officer corps. On this issue, the political leadership prevailed only in part. As a whole, the military leaders accepted and implemented the decision, but they also stubbornly fought an effective rear-guard action. They were apparently given the deciding voice in allocating military reductions and in shaping the force structure under the politically imposed man-power ceiling. The decision of July, 1961, to suspend the reduction of forces and to resume nuclear testing, though gratifying to the military leaders, was clearly a political decision related to the crisis unfolding over Berlin. Subsequent reductions in 1963–64 were grudg-ingly effected.

The Party is dominant—but not omnipotent—in Soviet society. The Party leadership, comprising the Presidium and the Central Com-mittee, is responsible for political decision-making; it also provides the arena in which policy conflicts are decided. The top leaders func-tion as Party representatives in their other assignments, but in the top Party councils they represent those other interests and institutions with which they are associated. If the interests of the Party are all-encompassing, so too is the range of interests which are brought to bear in its deliberations. Only a powerful minority of the top Party leaders are fully and exclusively identified with the Party machine, those in the Party's chief executive body, the Secretariat. All believe that the Party's requirements—for defense security, heavy industry, light industry and consumer goods, agriculture, ties with other Com-munist parties, and foreign policy—must be met; but, not surpris-ingly, they differ on the relative weight that should be assigned to each. Moreover, these interests not only complement one another, they also compete and conflict. Some leaders see a need for greater emphasis on heavy industry, others, on light industry; some believe a wider range of military capabilities is necessary, others believe retrenchment is possible and desirable in certain military fields.

Marshal Malinovsky is, of course, a long-time, loyal Party man, but he and his colleagues are chiefly concerned with military require-ments. It is as spokesmen for the military that their voices are heard in senior Party councils. Of course, Khrushchev and Brezhnev also want military security for the U.S.S.R., as well as military power which can be used politically to extend Soviet influence. But the political and military leaders have differed about the share of over-all outlays the military requires.

Sharp differences over many questions, including military policy and especially the size and shape of the military establishment, have arisen in the Central Committee. These came to the surface in the mid-1950's, in the Malenkov period, and again since 1960, when it became clear that the military leadership as a whole disagreed with Khrushchev's—and his successors'—policies of retrenchment, and with some of the related developments in the détente period such as the moratorium on all nuclear testing from 1958 to 1961, and later the August, 1963, treaty banning atmospheric nuclear testing. They probably were wary of Khrushchev's gamesmanship in the disarmament field—as were the Chinese. Above all, they disapproved of the unilateral military force reductions that were undertaken in 1960–61 and again in 1963–64.

All have been in favor of having a militarily strong Soviet Union. There may be differences, for example, over such questions as whether to install an antimissile system. But belief in a strong intercontinental offensive and defensive position is common to both the radical modernist and the conservative military schools as well as to the political leadership, despite any differences about details. What *has* been at issue is whether the requirements for waging and winning a general nuclear war, as they are seen by the military, need to be met. Khrushchev and some of his colleagues and successors evidently believe that these requirements need *not* be met, partly because they don't expect and don't want a general nuclear war, and also because theirs is a different attitude on what would be really decisive and necessary should a general nuclear war occur. From this standpoint, Khrushchev was always "radical" *beyond* the modernist school of professional opinion.

Khrushchev's sudden removal from power in October, 1964, was neither opposed nor regretted by the military leaders, who had been hard-pressed on military policy issues; but there is no indication that the military played an active role in the conspiracy to remove Khrushchev. Indeed, on the very eve of Khrushchev's downfall, a number of leading marshals praised Khrushchev's wartime role in their articles commemorating the twentieth anniversary of the liberation of the Ukraine. Had they known of his imminent displacement, they probably would have omitted such praise. Marshal Malinovsky was probably informed by the Party leaders shortly before they acted; we do not know. What we do know is that in the subsequent reshuffling of posts no career military men were promoted. (This contrasts with the rise of former secret police chief Aleksander Shelepin to full membership in the Presidium, and with the attainment of current KGB chief Vladimir Semichastny and of chief political commissar in the armed forces General Aleksander Yepishev to full membership in the Central Committee.)

In late September, 1964, Khrushchev used the occasion of a meeting of several score leading Soviet Government and Party officials to reveal elements of a new, major economic development plan. As can be seen even from the truncated version of Khrushchev's speech published in *Pravda* on October 2, he called for a drastic shift away from heavy–and defense–industry. The conservative Party leaders and the military chiefs, and even the usual supporters of consumer-goods industrialization, were not convinced by the wide sweep of Khrushchev's proposals. It is very likely that Khrushchev's intention to press for this radical shift at the November Central Committee Plenum contributed to the decision for his removal in mid-October. In this, as on many earlier occasions, the military were only a part of a coalition involving individual leaders and interest groups. No one can predict the alignments for future resource allocations. The 1965 budget was a middle-of-the-road compromise, with a modest 3.8 per cent reduction in the open defense budget.*

Coincidentally, only a few days after Khrushchev was deposed, Chief of the General Staff Marshal Semën Biryuzov was killed in an aircraft accident. Biryuzov was the most prominent military leader to support Khrushchev's reliance on strategic missile deterrence and counterdeterrence (though he may have favored a larger strategic missile force). After more than a month, the new leadership named as successor Marshal Matvei Zakharov—presumably Malinovsky's selection. Marshal Zakharov had been Malinovsky's chief of staff in the Second Ukrainian Front in 1944–45 and during the brief Manchurian campaign in the Far East. He had, moreover, served as Chief of the General Staff from the time of Sokolovsky's compulsory retirement in April, 1960, until March, 1963, when he in turn was replaced by Biryuzov—probably at least in part for his opposition to Khrushchev's pressures for more force cuts. On doctrinal matters, Zakharov, like Malinovsky, has been an "enlightened conservative." Each is in his late sixties—scarcely "new blood."

The Khrushchev era marked a transformation in military thought and in the military establishment. Political-military relations moved through several stages. At the end of the Khrushchev period, the military leadership was still excluded from the top councils, but its voice significantly influenced key decisions on resource allocations.

---

* For a discussion of the relation of the Soviet military budget to actual military spending, see Chapter 5.

Differences among military leaders have ranged from those who were so bold as to approach the Khrushchev image of a "new look" posture on the one extreme to very conservative men with a traditional image of war on the other. For example, conservative military judgment still holds that economic preparations must provide the requirements for months or years of military operations in a general nuclear war. The official compromise that has emerged—and it is constantly under review—can be called an enlightened conservative position.

The Soviet political system at the top has changed enough in the last decade so that different views are being expressed in various publications. All the leaders feel that they are dedicated to the best interests of the Communist Party and the Soviet Union, and they don't really distinguish between the two. Yet the views of some of the Party leaders whose chief interests and experience, and perhaps present support, are associated with the economic managerial group, differ from those of the military. In general, the most notable differences are those concerned with resource allocations.

Party control over the military is supreme. But in one sense the military is more the master of its own house than it would be if it had a civilian defense minister. The chief political-military issue of the mid-1950's was the role of party indoctrination and institutional control. The main issue of the 1960's concerns concrete military policy and programming.

It is not enough to say that the Party decides on policy and that the military (or the managers and engineers) implements it. The real situation is not so simple. Party leaders can—and do—differ on what is best or most needed for the Soviet Union. The Kremlin leaders share the view that "what is good for the Soviet Union is good for the world revolution." There can be—as there have been—differing views in Moscow as to what military posture the U.S.S.R. presently requires. The military leaders are among those who feel that they need a very strong and broadly balanced military posture, whereas prominent political leaders—Brezhnev and Kosygin, as well as Khrushchev—are agreed that the requirements of deterrence and aggressive counterdeterrence or blackmail, in short the political uses of military power, permit them to cut down on some parts of the military establishment which military planners would prefer to retain to meet all contingencies.

An analysis of the future of civil-military relations in the U.S.S.R. depends primarily upon a prognosis of the state of the political leadership and of the evolution of the Soviet society and state. Two things seem clear. First, the long-run tendencies toward the growth of professional interests (including the military) seem stronger than the prospect of a successful renaissance of Party *élan;* and second, when Khrushchev's successors from the Stalin regime and the various military leaders from the war period eventually fade from the scene, the new generation of military leaders will probably be more professional and less bound to the political leaders either by ideology or by the personal bonds of wartime service. This by no means implies direct conflict between the military and political leaderships; the military are not likely to try to assume a leading role in the political realm unless there is a collapse of the Party's rule. It does mean, however, that within another decade or so, military-political relations will be entering a new phase.

II

Military Considerations in the Formulation of Soviet Foreign Policy

4. Ideology and the Balance of Power

The question is often raised whether "Communism" is a cover for an essentially Russian nationalistic aggression, or whether the leaders of the U.S.S.R. are doctrinaire fanatics seeking only to further the expansionist aims of Communist ideology. Soviet strategic aims in areas adjacent to the U.S.S.R. have in many instances been similar to those of pre-revolutionary Russia; as a consequence, casual observers sometimes give undue weight to the first hypothesis. It was Russia's foreign policy to pursue these territorial aims as ends in themselves, behaving in a manner no more and no less imperialistic than its Western counterparts, limiting its objectives to the acquisition of warm-water outlets and the occasional conquest of neighboring states. Certainly the Czars did *not* assume that peace and stable relations with the rest of the world were impossible. This is the crucial feature that has distinguished Imperial Russian from Communist foreign policy.* The Soviet leaders have asserted, and their actions have seemed to confirm, that they consider the Soviet Union as a mere beginning, an embryo of a world Communist state or commonwealth of states, to which every people and country on earth must be added before the ultimate victory of the Communist revolution. In short, they aim, at least theoretically, at the annihilation of all independent power in the world.

Since the Communist ideology sanctions the pursuit of power, the leadership of the Soviet state can resort to complete political expediency without moral hindrance, rationalizing in terms of Communist ideological demands. Even if the asserted goals of Communism are submerged forever in the pursuit of power, there has been no need openly to question and reject the fundamentals of the ideology. Those elements of Marxism-Leninism that *do* correspond to power relations and power situations of the Soviet state are accepted and stressed, while those elements that are *not* applicable or subject to easy manipulation shrivel into ceremonial liturgy.

As we shall see in the present and subsequent chapters, significant

* This point has been more fully developed and illustrated in Chapter 1.

shifts in the application of ideology to current operative policy issues raise the question of a change in the basic relationship between Communist ideology and Soviet policy.

To return to the opening question, then, the Soviet leadership has always been oriented both by Soviet self-interest and by the dictates of ideology, inextricably combined to impel the Soviet power drive. This dual impetus to power resulted almost from the beginning in a dual foreign policy. Operating on two levels, this policy supports both the long-range goal of world revolution and the present security and aggrandizement of the Soviet state.

When the Bolshevik leaders seized power in 1917, they did not immediately recognize the diplomatic difficulties of their dual role as directors of the world Communist movement and rulers of the Soviet state. While acting as the government of one nation, they openly aided groups whose avowed purpose was the subversion of other governments. Thus, at Brest-Litovsk in 1918, the Bolshevik peace delegation damaged its bargaining position by trying to act simultaneously as representatives of a sovereign power and as Bolshevik agitators. Similarly, the first Soviet diplomatic mission (to Germany, in 1918) was expelled within the year for its revolutionary activities. This taught the Bolshevik leaders that the foreign policy obligations imposed by statehood in Russia made overt diplomatic activities incompatible with subversive ones. As a result, they created separate organs to implement their dual policy: the People's Commissariat (later Ministry) of Foreign Affairs, in charge of Soviet diplomatic relations, and the Communist (Third) International, or Comintern, in charge of the world Communist movement. Although the Comintern ostensibly had no connection with the Soviet Government except for its adherence to common ideology, it remained under the control of the Bolshevik leadership. Sometimes the separate organs were poorly coordinated, and inconsistent policies led to paradoxical situations. For example, in the German crisis of 1923, the Red Army supplied the Reichswehr with munitions at the very time the Reichswehr was crushing a Communist uprising in Hamburg. By 1928, however, complete coordination was effected. By this time, the Soviet leaders realized that their real power lay in the Soviet state and not in the world proletariat. Accordingly, Comintern policy became merely an adjunct of Soviet policy, convenient as a propaganda outlet and as a catalyst for occasional revolutionary action, but completely subjugated to the state interests of the U.S.S.R. When the realities of diplomatic life later demanded it, in May, 1943, the

Russians dissolved the formal Comintern structure, but they abandoned neither its aims nor its underground assets. Stalin openly explained: "The dissolution of the Communist International is *correct and timely* because it facilitates the organization of the common attack . . . against the common enemy—Hitlerism." That is, it facilitated diplomatic concord with the Western democracies.[1] In 1947, when the alliance had served its purpose and the Soviet postwar line of hostility emerged, an international Communist organ was resurrected in the Cominform. The Cominform, in turn, was dissolved in 1956 in the course of de-Stalinization.

The Soviet leadership has of course direct lines of communication with the various foreign Communist parties. In return for obedience to policy dictates from Moscow, the parties are supported in their overt and subversive activities. In his closing address to the Nineteenth Congress of the CPSU in October, 1952, Stalin acknowledged the practice of subsidizing the national parties and pledged continued Soviet aid.[2] In recent years, the relation of many foreign Communist parties to Moscow has changed.

The emergence of the Soviet state not only required the creation of a dual policy; it also necessitated a basic readjustment of Communist ideology to explain the role of the U.S.S.R. vis-à-vis the rest of the world. Let us see, then, how the Soviet leadership has conceived and utilized the Soviet Union's status as a sovereign state among nations.

Among the basic Marxian tenets that had to be readapted after 1917 was the concept of inevitable capitalist hostility, embodied in the theory of "class struggle." The new socialist state faced "capitalist encirclement"; the whole of the outside (capitalist) world was committed to unrelenting hostility toward the Communist state and an encircling ring of capitalist nations bent upon destroying the Soviet regime. The early Bolsheviks seized upon the inherited war with Germany (1917–18) and the subsequent Allied and Polish interventions in the Russian Civil War (1918–21) as proof of capitalism's hostile intentions; and the concept has remained in Bolshevik dogma ever since. A typical statement was contained in Stalin's address to the Central Committee of the Communist Party in 1937:

> Capitalist encirclement is no empty phrase. It is a very real and unpleasant feature. Capitalist encirclement means that there is one country, the Soviet Union, which has established the Socialist order on its own territories and besides this there are many countries, bourgeois

countries, which continue to carry on a capitalist mode of life and surround the Soviet Union, waiting for an opportunity to attack it, to break it, or at any rate, to undermine its power and weaken it. Our comrades forget this fundamental fact. But it is precisely this fact which determines the basis of relation between the capitalist encircling countries and the Soviet Union.[3]

According to Bolshevik theory, the capitalist encirclement presented a twofold threat. First, the intelligence services of the encircling powers attempted to spread internal dissidence within the U.S.S.R. This theme, although asserted earlier, was enormously intensified during the Great Purges of 1936–38, and again in the period of ideological rearmament following World War II. Whether or not the suspicion was sincere, it was a useful rationalization of internal disciplinary measures.

The second, and basic, danger was armed intervention from outside the Soviet Union. Stalin frequently made such statements as:

> The defeat of the first intervention did not destroy the danger of new intervention, inasmuch as the source of the danger of intervention— the capitalist encirclement—continued to exist. Neither would the danger of intervention be destroyed by the defeat of the new intervention if the capitalist encirclement continued to exist.[4]

Again, in his much publicized "Letter to Ivan Ivanov" in 1938, Stalin stated: "Only blockheads or masked enemies . . . can deny the danger of military intervention and of attempts at restoration [of capitalism] as long as the capitalist encirclement exists."[5]

This "danger" of armed intervention was not always considered imminent, but varied with the world political situation. In the Soviet view, a "breathing spell" or "temporary balance of forces" between the capitalist encirclement and the Soviet state came into being after the peace with Germany in 1918, and the defeat of the foreign military "interventionists" and White counterrevolutionary forces (1918– 22). It was clearly to the Russians' interest to postpone a recurrence of "intervention" while building and consolidating strength. This basis of Soviet policy was stated in *Izvestiya* in 1929 with a quotation from Lenin:

> The later the imperialist front attacks the Soviet Union, the longer can we peacefully build our socialist economy, the longer will the Communist parties of the West be able to close the ranks of the working class, the longer will the national revolutionary movement develop in the oriental states, and the better will conditions be for international

socialism to meet the *inevitable* attack against the Soviet state on the part of the capitalist encirclement.

Izvestiya continued:

> Therefore it is naturally the first and most basic principle of Leninist foreign policy to extend as long as possible the breathing spell which Soviet Russia first gained for herself during the Brest period. The extension of this breathing spell appears as the basic and most substantial formula of the foreign policy of the Soviet Union.[6]

Soviet diplomacy is credited with having preserved this delicate "breathing spell" or "temporary balance of forces" by the skillful utilization of "contradictions" among the imperialist states. By the Soviets' own definition:

> Soviet foreign policy is . . . scientifically based. It is flexible and tactically wise . . . [it] distinguishes the sharp contradictions between capitalist countries and utilizes them in the interest of the Soviet state. . . . A minute study of these contradictions and their roots is the necessary condition for the successful conduct of the foreign policy of the Soviet state.[7]

Aggravating and capitalizing upon the contradictions in the capitalist world requires flexibility and expediency, qualities often praised in Soviet writings: "Precise calculation of the relation of forces, the greatest flexibility and maneuverability, courage, firm and iron will in the execution of set tasks, have always played a decisive role in the successful realization of the foreign policy of the Soviet state.[8]

In the Soviet view, capitalist intervention was prevented for over twenty years by Soviet foreign policy's skillful manipulation of inter-capitalist contradictions, as reflected in the treaties of Rapallo in 1922, Berlin in 1926, with France in 1934, and with Nazi Germany in 1939. When the "inevitable attack" predicted by Lenin occurred in June, 1941, it was again Soviet manipulative skill, so the line goes, that enabled the U.S.S.R. to gain the Atlantic powers as temporary allies for the duration of the threat from Germany, and to neutralize the Japanese threat.

Throughout this period, the Soviet Union remained the sole "socialist" state, enclosed within a vast encirclement of imperialist states. But just as World War I had given birth to the first Soviet "socialist" state, so World War II was expected to create further "socialist" states in its aftermath.[9] With a good deal more manipulation—not to mention the presence of Soviet armies in Eastern Europe—this is precisely what occurred. As the Communists effected one coup after another in the satellites in 1947–48, a new theme emerged in the postwar line of Soviet policy, displacing though not eclipsing the theme of capitalist encirclement. This was the formulation of the "two camps"; now, the Soviet Union no longer stood alone but was surrounded by "friendly socialist states," or "people's democracies." Thus a "favorable alteration in the relation of forces" had prevailed between the capitalist encirclement and the Soviet Bloc, transforming them into "two camps" roughly equal in strength.

Andrei Zhdanov's speech at the formation of the Cominform in September, 1947, officially set the new course. He opened with these words:

> The end of the Second World War brought with it big changes in the world situation. The military defeat of the bloc of fascist states, the character of the war as a war of liberation from fascism, and the decisive role played by the Soviet Union in the vanquishing of the fascist aggressors, sharply altered the alignment of forces between the two systems—the Socialist and the capitalist—in favor of Socialism.

And later in the speech:

> The fundamental changes caused by the war in the international scene and in the position of individual countries has entirely changed the political landscape of the world. A new alignment of political forces has arisen. The more the war recedes into the past, the more distinct become two major trends in postwar international policy, corresponding to the division of the political forces operating in the international arena into two major camps: the imperialist and anti-democratic camp on the one hand, and the anti-imperialist and democratic camp, on the other.[10]

The concept of "two camps" was not new. As early as 1919, Stalin stated: "The world has decisively and unalterably split into two camps: the camp of imperialism and the camp of socialism."[11] Until 1947, however, it was a subordinate theme, accepted as an implicit and incidental aspect of capitalist encirclement. In the postwar Stalin period it largely replaced the encirclement theme. The accretions of the "people's democracies" in Eastern Europe, East Germany, and the Chinese People's Republic were heralded on all occasions as the "main weights" in the "favorable alteration of forces" between the two opposed camps. The idea was expressed repeatedly, as by Malenkov in the peroration to his address before the Nineteenth Party

Congress, "Comrades! The Soviet state is now no more a lonely island surrounded by capitalist countries."[12]

Until 1947, the Russians did not clearly designate a "leader" of the capitalist camp, although Great Britain and "the Anglo-American imperialists" were most frequently cast in that role. Since that time, however, the United States has explicitly been accorded the honor, "heading the camp of imperialism, as the center of attraction of aggressive and reactionary forces in the whole world." The Soviet Union was of course described as "heading the camp of socialism and democracy, as the center of attraction of all progressive forces struggling to prevent a new war and to consolidate peace."[13]

Although the theme of capitalist encirclement was subdued in the late Stalin years, it was by no means abandoned. Apparently, the new "balance of forces" of the late 1940's and early 1950's led some theorists even in the late period of Stalin's rule to discount Western "aggressive" intentions and to venture that the encirclement concept was now completely outmoded. In February, 1953, *Pravda* reacted as follows:

> Certain propagandists have engaged in an academic dispute over whether capitalist encirclement of the Soviet Union continues to exist or has faded into the past. Dogmatists and doctrinaire people have been found who have begun to assert that once the people's democracies friendly to us appeared on our western and eastern frontiers the question of capitalist encirclement was removed. Certain would-be theoreticians have even gone so far as to say that since the powerful camp of socialism has been formed, imperialism has ceased to be a danger to us. Such discourses are anti-Marxist and harmful.[14]

The perpetuation of the encirclement theme was useful in internal propaganda; for years, the dangers of encirclement served as the main justification for the sacrifices exacted from the Soviet people and for the disciplines of the police state. The theme was also retained in the rationale of the doctrine of "inevitable clash."

The Bolshevik leaders first bowed to the need for some form of coexistence with the capitalist world in March, 1918, when they signed the Treaty of Brest-Litovsk with the German Empire. This unorthodox compromise of the Marxian view was regarded by the "Left" Communists with strong misgivings, an attitude they maintained and frequently voiced until their fall from power in the mid-1920's.[15] Nonetheless, the decision had been made. Subsequently, Stalin did not hesitate to envision an indefinite—though *not* limitless —period of "peaceful coexistence with the capitalist encirclement."

Stalin's "peaceful coexistence," a vaguely formulated compromise that contradicted doctrine, was devised to legitimize the establishment of Soviet diplomatic relations, and later was adopted as an effective weapon in Soviet and world Communist propaganda. It was purposely elusive. In every one of Stalin's statements to foreign interviewers during the 1930's and 1940's about the possibility of peaceful coexistence, "he neglects to specify how long and on what terms."[16] The same comment applies to the frequent statements on peaceful coexistence directed to the Soviet people in the postwar Stalin period, especially after 1949.[17] One specific statement in Malenkov's report to the Nineteenth Party Congress in 1952 reveals the conditional and temporary nature of "peaceful coexistence" in the Stalinist conception:

> The Soviet policy of peace and the security of nations is based on the fact that peaceful coexistence between capitalism and Communism and collaboration are fully possible *if a mutual desire to collaborate exists, if there is a readiness to implement accepted commitments and to adhere to the principle of equality of rights and noninterference in the internal affairs of other states.* The Soviet Union always favored and favors today the development of trade and collaboration with other countries, irrespective of the difference of social systems. The Party will continue to implement this policy in the future *on the basis of mutual advantage* [italics added].[18]

It points out that coexistence is possible only if there is "mutual desire to collaborate," "readiness to implement accepted commitment," and "noninterference in the internal affairs of other states." The impartial observer cannot study the record of postwar history without seeing that the Russians simply did not fulfill their own criteria for peaceful coexistence but tried to conceal this by loudly proclaiming alleged failures by the "capitalist camp." And, by stating that this policy will continue in the future "on the basis of mutual advantage," the Russians make it clear that if it should cease to be to their advantage to continue peaceful coexistence, they would abandon it. Malenkov, in the same speech, inadvertently revealed what the Russians would consider an adequate fulfillment of the above-cited conditions for "peaceful coexistence." He spoke of "entirely new relations between states . . . built on the principles of equal rights, economic collaboration, and respect for national independence." Here was a virtual paraphrase of the stated prerequisites for peaceful coexistence—but this time Malenkov was offering the Soviet version of the relations between the U.S.S.R. and its satellites.[19]

The coexistence concept is closely linked to the concept of the "relation of forces," discussed in detail later in this chapter. In a 1925 Party report, Stalin directly referred to what he called "the *current streak* of peaceful coexistence" as "a certain *temporary* balance of forces [italics added]."[20] *Pravda* indirectly expressed the same idea in an editorial in 1952: "The *present* relation of forces between the camp of imperialism and the camp of democracy and peace makes the possibility of preserving peace and preventing a new war fully real [italics added]."[21] Thus, the relation of forces is viewed by the Russians not as an unalterable state of affairs but as the reflection of political realities that must be soberly calculated, and which can and must be manipulated in a carefully planned policy. Peace and peaceful coexistence emerged as a temporary Soviet policy, dictated by the present "balance of forces"—that is, by the "rough equality" prevailing between the two camps, which would make a war a disadvantageous and dangerous proposition. Peace was the tactical, not the strategic, goal.

The early postwar interim of "peaceful coexistence" was not allowed even a spell of genuinely—if temporarily—peaceful relations; instead, it brought the "cold war." In the 1930's, the Soviet Government was relatively so weak that pacific relations were the only course possible. But after the war, with no prospect of any effective "third force," the rough balance of the "two camps" permitted (or, to the Bolshevik, "required") a more aggressive policy. *Bol'shevik* assessed the situation in 1946, still in terms of capitalist encirclement:

it is not sufficient to guess at the schemes of the enemies, frustrate their plans and confine oneself to defense against hostile diplomatic activities. The conditions of capitalist encirclement require the application of extensive counter plans which would not only foil the enemy but would systematically improve the international position of the Soviet state.[22]

One such "counter plan" was the Soviets' massive propaganda campaign to divide the non-Communist world by presenting the Soviet Union as the ardent advocate of world peace, head of "the camp of peace and democracy" as well as head of the camp of socialism. Stalin commented that "the contemporary movement for the preservation of peace differs from the movement during World War I for the transformation of the imperialist war into a civil war" because "the latter movement went further and pursued socialist ends."[23] In other words, Stalin's peace campaign did not. In the light of this claim, it is interesting to recall Lenin's dictum on "peace programs" in 1916: "Every 'peace program' is a deception of the people and a piece of hypocrisy unless its principal object is to explain to the masses the need for a revolution, and to support, aid, and develop the revolutionary struggle of the masses."[24] It is tempting to conclude that the Stalinist "peace movement" was a hypocritical deception because it allegedly pursued peace for peace's sake, and disregarded "socialist," or Soviet, ends. There is, however, more reason to believe that the hypocrisy lay more in the latter allegation. The way the campaign was conducted; the specious issues to which it was tied (e.g., petitioning for atomic disarmament, while persistently refusing to implement an atomic-control program in the proper forum of the United Nations); the vilification of the West as the "warmongers" —these and other aspects of the campaign were certainly tactics "which would not only foil the enemy but would systematically improve the international position of the Soviet state."

The final proof of the temporary nature of "peaceful coexistence" was provided in Stalinist doctrine by the concept of the "inevitable clash." This idea was the logical outgrowth of the encirclement theme, and completes the circle of our analysis. In the Bolshevik view, since armed intervention by the capitalist nations was inevitable and their hostility implacable and undying, only one way was seen to resolve the danger for all time: "To destroy the danger of foreign capitalist intervention, the capitalist encirclement would have to be destroyed."[25] The new "balance of forces"—i.e., the greatly enhanced strength of the Communist camp since the war—did not eliminate the emphasis on capitalist "aggressive" intentions or the danger of capitalist intervention. As a writer in *Bol'shevik* stated in 1951: "The question of the conclusive victory of socialism . . . is the question of the liquidation of the capitalist encirclement which generates the danger of intervention."[26] Thus, a clash or series of clashes between capitalism and Communism was seen as inevitable, ultimately to result in the destruction of the one by the other system. Lenin, addressing the Eighth Party Congress in 1919, had said:

> We are living not only in a state but in a system of states, and *the existence of the Soviet republic side by side with imperialist states for a prolonged period is unthinkable*. At the end, either one or the other will win. And before this happens a series of the most frightful collisions between the Soviet republic and bourgeois states is *inevitable* [italics added].[27]

Stalin commented succinctly on this passage, "Clear, one would think!" and frequently quoted it in his pronouncements.[28]

This concept of inevitable clash was reiterated throughout the Lenin and Stalin periods of Soviet history. Ironically, it was in commemoration of the twenty-fifth anniversary of Stalin's first statement on the possibility of protracted "peaceful coexistence" that *Pravda,* in September, 1952, flatly declared: "The fate of the world will ultimately be decided by the outcome of the *inevitable* conflict between the two *worlds* [italics added]."[29] After 1949, Soviet leaders openly asserted that the approaching inevitable clash would spell "the liquidation of the whole system of world imperialism," "the graveyard not only of separate capitalist states, but for all of world capitalism."[30] One Soviet writer said that "the second half of the twentieth century will bring the complete victory of Communism throughout the world."[31] And by the end of the Stalin period, the Russians were no longer reluctant to prophesy the victory of the "world revolution" as the outcome of the next world war.

According to the proclaimed Soviet view, a new incidence of "imperialist" aggressive intervention has been prevented only by the existence of two crucial forces: the military might of the Soviet state; and, as in the prewar period, the internal contradictions and vulnerabilities within and among states of the non-Communist world. Stalin's last major pronouncement, his article in *Bol'shevik* on the eve of the Nineteenth Party Congress, aroused considerable interest because it stressed these inter-capitalist contradictions; in brief, he stated that "in practice" they are "stronger than the contradictions between the camp of capitalism and the camp of socialism," despite the "theoretically" greater severity of the contradictions between the two camps.[32] He offered as his primary justification:

> war with the U.S.S.R., as a socialist country, would be more dangerous to capitalism than war between the capitalist countries, for if war between the capitalist countries poses only the question of the supremacy of some capitalist countries over other capitalist countries, *war with the U.S.S.R. should certainly pose the question of the continued existence of capitalism itself* [italics added].[33]

In other words, such a war might well result in the total destruction of capitalism predicted by the Communists.

Despite this new theoretical twist, Stalin did not modify the basic theme of the inevitable clash between the two camps. Following on the heels of the above passage was a restatement of the old familiar theme: "In order to eliminate the inevitability of wars imperialism must be destroyed."[34] In the Bolshevik view, imperialism would be destroyed only by the inevitable clash of the two camps; hence the elliptical conclusion that war is inevitable. Once more, peaceful coexistence was underscored as a temporary phenomenon.

Stalin's dictum was widely interpreted as a directive to Communists to soft-pedal the aggravations between the Communist and non-Communist world, greatly intensified by the Cold War policy, and to concentrate instead on aggravating the "contradictions" within the capitalist camp. Stalin hoped the imperialist states would war among themselves; then the Soviets would enter at the moment most propitious for maximum gain at minimum risk. As Stalin had declared in 1925 to a closed session of the Party's Central Committee: "If war begins, we must not sit by with arms folded—we must enter, but enter last. And we must enter in order to throw the decisive weight onto the scales, the weight which can tip the scales."[35] This was the strategy pursued by Stalin in the early years of World War II, before Hitler's attack. His emphasis in 1952 on the inevitability of inter-capitalist wars gives reason to believe that the concept persisted in his long-range strategic planning.

From 1946 to 1953, Soviet policy pursued three major objectives to increase the relative power of the Soviet bloc, presumably for "the inevitable clash":

(1) the consolidation of wartime and postwar territorial and economic gains, and the strengthening of military power and potential (e.g., the fifth Five-Year Plan in the U.S.S.R.; the purges and the cautious militarization of the satellites of Eastern Europe, and, by proxy, of China);

(2) the attempt to fill any remaining power "vacuums" (e.g., Czechoslovakia in 1948; South Korea in 1950); and

(3) the stimulation and exploitation of all vulnerabilities or "contradictions" within and between the non-Communist states, and between colonial powers and their colonies (e.g., French fears of Germany; British-American differences; neutralism in Europe and Asia; civil war in Indochina; nationalist agitation in the Near and Far East.

The Soviet Union suffered important setbacks in all three sectors of its policy: It was confronted with increasing unrest in the satellites and the outright defection of Yugoslavia; it was foiled in most of its attempts to fill what it deemed to be power "vacuums"—in Iran (1946), Berlin (1948–49), Greece (1947–49), and Korea (1950); it saw that the inter-capitalist "contradictions" did not prevent a united defense effort and a vast increase in free world defensive capabilities.[36]

It was in this context that the post-Stalin era opened.

But let us first examine the theoretical underpinnings of the Stalinist ideology.

The analysis of any concept is inevitably complicated by the need to separate the mental processes of the originator and the investigator. The concept under examination remains, and must be treated, as essentially a living precipitate of the environment in which it was born and nourished.

Objectivity itself is such a concept, and recurrent Soviet attacks on "bourgeois objectivity" should caution those rash persons who see Soviet ideas and actions from the myopic viewpoint in which objectivity is always the midpoint between unhappy extremes.

The degree to which language is the passive instrument of its employers or the unconscious tyrant of their thought process is a disputed issue; what cannot be disputed by the serious student of social relations, particularly of comparative intercultural conceptions, is that language does bear a significant role in relation to thought patterns. It is essential, in analyzing a "foreign" conception, to realize that lack of explicit reference to a specific word-symbol need not reflect a lack of cognizance of this process, or of thinking which implicitly, even if unconsciously, employs the concept.

Terminological differences or even apparent conceptual gaps are not necessarily indications of difference; ideas may assume very different formulations, and published writings may not always reflect ideas or motivations, even when there is no conscious effort to conceal them. Accordingly, an extensive perusal of several million words of Soviet expression, including both random and selected expressions by Soviet leaders and the Soviet press, was funneled under examination for the analysis in this chapter. The selected writings comprised the most important writings and speeches of Lenin and Stalin, including the reports to Party Congresses. The general sources were Soviet histories, works on diplomacy, and military writings. An effort was made to obtain balanced representations from various periods of Soviet history from 1917 to 1951, when this analysis was originally prepared. Changes of application in the post-Stalin era are discussed later in the chapter.

The precise Soviet terminology used in discussing the "balance of power" is important. Careful attention must be paid to the context of expressions, for shades of meaning reveal possibly important nuances.

"Power" has come to be recognized, or accepted, as a dominant factor in Western political science. Its meaning is confused, but to attempt the task of unraveling the tangled threads of thought would only render us the disservice of erroneously simplifying this complex and varicolored Western conception. It combines physical, moral, spiritual influence, and other forms, and almost always combines an amalgam of content irreducible to one common denominator such as "military force" or "authority" or even "force." This very vagueness and broadness of meaning is significant. The Russian language has no term of equal connotation; the implications of this simple fact are vast. Seven fundamental Russian meanings of "power" are listed and defined below, and although each also has a direct English translation other than "power," it must be kept in mind that there is no single all-embracing term equivalent to our word "power."*

(1) *Vlast'* is defined by the Ushakov dictionary as "the right and ability to submit something to someone"; or as "dominion," "authority," "rule," or "power." It is used in the famous slogan of 1917: "All Power to the Soviets."

(2) The words *moshch'* and *moguchestvo* mean "power" in the sense of might, potency, and powerfulness.

(3) *Derzhava* expresses "power" in the sense of sovereignty, and is used in the phrase "The Great Powers."

(4) *Polnomochie* means "power" in the sense of delegated complete authority, as to a diplomat for negotiating settlement of a particular issue.

(5) *Sposobnost'* means "power" in the sense of talent, ability, or capability.

(6) *Voiska* is used to express the specific restricted meaning of troops or military "forces."

(7) *Sila*, the most general term, means "elemental force," "strength," or "vigor." It is used variously, as in "water-power," "force of gravity," and "armed forces."

The direct equivalent of the term "balance" is the word *ravnovesie*, which means "balance" or "equilibrium." The Ushakov dictionary defines a "political balance" (*politcheskoe ravnovesie*) as: " a comparative stability of the general relation of forces in the political struggle; for example, in the struggle of parties, governments."

To express the idea of manipulative balancing, the act and the process, the verbs *uravnovesit'* and *uravnoveshivat'* are used, the

* The fundamental reason for this is the absence of an analytical framework of political science, as we know it, based on a study of power. Marxism-Leninism, while acutely conscious of influence and power, is restricted in its open analysis of politics to generalizations of the Marxian social-economic philosophy; this is another story.

resultant equilibrium being *uravnoveshennost'* and the state of counterpoised or neutralized balance being *uravnoveshivannie.*

The English use of "balance," as in the phrase "balance of power," meaning a preponderance, is always expressed unambiguously by the Russian term *pereves,* meaning an "imbalance."

"Balance" in the distended meaning of "distribution" is expressed by these other terms in Russian:

(1) *Sootnoshenie* means "relation," "correlation," "connection," or "relationship." (The term *otnoshenie* expresses relation toward or regarding something.)

(2) *Rasstanovka* means "arrangement," "alignment," or "distribution."

(3) *Gruppirovka* or "grouping," and *peregruppirovka* or "regrouping," sometimes express this conception.

Sootnoshenie sil, the "relation of forces," is the central Soviet concept regarding political phenomena.* This expresses the equivalent of an interpretation of the "balance of power," defining "balance" as distribution or relation, and defining "power" as quantitative forces. If "power" were meant to refer to a sovereign nation, *derzhava* would have been used; if military forces, *voiska* would have been used; if general "might," *moshch'* would be expected; but the non-ethical, implicitly quantitative term *sil,* meaning "of forces," is always used in expressions meaning equilibrium, imbalance, relation, and distribution.

The term *ravnovesie sil,* "balance of forces," is always used to describe the relation of forces in an equilibrium relation—and only in this situation.† This occurs rarely, in comparison with the number of instances in which the relation is not seen as pure counterpoise.

Similarly, *pereves sil* is used to express all instances of imbalance, and only such instances.

These Russian equivalents always express their respective meanings of "balance" or "imbalance" unambiguously.

For this analysis, the author located and examined two hundred and fifty instances of the terms defined above. It is interesting to note the relative frequency of different equivalents to the various meanings of "balance of power" in English. Of the 250 instances examined, 136 were the phrase "relation of forces" (*sootnoshenie sil*), 87 were other expressions of general distribution of forces, 17

---

* The terms *rasstanovka sil,* "alignment of forces," and *gruppirovka sil,* "grouping of forces," convey substantially the same meaning but are less frequently used.
† See again the Ushakov definition of a "political balance" cited above.

were "equilibrium" (all *ravnovesie*), and 10 were "preponderance" (all *pereves*). Illustrations are given here from Stalin's writings:

(1) The relation of forces:

at the present stage of development and with the present conditions of the relation of forces [*sootnoshenie sil*], the intensification of the class struggle and strengthening of the resistance of the capitalist elements in town and country is taking place.[37]

(2) The alignment (distribution) of forces:

From the history of Europe we know that every time when treaties are concluded concerning the alignment of forces [*rasstanovka sil*] for a new war, these treaties are called peace treaties.[38]

(3) The equilibrium of forces:

Lenin regarded the Manifesto of October 17 [1905] as an expression of a certain temporary equilibrium of forces [*ravnovesie sil*]; the proletariat and the peasantry, having wrung the manifesto from the tsar, were still not strong enough to overthrow tsardom, whereas tsardom was no longer able to rule by the old methods alone.[39]

(4) An imbalance of forces:

[Stalin is discussing an alleged struggle over markets between the U.S.A. and U.K. within the imperialist camp.] The overbalance of forces [*pereves sil*] in this struggle—and it is a definite overbalance— is on the side of the U.S.A.[40]

"Power" has no direct Russian equivalent, however, in the general ambiguous meaning in which it is used in "balance of power" in Western political parlance and analysis. Its Russian equivalent in this phrase is more restricted in scope, but not more definite in meaning, and while implicitly excluding certain meanings sometimes intended in the English expression, it is limited only by vague boundaries of quantitative nuance.

To investigate this concept further in its many meanings and aspects, it is necessary to look to the political context.

"Relation of forces" is the generally inclusive term in the distributional sense (equilibrium and imbalance being particular forms of alignment or relation), and hence it is the general concept which we are considering at present. Expressions, or the absence of expressions, of other connotations of "balance of power" will be specifically referred to in the discussion.

The Soviet elite, and some other claimants to Marxian "science," have always contended that the calculation of the relation of class forces is the basic scientific analysis which guides policy-making. Lenin once said that it was "the main point in Marxism and Marxian tactics."[41] On another occasion he remarked:

> We, Marxists, have always been proud of the fact that by a strict calculation of the mass forces and mutual class relations we have determined the expediency of this or that form of struggle.[42]

Again he said that "adopting a serious attitude toward the defense of the country means . . . strictly calculating the relation of forces."[43] To cite but one more statement of Lenin's, he wrote that:

> The fundamental task of proletarian tactics was defined by Marx in strict conformity with the general principles of his materialist-dialectical outlook. Nothing but an objective account of the totality of all the mutual relationships of all the classes of a given society without exception, and consequently an account of the mutual relationships between it and other societies, can serve as the basis for the correct tactics of the advanced class.[44]

Many similar statements by Bolshevik leaders, especially in the earlier years of the regime, could be cited.

It should be noted that expediential action on the basis of the calculation of the relation of force is permissible (and mandatory) for *tactical* actions, and at least theoretically does not affect the ultimate strategy or aims of Soviet Communism. As the 1919 Program of the Communist International stated:

> In determining its line of *tactics*, each Communist Party must take into account the concrete internal and external situation, the relation of class forces.[45]

Within this tactical scope, great flexibility is required.

> Tactics permit maneuvering, tacking, the transition from certain methods of struggle to others, alternate attacks and retreats on the basis of an exact calculation of forces.[46]

There can be but one correct "line" or policy at any given time on any given matter, that which is determined by a correct calculation of the relation of forces obtaining in the particular situation. Any deviation from this correct line is considered very dangerous, because it misleads errant supporters into "objectively" becoming opponents.

There are two kinds of deviation: underestimation of the hostile forces (with its extreme of failure to calculate them and an assumption of their nonexistence); or overestimation of the hostile forces (with its extreme of failure to calculate them and an assumption that they are too strong to be dealt with).

The "Left" deviation is termed "adventurism" (or in some contexts "dogmatism"), and the "Right" deviation is called "opportunism" (or in certain contexts *khvostism* or "tailism," when it connotes lagging behind events). Adventurism is taking an unwarranted risk without duly considering the strength of the hostile "forces," while opportunism is overlooking and not seizing a gain or advance which the objective relation of forces permits.[47] Both fail to calculate accurately the relation of forces and thus stray from the sole correct "line."[48] In the Stalinist epoch, this ceased to have much political meaning, since no one was permitted to express himself to the extent that he could attempt this calculation—except the sanctified leadership of Stalin—and deviationism became any expression other than that laid down in the Party line.

The Soviet view is that "the calculation of the relation of forces" in any given situation is the Marxian mode of determining policy, and carries an ethical compulsion to act accordingly. This calculation in fact imparts a "realistic" character to policy decisions. Advance, retreat, defense are all decided (at least theoretically) in terms of relative capabilities, and flexibility is permissible, and indeed required. All decisions based on this calculation are tactical, expedient, and do not consciously affect ultimate aims or intentions.

A calculation of the prevailing relation of forces would appear to be a more "scientific" method of policy determination than sheer intuition, but whence its Marxian essence? The concentration upon "class" hostility and its extension to Soviet vs. anti-Soviet (or counter-Soviet) hostility is apparently derived from Marxism. But granting that Marxian thinking may determine the opposing units the relation between which is being calculated, it simply does not define the "forces" or provide an algebra of decision-making that scientifically decides the opportuneness of action. The "forces" seem to be anything which affects freedom of action in advancing one's dominion by reducing that of the presumed enemy, and hence may be defined as the capabilities of struggle, physical and moral.

Two problems remain: Who is to calculate and ultimately judge

the correctness of calculation, and by what specific criteria is the relation of forces to be determined precisely enough to be "scientific"
and not subject to the fallibility of the calculator?

Theoretically, any intelligent and informed sincere Marxist would
seem to be an adequate medium for translating the Marxian calculation into decisions; after all, the Marxists disdain non-Marxian socialism or utopianism precisely because it lacks this scientific apprehen-
sion of the dialectic inherent in nature, far above any mortal abilities.
But in fact, this has not proved true. Persons who considered themselves sincere and genuine Marxists continued to disagree on matters
theoretically soluble by "scientific calculation" as long as freedom to
disagree was permitted. Bukharin, Trotsky, and Lenin were roughly
equal in intellectual ability, and each considered himself a totally
sincere and dedicated Bolshevik; yet each adopted different views
on the question of accepting the Treaty of Brest-Litovsk. The only
way out was for each to brand the others a non-Marxist on this particular calculation; and this occurred. Lenin's view, the most realistic, won out on this issue, and seemed justified by later events.
(Success is especially important in Bolshevik policy, since there can
be only one correct line at any time.) Many of the others later
capitulated and declared their failure to calculate the relation of
forces—not their *incorrect* calculation, which would seem logical to
the non–Marxist, but their total *failure* to calculate, despite their
statements of calculation at the time. This is but one, albeit an out-
standing, instance of total disagreement among Marxist calculators.

By March, 1921, "fractions," or organized expressions of dissidence
within the Bolshevik Party, were prohibited. The "majority" decisions
of the Central Committee (and its Politburo) were held correct and
binding on all Party members. Non-Party participation in decision-
making had, of course, been liquidated much earlier (in March, 1918).
Freedom of discussion, clarification of the relation of forces on any
matter under discussion, was permitted, and theoretically has never
been further limited. In practice, Stalin's rise to complete power,
which culminated in 1930 and was underlined by the blood purges
of 1936 to 1938, was attended by the eradication of permission to
disagree with the Politburo calculation of the relation of forces.

It is therefore apparent that the Marxian "scientific" character of
the calculation of the relation of forces is quite limited to the degree
of fallibility of the calculator, who assumes his calculations to be
the only correct ones, or at any rate rationalizes them as such. The
Bolshevik's former readiness to recognize mistakes was toned down in
Stalinist ideology. But denial of errors does not negate their ex-

istence. Such profound miscalculations as the anticipation of easy success in the Finnish campaign in 1939–40 are clear indications of the fallibility of Stalin and the Politburo. This again raises the question of the criteria of calculation.

Bolshevik ideology, even in its era of "frankness" before 1930, did not make explicit any criteria for calculation, because there were in fact no clear-cut indexes for decision-making.* What was the criterion, and probably remains so in its modified form, is the general Marxian "world view," with its many presumptions and presumed conclusions. This will be discussed later.

Several points concerning the criteria of calculations may be distinguished:

(1) Soviet ideology, while extolling the scientific, Marxian calculation of the relation of forces in determining policy, does not even imply what the criteria for calculating or for defining the forces are.

(2) Presumably the most able and sincere Bolshevik (genuine Marxist) can calculate best; but even this is not made explicit.

(3) Differences in calculation are not permissible, because there is always only one correct decision or line; they are not admissible, because this calculation is claimed as infallible Marxian "science."

(4) The calculation of the relation of forces is a most convenient means for internally and externally rationalizing the interpretation of Marxian ideology in pure "power" terms of political expediency. Its almost incidental use by Soviet leaders strongly suggests its currency in their calculations. It assumes maximization of advance, permits honorable retreat or a temporary "equilibrium," and does not limit freedom of action in any way, since only the top political elite is permitted to calculate, and yet it permits subjectively genuine (or consciously sham) restatement of loyalty to the old Marxian symbols.

There are relatively few explicit references in Soviet Communist, or in other Marxist, writings that illuminate the practical question of the degree of alterability or manipulability of the relation of forces. Certain historical actions are said to be impelled by the dialectic, owing to economic conditions that exist, but inevitability and proletarian policy-making are rarely focused together.

One clear statement of this issue (arising from a debate of policy formulation) was a statement by Bukharin at the Seventh Party Congress in March, 1918, debating "peace" with the Central Powers. His statement was not challenged by Lenin or by Bukharin's other oppo-

---

* There was an implicit recognition of limited ability to calculate. As Lenin remarked, "There is no battle in this world where all probabilities are known beforehand." (*Zvezda* [*The Star*], April 1, 1912.)

nents, who presumably thought it was unwarranted, but who did not attack the correctness of the theoretical point with its wide practical implication. Bukharin stated:

> Comrade Zinoviev stands on a completely fatalistic point of view. He says that now the real relation of forces is unpleasant, and nothing more. On that he is ready to quiet down, and proposes to others to do likewise. This position is absolutely inadmissible. Revolutionary Marxists have never said that the real relation of forces is such and such; our task in the capacity of realistic politicians consists in the fact that we constantly strive to change the relation of actual forces.[49]

The statement by Zinoviev to which Bukharin alludes is an example of the "fatalistic" view of inevitability. Zinoviev had said:

> No one can say how long this breathing spell will last. It seems to me that it is clear only that this peace, acquired by us at Brest, appears as a more or less exact photograph of that relation of forces which exists in the world arena . . .[50]

In Soviet thinking the relation of forces is manipulable to a certain ill-defined extent; the "balance of power" is not deterministic, but it is conditioning, and limits the freedom of policy-making to decisions made in accordance with a strict calculation both of the existing relation, and of the capabilities needed to cause a favorable shift from the extant relation. The degree of freedom depends upon the fluidity or rigidity of the opposed forces. Conscious, planned alteration of the relation of forces is obtainable only by great effort. As Professor Leonov remarked, concerning the recent war:

> *In order to alter radically the relation of forces* on the Soviet-German front to the advantage of the Soviet state, a tremendous straining [*napryazhenie*] of all forces of the country, the mobilization of all possibilities of our economy, was required [italics added].[51]

This military context shows clearly the Soviet conception of the manipulability of the relation of forces. As Major General Talensky has written: "Stalinist strategy has demonstrated a method of actively altering the relation of forces."[52]

To manipulate and yet to remain detached was the Soviet aim— one recognized as a principle of bourgeois diplomacy as well. Thus, concerning French motives in favoring a "greater Poland" in 1919, it was said that "The French imperialists wished to create a counterweight to Germany and to Soviet Russia," and also that Germany had at Versailles utilized the contradictions among the Allies.[53] And in 1939, Stalin interpreted British and French foreign policy as follows:

> The policy of non-intervention reveals an eagerness . . . to allow all the belligerents to sink deeply into the mire of war, to encourage them surreptitiously in this; to allow them to weaken and exhaust one another; and then, when they have become weak enough, to appear on the scene with fresh strength . . . and to dictate conditions to the enfeebled belligerents.[54]

This is what the Soviets feared of Western action, at least until the opening of the second front, and the Western Allies were severely criticized on this account.

However, this same tactic is laudatory in Soviet policy. As Stalin said in a speech to the Central Committee in 1925 (not made public until 1947):

> If war were to commence, then we must not sit by with idle hands— we must enter, but enter last. And we must enter for the purpose of throwing the decisive weight into the scales, weight which can turn the balance.[55]

Another aspect of maneuvering the relation of forces is that of realizing its potentials. Stalin showed a particular interest in distinguishing between potentialities (or opportunities—the Russian word *vozmozhnosty* may be rendered either way) and actualities. For example, in ending the NEP (the New Economic Policy, in effect from 1921 to 1929), Stalin once used this distinction to explain (or rationalize) his policy. He declared:

> Lenin does not say that N.E.P. gives us socialism ready made. Lenin merely says that N.E.P. guarantees the *possibility* of building the foundations of socialist economy. There is a great difference between the *possibility* of building socialism and the *actual building of socialism*. Possibility and actuality must not be confused. It is precisely for the purpose of transforming possibility into actuality that Lenin proposes that the country be electrified and industry, agriculture and transport placed on the technical basis of modern large-scale production, as a condition for the final victory of socialism.[56]

In reviewing these Soviet concepts, three points should be noted.
(1) The balance of power as the relation of forces is not considered to be totally deterministic in Soviet policy-making. It does not

deny the need for further decision by the leadership. The corollary effect is that leaders (who presumably make brilliant decisions) can be praised without endangering belief in the Marxian myth.

(2) The relation of forces is the basis for all decision-making, nonetheless, and is therefore strongly conditioning. Although it does not eliminate the need for decisions made by the calculator, it presents him with the material for calculation, and is the picture of reality which he interprets for policy decision. As we have noted, it may be so general in nature that the calculator, in fact, has considerable freedom and little guidance.

(3) Stalin's distinction between potentialities and actualities was usually used merely to rationalize some policy shift that he favored. It does not alter the general conception of the manipulability of the relation of forces, since calculation includes both actual and anticipated alignments of forces (in accordance with Marxian "dynamic dialectical movement," and in accordance with common political sense).

The relation of forces is the determining basis for advance or retreat, offense or defense, limited only by the finite manipulable opportunities. The close relation between Soviet military and political doctrines makes general statements on strategy almost interchangeable. As a Soviet general put it: "Strategy points the aims of the armed forces . . . these aims must be realistic. They must correspond to the relation of forces."[57] And as another Soviet general declared: "The strength of Stalinist strategy consists in its basis on the correct calculation of the real relation of opportunities, forces, tendencies, regarding them not as static, but dynamic, in development."[58]

The relation of forces in strategic decision-making is the estimated balance of relative capabilities at any moment of calculation. As a Soviet military manual stated: "The relation of forces is clarified by the comparison of one's own forces and capabilities with the forces and probable capabilities of the enemy."[59] This over-all estimation of the situation is usual in all armies;[60] its systematic use in political affairs is not usual, since international politics are not ordinarily viewed as pure conflict, and in this the Soviet view is distinctive.

In the case of a favorable relation of forces, one in which the Communists have the capability for effective advance, advance is mandatory, with the single reservation that this be viewed strategically (that sometimes potential tactical gains must not be realized because they are strategically inadvisable).[61] This stress on "advance" in the Bolshevik code of operations, and in Soviet policy and actions, is of supreme importance. Not only is advance *permissible* where possible, but *required*. Advantages proffered by the favorable relation of forces must be seized.[62]

In a case of defense, in an unfavorable relation of forces, the alteration of the relation to permit the assumption of the offensive is required. Again, to quote a Soviet general:

> In strategic defense one of the combatants, as a rule, faces an unfavorable relation of forces. . . . The fundamental aim of strategic defense in this situation consists of securing the conditions for an alteration of the relation of forces to the advantage of the combatant, to prepare the necessary prerequisites for the transition to offensive action, for the seizure of the strategic initiative.[63]

In situations of an adverse relation of forces, retreat may even be required as the temporary strategy. This same source has stated: "Naturally *the unfavorable relation of forces* for us in the first period of the Great Fatherland War *necessitated the retreat* of our troops into the depth of their territory, losing space."[64]

Retreat is undertaken—aside from minor local "ambush" withdrawals or withdrawals from "probing" (*proba sil*) to determine the relation of forces—only as the necessary consequence of an adverse shift in the relation of forces. The first such instance in Soviet Russia occurred almost immediately, and after bitter internal dispute, Lenin's view of necessary retreat (by acceptance of the German-proffered Treaty of Brest-Litovsk) prevailed. In this intra-Party debate Lenin declared:

> And adopting a serious attitude towards defense of the country means preparing thoroughly for it, and *strictly calculating the relation of forces*. If our forces are obviously small, the best means of defense is *retreat into the interior of the country*. Whoever regards this as an artificial formula, made up to suit the needs of the moment, is advised to read old Clausewitz, one of the greatest authorities on military matters, concerning the lessons of history in this connection. The "Left" Communists [i.e., those opposing the peace of Brest-Litovsk], however, do not give the slightest indication that they understand the significance of the question of *the relation of forces* [italics added].[65]

As he explained, "I want to concede space to the momentary victor, in order to gain time"; "We must not tie our hands in one strategic maneuver. All depends on the relation of forces. . . ."[66]

Stalin also recognized this. As he put it, "Retreat under certain unfavorable conditions is as legitimate a form of warfare as the offensive."[67] In *Foundations of Leninism*, Stalin wrote: "A proper retreat when the enemy is strong, when retreat is inevitable, when to accept battle forced upon us by the enemy is obviously disadvantageous, when, with the given relation of forces, retreat becomes the only way to ward off a blow. . . ."[68] Again, in his *History of the Communist Party of the Soviet Union (Bolsheviks)*, Stalin avowed, in relation to political and military strategy, the need to be able to retreat properly as well as to advance.[69]

The Soviet world view of international politics is based on the Marxian idea of a basic and inevitable conflict between exploiters and exploited. Originally conceived in terms of class struggle, the October Revolution lent a new territorial dimension to the struggle, and the acquisition of a "proletarian motherland" shifted conflict from internal subversion to external war. The class struggle remained theoretically primary, but it was soon reformulated in new terms. Stalin was among the first to do so, in a little-known article in *Izvestiya* on February 22, 1919, in which he stated: "The world has decisively and unalterably split into two camps: the camp of imperialism and the camp of socialism."[70]

Struggle was clearly apparent. First the German war had to be liquidated, then the foreign intervention and the Civil War. By a series of circumstances, the Bolshevik regime emerged in control of a vast part of the Russian Empire, and at "peace" with the rest of the world. As an early Soviet historian termed this, "a certain equilibrium [*ravnovesie*] settled between the Soviet Union and the capitalist encirclement."[71] This same writer continued:

> But by its [the Soviet regime's] very existence, the struggle is maintained. The fundamental contradiction remains. The decaying capitalist encirclement strives to contaminate the healthy Communist kernel. But the Communist kernel is able by its own growth to cast down the decaying surroundings, and by itself to fill up the whole encirclement, the entire globe. Thus the struggle is maintained. Only it has taken new economic-diplomatic forms in the place of wars. And so—until a certain time . . .[72]

Stalin formulated this official explanation at the Fourteenth Party Congress (1925), in reviewing the preceding period:

> The most fundamental, novel, most decisive, and most pervasive of all events for this period in the realm of foreign relations was that between our country which is building socialism and the countries of the capitalist world. There has been established a certain temporary balance of

forces [*ravnovesie sil*]—a balance which is defined by the current streak [*sic*] of "peaceful coexistence" between the land of the Soviets and the countries of capitalism. That which we once considered as a short breathing spell after the war [Brest peace] has extended itself into a whole period of breathing space. From this has come this certain balance of forces [*ravnovesie sil*] and this period of "peaceful coexistence" between the world of the bourgeoisie and the world of the proletariat.[73]

The entire idea of "peaceful coexistence" thus originated as "a temporary equilibrium in the relation of forces." This is clearly expressed in numerous later statements of coexistence, which never refer to permanent coexistence. As Stalin wrote in the *History of the Communist Party of the Soviet Union (Bolsheviks)* in 1938: "To destroy the danger of foreign capitalist intervention the capitalist encirclement would have to be destroyed."[74]

The relation of forces between the U.S.S.R. and the capitalist world is the basic determinant of Soviet foreign policy. "The foreign political situation of the Soviet Union has always been defined by its economic, political, and military might, and the relation of forces between the world of Socialism and the world of capitalism."[75]

In the post-World War II Stalin period, the theme emphasized was less "capitalist encirclement" than "two camps,"* socialism (the U.S.S.R. and its satellites), and capitalism (the free world). *Bol'shevik*, in an editorial in 1946, stated that: "The historic victory over Hitler Germany and its accomplices has altered the relation of forces in the international arena . . . ,"[76] a theme often repeated since that time.

The possibility of peaceful coexistence was restated even in the Stalin period, but the great danger of war was even more strongly stressed at that time. It was often stated that the inevitable world conflict would mean "the liquidation of the whole system of world imperialism."[77]

During the late Stalin era, the Soviet leaders expected war, a victorious war for "socialism," that is, for Soviet power. Their public claim to total world victory may have proceeded from the conviction that in another war their side, though greatly weakened in the process, would prevail and that world power was distributed in a bipolar pattern (a development "foreseen" by, and compatible with, their ide-

* Several formulations are used: two "camps" (*lageri*), "directions" (*napravlenii*), "tendencies" (*tendentsii*), "courses" (*kursi*), "systems" (*sistemi*), "worlds" (*miri*). "Camps," "systems," and "worlds" are all frequent.

ology). If they entertained highly classified and probably internalized doubts as to the real outcome of such a war, that much they did see as the course of history. Moreover, the suffering of the Russian people in World War II, and the continued consumer and political deprivations, made the prospect of genuine peace in the measurable future (i.e., after one more great world war) a useful, perhaps necessary, promise.

The history of Soviet diplomacy can readily be explained in the general terms of their claimed ideology. The fears of capitalist encirclement as expounded above, the techniques of utilizing contradictions in the hostile camp, and above all, the sharp delimitation between the Soviet Union and all the rest of the world, have been eloquently expressed in the policies of the Soviet Union. Peace is the genuine desire of those who believe that they are the weaker side of a precarious equilibrium; nor does this contradict their long-range aim of destroying the hostile counters in the world scale. The world has seen only too clearly that formal peace may be coordinate with Communist subversion, coups, and satellite aggression—all this while the Soviet Union ardently championed and, for the time, genuinely sought world peace.

Capitalist encirclement and the international equilibrium of forces between it and the Soviet state became the emphasis of Soviet ideology. As noted at the outset of this chapter, those elements of Marxism-Leninism that do correspond to power relations and political situations of the Soviet state are intensified and accepted, while those elements that cannot easily be manipulated by the political leadership tend to be discarded. That this is not good Marxism is all the more fortunate for the Soviet leaders, for it tends to make Soviet operative ideology more realistic and viable (although not necessarily more "correct" or justified) policy.

The Soviet emphasis on advance, in using all opportunities to further their power, is sanctioned by their ideology, so there is no deterrent to complete political expediency. Maneuver, retreat, pause—all are tactics in the general strategy of advance; the calculated relation of forces determines the limitation of advance. Thus, "Soviet foreign policy soberly calculates the presently effective hostility of the capitalist encirclement to the U.S.S.R."[78] History, however, is dynamic, so this situation fluctuates. (That the Soviet Union has greatly increased in its relative and absolute power since World War II serves to intensify conviction in illusory ideas as to the source of this change. This should not be construed to suggest that they fail to appreciate the cold bases of forces, and of propaganda, which are the real source of their own strength; quite on the contrary, these are "forces" to be calculated and maximized.)

Necessarily, any balance of power must theoretically be temporary, insofar as Soviet aims are concerned.* It cannot be part of the goal, because the goal is clearly universal "monolithic" control. Although a balance of power (*ravnovesie sil*) may be sought tactically, it cannot be sought as an ultimate aim. Nor can there be a distribution-balance of power (*sootnoshenie sil*), since the foe must be totally annihilated.

In the absence of any comprehensive Western analysis of the concept of the balance of power, the Soviet conception cannot be precisely compared with it here. The English-language term "balance of power" comprises four different meanings of distribution. Soviet thinking also encompasses these four meanings, but uses different terms.

(1) A general relation or distribution of power is expressed by the terms *sootnoshenie sil, rasstanovka sil,* or *gruppirovka sil.* It may in context sometimes denote a preponderance (by reference to a "favorable" or "unfavorable" *sootnoshenie sil*), but continues always to express a general distribution of forces.

(2) An equilibrium of two units is always a *ravnovesie sil.* This true "balance" is always considered temporary, and is usually explicitly stated to be such. Politically, this means that a maximum advance (or minimum retreat) has been effected, and that for the time being a static situation prevails.

(3) The idea of an equilibrium of two equal units, with a detached mobile balance, is not frequent, but is used to describe situations in which an "active neutrality" (i.e., neutrality as a positive policy of calculated advantage) will permit later decisive commission, as in Soviet policy in the period from 1939 to 1941. The more usual idea in Western thought, that the balancer (for example, Great Britain in the nineteenth century) should remain uncommitted indefinitely (unless threatened) so as to augment gains by continually exerting pressure on the two "balanced" counters, is not seen in Soviet thought. The detached balancer and the "equilibrium" are only temporary measures in the appropriate situation, and not permanent goals or expectations.

(4) A favorable imbalance (preponderance of power) is always a *pereves sil,* and of course represents an advantageous situation requir-

---

* This reflects the Marxian idea that the dialectic of history is dynamic and constantly in flux, thus denying any "static" balance. While Soviet ideology does *not* express these terms, it may be influenced by the earlier ideological considerations expressed.

ing further advance. Thus, it is more than likely that the Soviet leadership, convinced as they seem to be (at least in public statements since 1947) that a great *pereves sil* has redounded to their "camp" since the war, consider that a "potentiality" for advance exists, and must therefore be realized—hence the aggression (by coup, occupation, and proxy attack) in Eastern Europe and Asia in the period from 1947 to 1950, and the largely abortive indirect advances after 1957. Such advance fits the terms of the Soviet conception of the balance of power, and could have been predicted by anyone who correctly understood this conception.

A favorable imbalance means a potentiality for advance, and if the Russians feel that they hold this advantage (locally or universally), they will advance; if they conclude that the enemy holds such a *pereves*, they will retreat. American policy, therefore, must be calculated from the Soviet as well as the American viewpoint to make the maximum use of situations in which the Russians can be "contained" or forced to retreat.

A different aspect of the "balance of power" is the degree to which world events can be maneuvered or manipulated. It seems clear that from an operative standpoint the Marxian expectation of inevitable victory does not strongly affect policy-making. In the short run, the Soviet approach to policy decisions is based on the manipulation of politics. It is limited by the requirement of a "calculation of the relation of forces," but ambiguity about the forces involved and the criteria of calculation make it, in effect, a purely expediential *Realpolitik*.

Thus, inevitability in goal-expectations and, probably to a limited degree, in defining the forces calculated does not interfere with an extremely high degree of permissible manipulation of policy. It is perhaps the supreme tragedy of our time that the Soviet leaders' misapprehension of the world in which they live has been a self-fulfilling prophecy.

Officially and generally, the attitudes of the West immediately after World War II were that lessened hostility and peace with Russia would naturally follow the defeat of the common foe. The Soviet Union was therefore granted large concessions in recognition of its great losses in the common struggle, and as "proof" that the West was ready to cooperate in establishing a common peace among the then "united nations."

The Soviet leaders' view of this phenomenon could only have been that they were fulfilling a potential in the gigantic *pereves sil* that had come to them vis-à-vis the "capitalist" world. Moderate opposition from the West during the consolidation process in Western Europe was to be expected; more effective opposition was felt through the Truman Doctrine, Marshall Plan, Berlin airlift, and Korean War (and more recently over Berlin and missiles in Cuba).

Meanwhile, the Western world had been rudely jolted by the crude "advances" of the Soviet Union, notably the coup in Czechoslovakia, the Berlin blockade, and the invasion of South Korea. The West reacted instituting a series of countermeasures—the Truman Doctrine being the first explicit one.

This met Soviet expectations; had not their supposition been that the West would initiate "Truman doctrines," etc., when it could? The actual appearance of *counter-Soviet* measures were seen as the anticipated *anti-Soviet* actions, seeming to confirm the policy of utilizing all potentialities for advance.

The "balance of power" may also be viewed from an ethical standpoint, superimposed on those previously discussed. The Soviet view does not premise alternatives of ethical and unethical except in terms of expediency.[79] All actions that expedite advance or minimize retreat (or in any manner advance the Party power) are ethically not only permissible, but required.

The Soviet conception of "balance of power" excludes any balance as permanent; any equilibrium or relation is of indefinite but temporary duration. But no time limits are set on the "inevitable" historical processes; to do so would be incompatible with the Soviet concept of calculated policy. Over an extended period of time, Soviet conceptions may mellow and change with new leaders, and under new conditions. Has such change been occurring in the post-Stalin period?

The present Soviet leaders continue to view the world and the course of international politics and world history through Marxist-Leninist eyes. But the extraordinary flexibility of Marxist-Leninist ideological prescriptions on policy actions permit extensive alterations of national strategy *without* requiring Communist leaders even to pose to themselves the question of "discarding" or fundamentally reconsidering "the ideology." If a Communist leadership bases its policies and actions on a "scientific," Marxist-Leninist calculation of what is expedient under the given relation of forces, it may reach very different conclusions from those reached by earlier Marxist-Leninists under other circumstances. Thus, in giving the Party's eulogy to Lenin on the 95th anniversary of his birth in April, 1965, Party Secretary Pëtr Demichev declared: "We would not be acting according to Lenin were we not to assess realistically the relation of world forces."[80] So, too, Khrushchev once stated quite frankly:

> One must not, without account of the concrete situation, without due account for changes in the relation of forces in the world, repeat that which was said by the great Lenin under entirely different circumstances. . . . We live in a time when Marx, Engels, and Lenin are not with us. . . . On the foundations of the teachings of Marxism-Leninism *we must think for ourselves*, deeply study life, analyze the contemporary situation, and draw such conclusions as will bring advantage to our common cause of Communism [italics added].[81]

Today, the Chinese and Soviet Communists are trading accusations of "treason" and "betrayal of Marxism-Leninism." And their sharply conflicting ideological positions are based on very real differences in interests, policies, and aims. But today there is no single omnipotent central authority that can resolve differences and liquidate those who deviate and are un-Marxist (that is, the losers). Lenin had the authority, and Stalin the cold power, to enforce *the* "correct" line. Under Khrushchev, this position slipped irretrievably (though, to be fair, one must recognize that it would have occurred under any other man —even Stalin had his Tito). Neither a Brezhnev nor a Mao can do more than advance a claim to the correct reading of the "scientific" universal key to a Leninist general line, and impugn all other claimants. But neither of them can vanquish or ignore the other because neither is a Trotsky in exile, or a Molotov in retirement, or an isolated Balkan exception. They each represent a major power whose mainstream of policy is set on its own course, with or without them personally.

And World Communism as a movement? Whose World Communism—with split and warring rival parties in many countries, coalitions of pro-Muscovite and pro-Peking parties (or factions), and a growing army of parties (some ruling independent countries) which don't want ever again to become satellites or mere extensions of *any* Center? It is now clear even to the sadder but wiser current leaders in the Kremlin that it will be a long time before there is another conclave of the world's hundred Communist parties—if indeed there ever is one again. And the ambiguous compromise Declarations of 1957 and 1960—to which, in their pursuit of legitimacy, the contenders are each desperately attempting to lay claim—are more a bone of contention than a bracing backbone.

Communism as an ideology is eroding. But erosion is a matter of degree; it affects intensities of belief, ranges of expectations, and, above all, the tempering of doctrine to expediency. In the final analysis, concrete expectations, objectives, policies, and actions are the real stuff of politics. Long-run expectations and goals do matter, but they matter most as they affect one's acts. And if present circumstances— the relation of forces in the nuclear age—call for peaceful coexistence as *the general line* for socialist states and for the international movement (as the Soviets claim and the Chinese deny), we of the West should welcome the challenge—unless we share the expectations of the Communists that "Communism" will become much more productive, democratic, and popular than rival forms of state and economic organization in the world.

It would be both erroneous and dangerous to conclude that Communism has eroded into passive-ism or pacifism. The Soviet leaders remain Communists. But they no longer head a monolithic "camp" in any politically meaningful sense, and their Communism bears little resemblance to that of Lenin or Marx. Shrewd, deceitful, powerful, and aggressive, the Soviet and Chinese states continue their "protracted conflict" with all rivals (now including each other).

It is not the purpose of this chapter to survey and interpret the development of recent Communist views on war, peace, and revolution* or to review the uses of military instruments of policy.† This discussion has sought to focus on the crucial interconnection between ideological motivations and policy determination. Particular attention has been given to analysis of the Marxist-Leninist approach in theory and in its early development. Major changes in the post-Stalin period (examined in later chapters) have occurred within the theoretical framework of the *role* of ideology in guiding policy described earlier in this chapter. Ideological guidelines, however, have been substantially revised.

The Twentieth Congress of the CPSU in February, 1956, declared that war is not inevitable. The Twenty-first Congress in January, 1959, concluded that the victory of socialism in the U.S.S.R. was "final," even without the end of capitalism. At the Twenty-second Congress in October, 1961, it was revealed that "Communism" could be built in the U.S.S.R. while capitalism remained in the world; that peaceful coexistence with capitalist states was the *general line*; that war was not only not inevitable, but also not desirable or even permissible as a means of advancing socialism; and that peaceful transition of capitalist countries to Communism was feasible and preferable to armed revolution. The dogma that the class struggle would intensify (lead-

* See Chapters 10–12.
† See Chapters 6–9.

ing to war or to civil war-revolution) as the final victory of Communism came nearer was discarded.

The post-Stalin Soviet leaders have not always agreed on the advisability of publicly revising ideological prescriptions, but there seems to have been near unanimity on the substance of the revisions. The one exception, the one unreconstructed Bolshevik, was Vyacheslav Molotov. Stripped of all power long before, old Molotov nonetheless wrote a secret letter to the Twenty-second Party Congress arguing that "without serious conflict, without war, advance toward Communism is impossible." He denied the possibility of avoiding world war, and argued that peaceful coexistence should be regarded as "only a temporary tactic" and "an aspect of the Cold War" rather than as the general line of the Communist Party and Soviet Union.[82] But such *chinoiserie* found no takers among the Soviet leaders, and Otto Kuusinen, the still more venerable Bolshevik member of the Party Presidium, complained that Molotov's platform had been concocted in the hope that "some miserable tiny fish might bite, if not here in our home waters, then at least *in someone else's waters.*"[83] But the Chinese didn't need Molotov to tell them that Khrushchev, Brezhnev, and the other Soviet leaders had discarded Marxism-Leninism—as the Chinese knew it.

Khrushchev, his colleagues, and his successors have continued to calculate the balance of power in terms they regard as live and valid Marxism-Leninism, taking account of the power factors in the relation of forces in the world today.

5. The Geostrategic Arena, Economics, and Technology

Ideological and political considerations provide an outlook on the world, conceptions of political action, and motivations and objectives of national policy. Policy is based on calculations that spring from such factors. But policy calculation and decision must take account of the geographical and economic context within which national power is generated and from which the instruments of power are fashioned. All elements contributing to national power combine to create the particular strategic assets and liabilities of any country. The balance of these strategic assets, however, can be measured usefully only in terms of the corresponding power of other states and in the light of the political relationships among various states. In short, there is a geostrategic arena, deeply affected by economic and technical factors, within which international politics operates and which strongly conditions the range of military and other instruments of foreign policy.

Geography is sometimes regarded as a relatively unchanging factor, but in fact it is one dimension of a single dynamically changing world. Space, terrain, natural resources, ecology, and virtually all other aspects of geography assume ever new significances as new political, economic, technological, military, and other developments take place.

Transportation, for example, is a key element in strategy that is deeply affected by technological change. The significance of terrain differs radically if armies are motorized rather than on foot or on horse, in an age of aircraft, or in an age of missiles and space vehicles. Development of rapid communication also drastically affects geostrategic considerations: Not only can a field commander be rapidly informed of a wide range of military developments, but entirely new possibilities of direct political command and control of military power can be applied.

Natural resources provide essential raw materials for the manufacture of weapons, equipment, and other strategic items, and their importance changes rapidly. Oil, uranium, and manganese have acquired radically new significance with the advent of the gasoline combustion engine, nuclear explosives, and weapons using alloy steel. The levels of economic, scientific, industrial, and technological development also have a critical impact: for example, without a gaseous diffusion plant or other means of enrichment, natural uranium cannot be used to make a nuclear weapon. Resources must of course be converted into instruments of military and other power in order to exercise their full influence in international political relations.

If it efficiently contributes to running a modern society and economy, population as a resource is an asset, but it may be a liability if it is politically alienated or it requires nearly all its energies just to meet minimum fundamental needs of survival. The degree of social and political cohesion is highly relevant, and popular responsiveness to concerted action may depend on morale and political allegiance as well as on standards of living and levels of technical education.

Other elements of geography, economics, transportation, political organization, and technical-industrial levels also contribute to, or detract from, national power.

For the purposes of this study, the basic factors of national power are relevant in two respects, which we shall now examine: In their own formulations of national policy, what role do Soviet leaders assign to geostrategic and economic-technical elements of national power? And what are the basic geostrategic and power strengths and weaknesses of the Soviet Union in the present balance of world power?

Although they are not "geopoliticians" in the classical sense, the Soviet leaders are well aware of the geographic-strategic advantages and limitations of the U.S.S.R. and of the distribution of power in the world generally. As it originated in the writings of Sir Halford Mackinder in the early years of this century, and as it was further developed in Germany by Professor Karl Haushofer in the interwar period, geopolitics was premised on a geostrategic determinism in history. Geographical considerations were ultimately determining historical factors, both in motivating states in their international relations and in deciding which states would prevail in international conflict. According to the dominant school of geopolitics, whoever controlled the Eurasian "Heartland" (the area from Germany to the Urals) would dominate the Eurafroasian "world island" and eventually the whole world. Attracted to *Geopolitik*, some Nazis rationalized their aggressive designs in terms of *Lebensraum*. The Soviet leaders, however, as Marxists, still believe that political forces, based on "class" interests (derived from the ownership of the means of economic production) are the ultimately motivating factors in world politics.

Although they reject "geopolitics," the Soviet leaders keenly appreciate the importance of concrete geostrategic constraints and opportunities. They regard the U.S.S.R. primarily as a European power, but also as an Asian power, a Middle Eastern power, and a global power. But they recognize their limited ability to extend their presence beyond the oceans and across the geographical-political barriers that still keep the Soviet Union apart from most of the rest of the world.

The collapse of Germany and Japan in World War II gave the Soviet Union new opportunities. From 1945 through 1948, the Soviet leaders extended their power as far as they deemed prudent in Eastern and Central Europe. In 1946, they also attempted unsuccessfully to gain a foothold in Japan and to gain trusteeship over at least one of the former Italian colonies in Africa. In China, they played both sides of the street, but the decision in that country was made by the victory of the Chinese Communists. At the close of this period, Soviet expansion was further limited by the unsuccessful Berlin blockade and the unsuccessful North Korean invasion to seize South Korea. Soviet expansionist moves in the latter half of the 1940's were based on political, military, and geostrategic calculations, but they were not reflexes of geopolitical determinism.

"Geographic conditions and factors, space and time, have played and continue to play an important role in armed conflict," the Russians note.[1] They recognize in particular the important interrelation of geographical considerations with military-technological developments, as well as with shifting political conditions.

As Marxists, the Soviet leaders ascribe a fundamental importance to dialectical materialism and to economic determinism in history. In short, they tend to appreciate fully—and perhaps to overstate—the significance of the material factors of power. However, as Marxist-Leninists, they also tend to emphasize the importance of "class" outlook, to overestimate morale, economic efficiency, social-political cohesion, and other nonmaterial factors of states belonging to the "socialist system," and to underestimate those of other states.

There is growing impressive evidence of failure of the Communist states to exceed or even to match the economic achievement of a number of "capitalist" economies in North America, Western Europe, and the Pacific, but the Soviet leaders stubbornly persist in slanting the evidence even to themselves in order to avoid facing the continuing failure of the facts to meet their ideological preconceptions.* The Soviet victory over Nazi Germany continues to be widely acclaimed as "convincing proof of the superiority of socialism over capitalism—one of the most important lessons of the war."² This claim, of course, completely ignores the fact that Nazi Germany was not typical of "capitalist" states, that the capitalist Western powers were also victors, and that their economies grew more rapidly in supporting not only the war efforts of their own armies, but also in providing through Lend-Lease a not insignificant portion of the material requirements of the Red Army.†

* In 1962, the value of gross national product (GNP)—the sum total of economic goods and services, public and private—for the U.S.S.R. had reached $256.3 billion, while that of the United States was $551.8 billion (and the United Kingdom, France, West Germany and Italy together had $324.1 billion). While absolute levels of economic production and activity are extremely important, from the political-ideological standpoint the most significant indicator is the *rate of growth* of GNP. Soviet economic growth has been creditable, and has—at least until recently—exceeded that of the U.S. It has not, however, been as great as that of West Germany, Italy, or Japan. Moreover, the rate of increase has been declining. Thus, while the Soviet per capita economic growth rate averaged 5 per cent for the years 1950 through 1958, it averaged only 2.8 per cent for 1958–62. The U.S. growth rate rose from 1.2 per cent average in 1950–58 to 2.5 per cent in 1958–62, thus showing a more favorable trend (to say nothing of the greater actual volume of the U.S. product, since the GNP base is twice as great as the Soviet one). During this same period, West Germany averaged 6.4 per cent increase 1950–58, and 4.9 per cent 1958–62; Italy rose from 5 per cent in 1950–58 to 6.6 per cent 1958–62; and Japan rose from 5 per cent in 1953–58 to a phenomenal 12.2 average annual growth 1958–62. (These data are taken from *Annual Economic Indicators for the U.S.S.R.*, Joint Economic Committee, U.S. Congress, U.S. Government Printing Office, Washington, D.C., 1964, pp. 95–96.)

† Soviet sources rarely acknowledge Lend-Lease aid from the U.S. and the U.K. in World War II. Marshal Malinovsky has referred to it, and even admitted that it "had a certain positive significance," though he quickly went on to add that "by the scale of the conflict it was not so great and of course was not decisive" (Malinovsky, *Velichie pobedy* [*Great Victory*], Moscow, 1965, p. 23). Professor K. Terekhin has said that Lend-Lease provided only 4 per cent of "the material resources expended by the Soviet Union on its war effort," though he admitted the receipt of over 400,000 trucks was especially helpful (TASS, *Radio Moscow*, April 20, 1965). Yet another Soviet military historian has given a more accurate indication by citing actual—and probably substantially correct—figures for overall Soviet wartime production, and U.S. and U.K. wartime assistance to the U.S.S.R., in key general weapons categories. Thus the U.S.S.R. produced during World War II a total of 136,800 aircraft—the U.S. and U.K. provided 18,700; the U.S.S.R. produced 102,500 tanks—the U.S. and U.K. gave 10,800; the U.S.S.R. produced 489,900 artillery pieces—the Western Allies provided 9,600 (Prof. G. A. Deborin, *Voprosy istorii*, April, 1965, p. 11). These figures do not,

According to the Soviet view,

> It is obvious that the socialist organization of production has incontestable advantages over capitalist organization. . . . An economy which is subordinated to a single plan and to a single will is capable of utilizing material and human resources in a most complete and purposeful way, and it will ensure the coordinated functioning of all cells of the organism of the national economy. Precisely the socialist system of public production, and not the private capitalist system with its internal contradictions, is capable of withstanding extreme exertions and commands the real potentialities of providing the maximum production to the armed forces in the shortest possible time.[3]

Thus do the Russians contend that their system is superior in utilizing economic potentialities for the conduct of war. What do they consider the role of economic considerations in winning war?

The Soviet view, as expressed in various contexts over recent years, emphasizes the continued—indeed the increased—importance of the economy in nuclear war. Thus, "Under contemporary conditions the role of economic conditions and factors in the preparation and conduct of war has increased sharply. The economic factor, as the most important index of the military power of a state, has assumed especially great importance."[4] Indeed, as another Soviet military writer has put it,

> Under the conditions of nuclear war the significance of economic potential has been enhanced . . . there must be a strong economic base capable, in case of a prolonged war, of sustaining colossal pressures, of maintaining its survivability, and of ensuring the military needs of the state for the necessary length of time.[5]

This "necessary length of time" is intentionally vague. Some years ago, in 1957, in a rare explicit statement neither reaffirmed nor modified since, Major General (then Colonel) Lagovsky stated: "The basic thing that strategy must establish is the requirements of the armed forces for *the first year* of the conduct of military operations."[6] What does this kind of thinking mean on the role of the economy in nuclear war?

Soviet military theoreticians have not been consistent or clear in

----

of course, tell the whole story; while the West provided a little under 15 per cent of the Soviet aircraft, it provided the wartime medium bomber with which the Soviet Long Range Air Army was largely equipped—the B-25. On the other hand, it is true that most Western matériel arrived after the crucial turning point of the battles of Stalingrad and Kursk in late 1942 and mid-1943.

describing the role of the economy during a nuclear war. On the one hand, there is at least some recognition of the need to depend substantially on stocks of matériel produced before such a war. However, there is also a continuing belief that wartime production would be feasible and could be of very great significance. Colonel General Shtemenko, Deputy Chief of the General Staff, has stated: "The national economy will not have much time to reorganize itself during the course of military operations, as it did before. Everything necessary for work under war conditions must be prepared in advance. The *potential* of industry, agriculture, transportation, science, and culture will be utilized even more fully in the interest of victory."[7] He thus implies an important continuing role for wartime production. And others go further.

The role of economic support for military operations obviously depends on the nature and duration of these operations. Prior to 1960, Soviet military doctrine firmly posited a long war, even with wide use of nuclear weapons. The general conclusion of the military doctrine deliberations of the first half of the 1960's is reflected in the following passage from a statement by Marshal Malinovsky:

> Now no one can deny the possibility of a short quick war, above all because the very first surprise nuclear missile strike can deal unheard of destruction, destroy an enormous number of troops in their barracks, and annihilate a significant portion of the population of major cities. At the same time, it is completely clear that, depending on the conditions of the outbreak of war, the armed conflict will not be limited only to nuclear weapons strikes. It can be protracted, requiring a long and sustained effort by all the forces of the army and the country as a whole.[8]

The idea that general nuclear war might be either brief or long was seriously challenged only once, when Marshal Sokolovsky and Major General Cherednichenko contended, in August, 1964, that "a thermonuclear war cannot last long. Hence, it is necessary, in our opinion, above all to make prepartions for a short war."[9] However, in the period since the ouster of Khrushchev there have been a number of authoritative restatements of the view of the Soviet military leadership that a future general nuclear war may be protracted, and would in any case require the engagement of large-scale ground armies.

In March, 1965, *Red Star* noted editorially that there was considerable interest—and by implication some confusion—over the question of duration of nuclear war. It commissioned a well-known writer on questions of military doctrine, Colonel V. Larionov, to prepare an article on this subject.[10] Larionov emphasized the distinction between a "swiftly moving war" and a "short war," arguing that a nuclear war would certainly be a swiftly moving war, but not necessarily a short one. He also observed that while some Western military theorists argue that it is not possible to undertake preparation simultaneously for both a long war and a short one, the United States was nonetheless building its general-purpose forces for the conduct of protracted operations, while maintaining strategic nuclear forces for a swiftly moving and presumably short war.

But the most interesting and notable reaffirmation of Soviet doctrine appeared in another article in the same month written again by the team of Marshal Sokolovsky and General Cherednichenko. Whether directly connected with the fall of Khrushchev, or whether they had a change of judgment or were persuaded to change their position, they drastically revised their judgment of the previous summer. They now stated that in addition to preparing necessary ready forces for the beginning period of a war, "at the same time, it is also important to effect promptly mobilized deployment of mass armed forces in the event that they were required during the course of the war, and to take steps to prepare the entire population of the country, the economy, and the transportation system to support the vital activity of the country under conditions of the aggressor's nuclear attack. . . ."[11] And they affirmed that mass ground armies would be needed for the successful prosecution and conclusion of a general nuclear war.

The Russians recognize that

> Of course the role of economics, and especially of military economics, will depend to a great extent on the conditions of the outbreak of a war and on its duration. But under all circumstances, whether a war is swift moving or protracted, economic preparation for the repulse of the aggressor, and the competence of the economy to provide the armed forces with all requirements, will play a primary role in the course and outcome of the war.[12]

Thus, if a war were swift and brief it would "obviously be conducted with previously produced arsenals of arms and munitions." But "to build one's calculations only on the swiftly moving character of war would be incorrect. War can also be protracted. Therefore the economy must be ready *in a timely manner to replace losses and supply the armed forces with the necessary means out of current production.*"[13] Accordingly, while stocks must be built up in peacetime, so too must preparations for extensive *wartime* production.

Nuclear missile war requires the timely stocking of the necessary reserves of military equipment and matériel. During the war these reserves must be built up and, moreover, replace losses of weapons and equipment. Cadre military industry alone is, of course, not capable of meeting this complex task. Making up for the enormous losses in military equipment and providing for all the requirements of the armed forces for the conduct of war and achievement of victory over the enemy requires not only the distribution of finished goods, raw materials, electrical energy, fuel, manpower, and finances in the interests of the war, but also the conversion of civilian industry, agriculture, and transport for accomplishment of state tasks for meeting the needs of war.

Under contemporary conditions, with the appearance of a real threat of the use of new means of mass destruction and annihilation, problems of ensuring the survivability of industry, especially heavy and military industry, and transport and means of communication, assume particularly great importance. While in past wars industry and transportation resources located in zones beyond the reach of the land and air power of the enemy could without interruption produce for war needs, today their geographical disposition is no guarantee against nuclear missile strikes. Therefore, the survivability of industrial installations will depend not only on their territorial dispersal, but also on duplication, and on the active application of other measures of defense against atomic attack.[14]

Soviet views in the mid-1960's on the continuing need and ability for wartime functioning of the economy in nuclear war are based on recognition of the fact that, in Marshal Malinovsky's words, "Along with groupings of troops, industrial and administrative centers, communications centers, and all that feeds a war will become the targets of destructive nuclear strikes."[15]

"Economic potential," according to a recent authoritative Soviet military source, "plays a most important role in deciding the outcome of wars. The military power of a state depends directly on the economic potential of that country."[16] Indeed, it has long been a tenet of Soviet doctrine that "the level of military power of a state is determined by the condition of its economic, morale, and military potentials."[17] Of course, "potentials" must be developed, and the military leaders have come to stress this theme as they have felt the pressure of constraints on military expenditures. Marshal Malinovsky thus has had occasion to stress that "military power is not automatically created by the progress of the economy."[18] We have earlier reviewed disagreements between the political and military leaders over the proportion of resources which should be devoted to the military establishment.*

It is of interest that in February, 1965, just a few months after Khrushchev's fall from power, his successors raised the seven important state committees concerned with defense production (defense technology, aircraft technology, radio, shipbuilding, electronics, medium machine building (cover for the nuclear weapons industry), and general machine building (perhaps the missile industry) to the status of ministries. Originally, and presumably at the instance of Marshal Zhukov as the then Minister of Defense, these establishments had been retained as ministries when (in May, 1957) virtually all other production ministries were reduced to state committee status. (It was only in December, 1957, after Marshal Zhukov's ouster, that these, too, were reduced to such status.) And now they have been restored to the level of centralized cabinet-level ministries.

The general reorganization of the Soviet economy, especially the decentralization effected in the creation of regional economic councils in the late 1950's, may have been designed in part to provide a more viable basis for meeting conditions of nuclear war. Indeed, in November, 1957, Khrushchev declared that the reorganization of industrial management "improves our strategic position." He added that while this was "not the main aim of the reorganization, it is nonetheless a very considerable one."[19] It would, however, be wrong to overestimate the extent to which such considerations enter into Soviet economic policy and organization, especially in the 1960's.

Economic factors, like geographic ones, are strongly influenced by technological demands, achievements, limitations, and prospects.

"Tumultuous scientific-technical progress has evoked radical changes in the development of military technology. Weapons have been created which have enormous destructive power. The army and navy are equipped with nuclear missile weapons. Soldiers are now confronted with radio-electronics, jet technology, and atomic engines. This confronts them with the task of deep study of technology, to know how to exploit and adapt it." These words were used by Marshal Malinovsky in June, 1965, in describing the impact of technological change on military affairs. Nonetheless, he added that "The high ideological awareness of our troops is the strongest and most powerful weapon of our army. Our undoubted superiority over the armies of the imperialist powers is based on this fact."[20] This state-

* See Chapter 3.

ment reflects the balance that Soviet military spokesmen (and theo-reticians) must maintain between recognition of the importance of technical military developments and continued stress on the ideo-logical and morale factors to which they continue to attribute a crucial significance.

While Stalin had pressed hard the development of certain lines of military technology, it was not until the release of military theo-retical expression after his death that extensive and thoughtful atten-tion was given to the role of science and technology in military affairs. Without reviewing the conclusions of Soviet military writers, we should note that scientific-technical considerations have now been given continuing attention for over a decade.[21] While ideological-political influences still are evident, there no longer is a compulsory line which unduly inhibits or precludes due regard for such technical considerations. The study of the tactical and strategic implications of new and potential weaponry and equipment (e.g., computers) is under way in the Soviet Union, as in the West.

On the global strategic plane, geographical, economic, and tech-nological developments—coupled with political changes—have tre-mendously affected the position of the U.S.S.R. In the latter half of the 1940's, the Soviet Union was totally incapable of offering any threat to the new chief rival for world power—the United States.* The Soviet Union could therefore do nothing more than hold West-ern Europe hostage against precipitate U.S. action, although not as a hostage to deter the United States from *all* counteraction to Soviet moves. And in fact, while the Russians maintained a *relatively* much more powerful façade of military power by keeping substantial mobil-ized forces, her military potential was incomparably weaker. In the first few years after 1945, indeed, the Soviet armed forces were a quite visible but thin crust over a very weak base of strength. (All of this is quite apart from the American nuclear monopoly in the 1940's which was politically but not militarily as important at that time as most people assumed.)

In the mid-1950's, the Soviet Union acquired a modest intercon-tinental nuclear capability with jet bombers. This added a relatively small percentage of the American population to the European hos-tage and thus to the Soviet deterrent, but it did not significantly affect the military balance. Meanwhile, the Korean War had led to a very great strengthening of American military power and of NATO.

---

* To say this does not, of course, imply that the United States aspired to gain world domination, as did the Soviet Union; the world power position of the United States—and of no other power—stood as the obstacle to Soviet expansion.

By this time, however, apparently rather suddenly, in 1955, the Russians realized the extreme vulnerability of their whole position to the now militarily very powerful American strategic nuclear bomber force.

By the time of the first Soviet ICBM test and the first Sputnik, in August and October, 1957, the Soviet Union was actually in the lead in this one new and important branch of technology. However, the "missile gap" of the 1960's turned out to be in favor of the United States rather than the Soviet Union, and this transitory technical precedence was not converted into a military advantage by the Soviet Union.*

By the mid-1960's, the Soviet Union was well on the way to building up a major "second-strike" (i.e., relatively invulnerable, and capable of surviving a hostile first attack) missile capability to deliver heavy thermonuclear strikes on the United States. However, the American second-strike (and still more the theoretically possible first-strike) capability remained much larger, was growing more rapidly, and was less vulnerable.

Thus, technological and geostrategic changes removed a former glaring inequality and weakness of the Soviet position, but they do not offer any prospect of gaining military "superiority" or of offsetting the continuing assured American retaliatory deterrent capability.

It is not the purpose of this discussion to review specific technological developments or prospects, which now extend—literally—out of this world. But while various possible future developments may radically change means of waging war, none appears likely to upset the most fundamental influence of all.

The supreme achievement of military technological advance has undoubtedly been the virtual exclusion of war as an instrument of political choice. War, general nuclear war, is not impossible, but it is not a rational "choice" except as an ultimate defensive recourse. Indeed, strenuous efforts are made to avoid it. Even limited wars carry such great dangers of "escalation" to total war that they, too, are rarely chosen (though they do occur from time to time). This determination to avoid war between the major powers has been the most profound effect of the revolution in military technology.†

The geographical, economic, and technological considerations we have briefly examined in this chapter all contribute to determination

* This subject is discussed in Chapter 6.
† Chapter 10 analyzes Soviet views on war and peace.

of the shape of Soviet military power—to decisions on force levels and composition, and on resource allotments to the military establishment. However, they remain conditioning and limiting factors—presenting certain opportunities, and constraints—on possible strategic programs. The ideological framework that we studied earlier establishes certain broad guidelines, and the geostrategic arena and economic base, as we have here noted, set out certain influencing considerations, but the objectives for which military power is actually designed depend on other politico-military policy aims, to which we turn in the following chapter.

6. Deterrence, Counterdeterrence, and Disarmament

Nations have always prepared for war, expecting that sooner or later war would occur. Sometimes, they have sought war; sometimes, they have prepared poorly for that contingency; sometimes, they have prepared well even while seeking to preserve peace. But today, the great powers, above all the United States and the Soviet Union, base peacetime military preparations on the realization that an unlimited general war would be calamitous beyond description for all. Global thermonuclear war is not "unthinkable"; its conscious choice would be.

Deterrence has superseded defense as the key to security. Defense, retaliation, a "war-winning" capability, or even a "damage-limiting" capability—all strategies of war—are now secondary to deterring or preventing war. A potential aggressor might not initiate a war if he recognized some critical weakness in his capacity for war or saw the likelihood of stimulating a superior coalition of otherwise disunited opponents. Nor would he start a war if he only could advance his interests at too great a cost, or if he recognized that he might fail. Deterrence is based especially on maximizing the last two inhibiting factors. *A deterrent is a capability for counteraction designed to prevent a potential opponent from taking certain actions he might otherwise undertake because of the risk of incurring greater losses than gains.* Deterrence is fundamentally defensive; it involves pre-emptive or prophylactic measures to dissuade an enemy from launching an offensive action, rather than the traditional waging of defense once a war has begun.

For some years, deterrence has been the chief strategy not only of the United States and NATO, but also of the U.S.S.R. The Soviet leaders want to attain and maintain a defensive and retaliatory military power that can deter any opponent from launching an attack or compelling a retreat. At the same time, they want to use their military power as a "counterdeterrent" political weapon—that is, to deter the United States from resorting to its military deterrent as a way of preventing Soviet use of nonmilitary economic, political, subversive, or even of proxy limited-military instruments. In other words, for the Soviet Union deterrence is a double-edged sword, capable of offense as well as defense.

Mutual deterrence is the ability—mutually recognized—of each side to destroy the other, no matter who strikes first. Strategic thinking usually lags far behind actual power changes; mutual deterrence, however, was articulated by President Eisenhower in 1953, ten years before the Soviet Union acquired a reliable and effective intercontinental striking capability. Now, in the mid-1960's, the U.S.S.R. is acquiring an effective "second-strike" capability—a capability to retaliate with a crushing strike on North America even in the hypothetical event that the United States struck first in a surprise blow. This will not, of course, invalidate the continued perfection of the larger United States second-strike capability. What it means is that the Russians will gain a stronger prop for their side of mutual deterrence, despite continuing U.S. strategic superiority.

Requirements for deterrence, and for hedging against the still possible contingency of waging war, are viewed differently in the Soviet Union and in the West. Before 1961 especially, the Russians criticized American theories of deterrence; but by now, Soviet understanding and acceptance of the concept are clear. As Marshal Malinovsky has put it, ". . . we are not proponents of the well-known military aphorism 'the best defense is offense'. . . . We advance another position: the best means of defense is warning the opponent of our strength and readiness to destroy him at the first attempt to commit an act of aggression."[1]

Deterrence depends upon the world balance of power. As a Soviet military discussion has put it:

> The Party views peaceful coexistence not as a result of arbitrary wishes and decisions of certain parties or governments, but as *an objective necessity resulting from the contemporary relation of forces* between the two systems, and the only alternative to a world thermonuclear war [italics added].[2]

The pursuit of peace, through maintenance of deterrent military power, characterizes the Soviet as well as the United States approach. In addition, since 1961, the Soviet claim to military superiority for the socialist camp has been broadened to a claim of general superiority for "the camp of peace." Thus the Soviet claim now includes other factors that affect the general balance of the "relation of forces."

To take advantage of the strategic nuclear stalemate, the Soviet Union seeks more actively to pursue policies to its advantage and contrary to the interests of the Free World. If the United States and its allies were to have a strategy and a corresponding military capability and political posture primed *only* to deter the enemy by threat of total—but mutual—destruction, the Soviet leaders might calculate that for lesser provocation than direct attack upon the United States (or NATO) total retaliation would not be made. A deterrent must be credible, and the Soviet leaders might not always believe the United States would risk nuclear devastation in order to save a distant ally.

Recognizing that the threat of retaliation by total destruction may deter only total wars, the United States began, in 1961, to implement a strategic concept stressing preparations for flexible response. "Total" deterrence, and the maintenance of the forces necessary for it, is alone not sufficient. To deter from lesser threat, or, failing deterrence, to meet lesser military challenges, a flexible strategy supported by capabilities for measured retaliation or confrontation is essential, to provide the basis for strategic choice. United States military policy and posture provide for local use of conventional forces, or, if necessary, nuclear weapons, to meet local aggression and provocation. But, since the Communist aim is to obscure the political basis for response, aggression is not always clear-cut (but may appear as a civil war or in some other guise), and the problem of meeting such aggression is therefore difficult.

It is probable that the Soviet Union figures on *by-passing* military confrontation altogether. After all, it is good Marxism and defensible Leninism to place major expectations on internal revolutions and even on peaceful transition to socialism. And from this perspective, the Russians believe that "the imperialists cannot hold back the course of history by military means."[3] Counterdeterrence is only an auxiliary instrument for constraining Western resort to military means to meet nonmilitary moves.

Only now, in the shadow of nuclear war, is attention being focused *primarily* on the management and use of military power short of war. Deterrence is its cardinal use, but it is by no means the only one. Counterdeterrence is the other, offensive, side of the coin. And there are other forms of military pressure which, within limits, may still be exercised, often in subtle ways. Field maneuvers are often used as military—or political—demonstrations; for example, the Russians and East Germans scheduled maneuvers in April, 1965, which necessitated closing the Autobahn to West Berlin just when the Bundestag of the Federal Republic met in that city. Fighter aircraft even "buzzed" the Reichstag building so noisily that the meeting was impeded. Political application of military power can take many forms: providing arms to other countries; advertising power by parading new armaments; publicizing scientific or technological achievements with military overtones (as in space activities); and many others. Those applications of greatest effect, and greatest risk, involve politico-military confrontations.

During the Suez crisis of November, 1956, the Soviet leaders began to "rattle their rockets," threatening Soviet military retaliation against the West's local uses of military power in other countries. Indirectly, the Russians threatened London in a note (later broadcast) to the British on November 5, asking what position Britain would have found itself in if it had been attacked by rockets possessed by unnamed countries. The United States promptly replied that any rocket attacks on Britain or France would be met by American retaliation on the U.S.S.R. Only *following* the cease-fire did Moscow then threaten that Soviet "volunteers" might aid the Egyptians.

In October, 1957, the Russians spun a tale of a military threat from Turkey to Syria, and again threatened that in case of an attack the U.S.S.R. would not remain passive. Military maneuvers in the Black Sea and Transcaucasus were announced with much fanfare. But while there was a genuine internal crisis in Syria, there was no Turkish threat; the Russians had created a straw man so that later they could claim credit for having averted an attack—an attack that had never been planned.

In July, 1958, unrest filled Lebanon, Jordan, and Iraq. In Iraq, the King and Prime Minister were killed and a revolutionary military dictatorship established. Lebanon and Jordan appealed to the United States and the United Kingdom for military aid, and the next day American marines landed at Beirut and British airborne troops landed in Jordan. The Russians again announced maneuvers in the Transcaucasus and in Bulgaria, with Soviet airborne troops participating in the latter. Despite their fulminations, the Russians had to content themselves with making only vague threats against any intervention in Iraq—clearly not intended by the West—by calling for a summit meeting.

Shortly thereafter, the Russians again felt called upon to make verbal threats as a supportive gesture to the Chinese Communists in their artillery bombardment of Quemoy. On September 7, 1958, Khrushchev threatened that an American attack on China would mean war with the U.S.S.R., but he neither provided tangible support for the Chinese Communists in their unsuccessful attempt to take Quemoy nor defined what would constitute "an attack on China."

In November, 1958, the Russians demanded that West Berlin become a "free city" within six months. They renewed the demand in 1959. Again, in June, 1961, the Soviet Government publicly demanded a German peace treaty—with access to Berlin turned over to the East German authorities—by the end of that year. These threats again failed. It is now more than seven years since Khrushchev demanded a "free city" within six months; the Soviet threats have been completely ineffective.

In Cuba, in July, 1960, the Russians gingerly used their counter-deterrent by saying that "figuratively" their rockets protected that country. Subsequently, in July, 1962, Khrushchev claimed credit for the failure of the 1961 Bay of Pigs invasion by saying that Soviet rockets, in the U.S.S.R., had deterred the United States. This claim was nullified by the *later* Soviet claim, made after the removal of Russian missiles from Cuba in November, 1962, that those missiles had been introduced into the island only to defend Cuba from invasion.*

Time and again, Soviet leaders and spokesmen have said that *any* attack on a socialist state would bring a crushing retaliatory blow. Yet in August, 1964, when the United States retaliated for North Vietnamese patrol boat attacks by attacking their bases in North Viet-Nam, the Russians made no move. Finally, in February, 1965, in response to North Vietnamese armed intervention in the Republic of (South) Viet-Nam through the Viet-Cong—and at a time when Premier Kosygin was in Hanoi—the United States began almost daily bombing attacks on North Viet-Nam, and the Russians did not retaliate. From these and similar cases,[4] a common pattern emerges: Soviet threats have always been vague, with loopholes for withdrawal; invariably, they have been made only when Moscow was certain that

---

* An even more startling inconsistency in the Soviet position was provided by an official statement in *Pravda* on September 12, 1962, only a little over a month before the missile crisis: "The Government of the Soviet Union has authorized TASS to state also that *there is no need for the Soviet Union to install in any other country—Cuba, for instance—the weapons it has for repelling aggression, for a retaliatory strike.* The explosive power of our nuclear weapons is so great, and the Soviet Union has such powerful missiles for delivering these nuclear warheads, that *there is no need to seek sites for them somewhere beyond the boundaries of the Soviet Union* [italics added]." This position was belied by the Soviet action in September-October, 1962.

the Western power or powers were not going to undertake the actions its retaliatory threats pertained to; and, in the few instances when the opponents have acted, Soviet retaliation did not follow. Even so, the Soviet Union has in some cases gained political capital from such "ballistic blackmail."

Such confrontations are not without risk. It is clear, however, that the Russians have attempted to make political gains from military counterdeterrent threats, though circumscribing the threats so as to minimize or evade the implied commitments.

Two especially significant cases of politico-military confrontation were the Berlin crisis of June to October, 1961, and the Cuban missile crisis of October-November, 1962. Underlying both was the so-called missile gap shift in the over-all strategic military balance.

The Soviet diplomatic campaign to change the status of Berlin had been intermittent since November, 1958. But soon after Khrushchev and President Kennedy met at Vienna on June 3 and 4, 1961, it entered a new phase of public confrontation. In a major televised address on June 15, reporting on the Vienna meeting, Khrushchev again demanded a German peace treaty and "free city" status for West Berlin before the year's end.

Perhaps Khrushchev misunderstood President Kennedy's readiness to establish good relations with the Soviet Union, although the President was quietly firm in their talks. Perhaps Khrushchev mistook for weakness the decision not to commit American forces directly to aid the Cuban *émigré* force in the Bay of Pigs invasion two months earlier. In any case, he realized that the impression of Soviet strategic strength was a waning asset, and he saw the United States embarked on a program to redress weaknesses in conventional military power. It may not have been that a push on Berlin was so promising at that time but that whatever chances there were would be even less promising in the future.

On July 8, 1961, Khrushchev announced an increase of 3.144 billion rubles ($3.4 billion) in the Soviet defense budget, and suspension of the large-scale reduction in the Soviet armed forces, which had begun in January, 1960. The Soviet increase in defense spending was precisely equivalent to the United States increase of $3.4 billion in defense expenditures, which had been announced by President Kennedy on May 25. The suspension of force reductions also demonstrated an intention to maintain a higher degree of combat readiness. Thus began the use of military moves to affect the Berlin situation.[5]

Soviet Air Force Day, July 9, was the occasion for displaying a number of new aircraft, including a supersonic medium bomber. Although Air Force Day is an annual celebration, 1961's was the first in five years in which there was a display of new and experimental advanced-performance aircraft. Navy Day, on July 30, also featured the first public display, at Leningrad, of missile-launching destroyers, submarines, and patrol craft.

President Kennedy, in a major address on July 25, restated Western determination on the Berlin issue. He outlined a number of major measures of military build-up including: a $3.25-billion increase in defense expenditures, an increase of the armed forces by 225,000 men; and authorization to call up an additional 250,000 reservists at any time. The President also provided that certain air and naval units previously scheduled for retirement be retained in service. He emphasized the need for boosting nonnuclear capabilities: "about half the total sum is needed for the procurement of non-nuclear weapons, ammunition, and equipment." At the same time, President Kennedy referred to steps taken earlier to put 50 per cent of all strategic bombers on ground alert. Finally, he directed attention toward civil defense, and transferred some of its functions to the Department of Defense.

On August 7, Khrushchev replied in a speech which paralleled, point by major point, the President's speech of July 25. He spoke of the catastrophic consequences of a nuclear war in terms not usually heard by a Soviet audience, and attributed motives of military pressure to the United States.

Meanwhile, a Warsaw Pact meeting was held in late July and early August. On August 10, Marshal Ivan Konev was recalled from retirement to be Commander in Chief of the Soviet forces in Germany. On August 17, in a classical military "demonstration," foreign military attachés in Moscow were invited to observe a Soviet field exercise featuring employment of mock tactical nuclear weapons. This was the first time since World War II that American and Allied attachés were invited to observe Soviet field maneuvers.

Western military measures were undertaken that paralleled these Soviet moves. On August 8, the three training divisions of the U.S. Army were ordered into combat-ready status, and it was announced that 270 B-47 medium bombers scheduled for retirement would be retained in service. Dispatch of modest French and British reinforcements to West Germany was announced on August 17. Immediately, the U.S. Navy disclosed plans to increase the active fleet by 5 per cent. After the Communists closed off East Berlin on August 13, Vice President Johnson went to Berlin on August 18, and on August

19, a U.S. Army battle group was sent there. On August 14, the Navy declared that reserve officers due for release would be retained. On August 16, it was announced that soldiers due for release in the eight months following October 1, 1961, would be kept on active duty for four extra months, and that 23,000 Army reservists were being alerted. On August 25, over 76,000 reservists were called to active duty. On the 27th, it was announced that the Marines would reach their planned strength of 190,000 by December 1. On August 30, General Lucius Clay was sent to assume command again in Berlin. On September 9, an order to dispatch 40,000 troops to Europe, and to cease sending dependents there, was made public.

The Russians responded to President Kennedy's July 25 program and the subsequent moves toward implementation during August with a new series of major measures to "match" the U.S. program and a new campaign to emphasize Soviet strategic nuclear and missile strength. On August 30, a formal decree was published temporarily retaining on active duty those servicemen due for annual release. The next day, the U.S.S.R. announced the resumption of nuclear testing. This move had evidently been under consideration for some time, and was not surprising, given Soviet inferiority in nuclear weapons technology. Although contingent preparations for testing must have been made earlier, the actual decision may only have been made after the President's speech, in late July or early August. The first nuclear test in the series was held on September 1. That day, it was announced that maneuvers would take place in certain closed areas of the Arctic from mid-September to mid-November. On September 8 and 9, another Warsaw Pact meeting was held. On the 10th, it was announced that there would be ICBM firings into the Pacific between mid-September and mid-October; this was accompanied by a multimegaton thermonuclear test in the Arctic. And, in mid-September, several belligerent articles by Soviet marshals were published.

The United States did not consider it necessary to match Soviet nuclear-missile demonstrations, though nuclear testing was soon resumed. The earlier program continued, including alert status for the Strategic Air Command. On September 19, the United States called another 73,000 reservists to active duty, including two National Guard divisions, and a new Strategic Army Command, incorporating the Air Force's Tactical Air Command, was established. The temporary reinforcement of the U.S. Air Force in Europe by over 200 fighter aircraft was revealed on September 8 and 28.

Allied measures to increase military strength were also announced.

Two divisions returned to France from Algeria, and the United Kingdom revealed plans to build a reserve division from other existing units by retrenchment of overseas deployment. The Federal Republic of Germany decided to retain 40,000 men due for release and to extend the draft term to eighteen months.

Along with the planned military measures, at least one unplanned demonstration occurred: Two West German fighters flew to West Berlin on September 14—without being challenged by East German air defenses. Two days later, two Czech fighters crossed ten miles into West Germany, apparently in token reprisal.

Both sides publicized maneuvers. NATO exercises Check Mate (held in Central Europe, September 12–15) and Check Mate II (held in the Mediterranean, Greece, and Turkey, September 16–21) were given prominence—especially in Soviet press denunciations. In the course of Check Mate II, a U.S. aircraft carrier and cruiser visited Istanbul, and two U.S. destroyers entered the Black Sea.

On September 25, Warsaw Pact maneuvers for October and November were announced, though scale and locale were not specified. A major Warsaw Pact command post exercise, involving several satellite armies, with large-scale field maneuvers, took place, ending on October 11.

In early October, most East European Communist countries announced extension of active duty for servicemen about to be discharged. The extension was for the period "until a German peace treaty was signed," but cutbacks were quietly made some months later even though a peace treaty was never signed. In East Germany, there was no reference to a peace treaty, but the extension was to be effective "for about six months."

The chief Soviet military moves in October were nuclear and missile tests. On the 13th, the period of missile testing in the Pacific range was extended to the end of the month. In his speech to the Twenty-second Party Congress on October 17, Khrushchev announced the forthcoming test of a 50–MT weapon. Following a 30–MT trial run on the 23rd, a 57–MT test was held on October 30, climaxing (though not concluding) the 1961 Soviet nuclear test series.

On October 11, the United States announced the reinforcement of its forces in Europe by another 10,000 men, including a reinforced regiment and 50 more fighter aircraft. On the 14th, a massive continental North American air defense exercise, "Skyshield," was held.

In a major speech on October 2, U.S. Deputy Defense Secretary Gilpatric outlined the U.S. measures of military build-up that had been undertaken to meet the Berlin situation, and authoritatively indicated the degree of U.S. nuclear superiority. American press sources had indicated a new, lower U.S. estimate of Soviet strategic missile strength, and Secretary Gilpatric added an unprecedented evaluation that the United States was so superior in strategic strength that even a Soviet first strike could not prevent a U.S. second strike of equal or even greater might. Significantly, though Soviet commentaries pilloried the "threatening" nature of the speech, and Marshal Malinovsky cryptically referred to it in his speech to the Party Congress a few days later, Gilpatric's evaluation was not challenged.

By the end of October, the Berlin confrontation of 1961 was over. The proceedings of the Twenty-second Party Congress diverted attention and helped to obscure the collapse of the Soviet offensive on Berlin. True, the Communists had built "the wall" on August 13, restricting civilian movement between the two parts of the city, but this was a fall-back action for dealing with some of the more desperate problems of East Germany, rather than a strategy for evicting the Western Powers from West Berlin. It is not possible to measure the precise effect of each move and countermove in the politico-military confrontation; in combination, however, the Western moves persuaded the Soviet leaders that they could not get their way.

Because the extensive use of politico-military measures involves an increased commitment of resources and prestige, there is also greater reluctance to back down. The 1961 Berlin crisis is proof that this consideration can be overridden by recognizing the greater risks of proceeding still further.

The United States build-up in conventional forces supported statements of intent to resist any encroachments for which a nuclear response would have been unsuitable. At the same time, parallel moves to increase the strength and alert status of the strategic nuclear forces demonstrated readiness to prepare for nuclear war if resort to it became necessary. The unity of the NATO Alliance, and the undertaking of joint and parallel politico-military moves by the United States and the European NATO powers, upset any Soviet hopes to divide the Alliance by intimidation.

Most of the specific military measures undertaken in 1961, including augmentations in force levels and redeployments by both sides, were gradually rescinded in the year or so following the crisis period.

Failure in the 1961 campaign against Berlin intensified Khrushchev's dilemma. Trading in rocket "futures," he had attempted from 1958 through 1961 the overambitious task of dislodging the Western Powers from Berlin. During that period, "the missile gap," which Khrushchev had relied on, was becoming less and less convincing.

The missile gap was born of a Western fear that the Soviet Union would press for and attain at least a temporary advantage in intercontinental ballistic missiles, and thus threaten Western superiority in the strategic balance. Soviet priority in ICBM testing and in launching two sputniks into orbit in the fall of 1957 made this a reasonable fear. Aware of the complexities in translating an early advance in long-range rocketry into an operational capability, military and intelligence analysts were concerned that, with maximum effort, the Russians might produce large numbers of such weapons before comparable U.S. missiles could be operationally deployed. For the United States, the only course was to prepare for the worst possibilities.

Long before precipitating the Berlin crisis of 1961, Khrushchev knew that there would be no missile gap in his favor. Indeed, it was probably that realization which led him to make the final effort to use bluff—testing the mettle of President Kennedy and the cohesion of the NATO Alliance. Neither was found wanting. By the fall of 1961, the swollen image of a missile gap was punctured by disclosures from Washington. During 1962, it became evident to the world that, as Moscow and Washington already knew, the missile gap of the mid-1960's—in fact, a *widening* intercontinental missile gap— was in the favor of the United States.

Khrushchev was disappointed and chagrined by his failure to gain any concrete political dividends from the Soviet Union's priority in space exploration and rocket development. But beyond this, he was also harassed by his loss of prestige within the Party leadership at home and within the world Communist movement. Moreover, now his military men were concerned about the growing American strategic missile superiority.

Sometime in the spring of 1962, it was decided to offset the American missile gap by a daring "end-run" emplacement of intermediate-range missiles in Cuba. Castro believed this would be an irrevocable as well as tangible Soviet commitment to his regime, something he had been denied in being excluded from the Warsaw Pact. From the standpoint of the Soviet military leadership, this would transform cheap and readily available medium- and intermediate-range missiles into ersatz intercontinental missiles, of which the Russians had very few, and would complicate and down-grade the defenses of the North American continent. To Khrushchev, a dramatic improvement in the Soviet strategic military posture vis-à-vis the United States would mean great prestige for him and for the U.S.S.R. Still more important, by reducing Western confidence and cohesiveness, it promised to give him increased leverage for a new confrontation on Berlin. Also, it would have given Khrushchev satisfaction to emulate the United States by placing a base close to its borders, paralleling U.S. missile and air bases around the periphery of the Soviet Union. And—though this is sheer speculation—he may have visualized the possibility of trading the Soviet missile base in Cuba for the U.S. missile base in Turkey if the United States showed sufficient alarm and disquiet.

Instead, Khrushchev faced Washington's resolute determination to have the missiles removed from Cuba by whatever means were found necessary. Khrushchev's only choice quickly became one of either removing the missiles, under humiliating circumstances of U.S. escort under an effective U.S. naval quarantine, or having them destroyed by the United States.[6]

Earlier, the Russians had begun shipping large quantities of weapons to Castro. In statements on September 4 and 13, 1962, President Kennedy made it clear that the United States would not intervene in this military build-up, but would prevent the Castro regime from extending its aggressive aims by force or threat of force anywhere in the Western Hemisphere, and that "the gravest issues would arise" if *offensive* missiles were brought to Cuba. But as late as October 18, when Foreign Minister Gromyko gave his personal assurance to the President, the Soviet leaders denied any intention of placing offensive missiles in Cuba.

On October 22, President Kennedy disclosed that reconnaissance overflight had revealed that the Soviet Union was installing medium- and intermediate-range missiles, and jet bombers, in Cuba. He imposed a quarantine on any shipment of offensive weapons and equipment into Cuba, said that the existing weapons must be dismantled and removed, and to deal with any interim threats, he declared: "It shall be the policy of this nation to regard any nuclear missile launched from Cuba against any nation in the Western Hemisphere as an attack by the Soviet Union on the United States, requiring a *full* retaliatory response upon the Soviet Union."[7]

The United States received complete support from the OAS and NATO allies, set up an effective blockade, rapidly built up a large conventional force capable of occupying Cuba, assembled tactical air force units capable of destroying the missile sites with non-nuclear strikes, and placed its world-wide strategic air and missile forces on alert.

By October 28, the Soviet leaders knew they had only hours left in which to remove the missiles themselves or leave them to be destroyed. They fumbled the response, tried belatedly and unsuccessfully to trade Soviet missiles in Cuba for U.S. missiles in Turkey, and then agreed to remove the weapons. The missiles and equipment, and after some wrangling, the IL-28 jet light bombers, too, were withdrawn under U.S. naval surveillance. Castro balked at permitting on-the-ground verification—with the result that U.S. aerial reconnaissance continued, and the United States declined to give any formal assurance against invasion of the island.

What was the threat from the Cuban-based missiles? In military terms, the twenty-four MRBM launchers, with missiles capable of striking targets over 1,000 nautical miles distant (e.g., Washington, D.C.), and twelve to sixteen IRBM's with a range of 2,200 n.m., would have added the equivalent of nearly half the existing Soviet first-strike salvo against North America. The missiles would have brought under potential attack forty additional SAC bases and other prime targets which otherwise would not be vulnerable in a Soviet strike. Thus they would have served as a powerful addition to the small Soviet ICBM force, offsetting much of the Soviet strategic missile gap vis-à-vis the more powerful U.S. force. They would *not*, however, have given the Soviet Union a strategic superiority, and even if many more had subsequently been set up in Cuba they would not have countered the invulnerable American Polaris and the hardened Minutemen forces. The IL-28 jet light bombers were a less serious threat, though previously U.S. air defenses had not had to be deployed against possible attack from the south.

The United States easily won the Cuban missile showdown because, first, it had greatly superior strategic military power; second, it was determined to effect the removal of the offensive weapons by whatever means should prove necessary; and third, it had local ground, air, and naval superiority which permitted the quarantine, conventional bombing, or, if necessary, land invasion, in order to effect its will. The United States could have invaded Cuba without provoking Soviet counteraction, but preferred to stay within the original and announced purpose of its application of power rather than initiate an offensive action aimed at the Castro regime itself. The Soviet Union was thus given a line of retreat. It was a complete defeat for the Soviet Union, even though the United States did not choose to exploit its victory by eliminating the Castro regime or even by removing all Soviet military presence on the island or military assistance to Cuba.

Khrushchev cut his diplomatic losses fairly effectively, using as a smoke screen the myth of having introduced the missiles only to prevent an impending American invasion.

The Soviet Union was frustrated in the political and military aims that had led to the missile gambit. American strategic superiority was doubly confirmed; Khrushchev's ploy exposed the Soviet's need for such substitute intercontinental missiles; and its failure not only denied such missiles to the Russians but bore impressive witness to the American superiority that compelled him to capitulate.

The failure of the Soviet Cuban missile venture, coming on the heels of the failure in Berlin and the exposure of the myth of the missile gap, caused Moscow to renew its attention to *détente* and to explore areas of agreement on arms control measures. The Cuban confrontation had compelled the Soviet leaders to reckon with nuclear war—and they did not want another encounter in which to choose defeat as the lesser evil. Moreover, now there was no prospect of offsetting the continuing rapid American build-up in strategic missiles. Would there be an alternative in disarmament?

There has been a long, and superficially consistent, Soviet tradition of public support for disarmament. Lenin had opposed the idea before the Bolsheviks seized power, but on a number of occasions after 1921, the Russians led in championing disarmament.[8] In the 1920's and 1930's, and for about ten years after World War II, the Russians regarded disarmament as a field for propaganda exploitation.

But over the last decade, Soviet leaders have shown a readiness to consider some arms control measures, presumably to curb certain aspects of the arms race. For example, they have agreed to a partial nuclear weapons test ban, and to a ban on nuclear weapons in space, in order to eliminate these particular arms competitions. (Arms limitation must, of course, be regarded as the other side of the coin of arms build-up; it is a dimension of military policy.)

The use of military power as a political instrument is often more important than its relative war-making capacity. Thus Khrushchev, with a trumped-up capability, engaged in ballistic blackmail as long ago as the Suez crisis, in November, 1956. The limits of bluff are well known, and the Cuban missile crisis showed the inadequacy of a minimum deterrent in a confrontation provoked by an adventurous gamble.

Why did the Soviet leaders permit the missile gap to develop against them? They did not regard their first ICBM's suitable for large-scale deployment, and they did not believe it was necessary to enter on a crash program. They realized that the United States would not strike without cause. And they rightly believed that they could control the risks and would not press a challenge that would provoke the United States to that extreme resort. But they also believed, wrongly, that they could parlay their scientific and engineering accomplishments into a bluff military capability. They recognized that even a crash program could give them only a slim and transitory strategic missile superiority, one which would not provide any usable military options. Finally, and perhaps most important, the Soviet leaders judged that the political leverage they could have had for the time required to build a large intercontinental strike force would have been so costly as to curtail other programs. The West did not intervene in Hungary in 1956 although the Soviet Union had only a marginal and makeshift intercontinental capability; on the other hand, the West would unite in repelling and retaliating to any Soviet attack on a NATO member even if the Soviet Union had doubled or tripled its forces.

The same considerations have led to a deliberate but not maximum Soviet strategic missile program in the years since. In addition, by the mid-1960's the Soviet leaders were well aware of the fact that if they did set out to try to attain military superiority, the United States could easily match their efforts and they would never succeed in reaching that goal.

The Soviet Union is now acquiring a second-strike capability. But there is no foreseeable way for the Soviet Union to neutralize the U.S. strategic second-strike capability. This is the basis of mutual deterrence. The United States now has a superiority of more than four-to-one in ICBM's alone—with almost all of them "hardened" to withstand nuclear attack. Soviet military men know this, but compulsively try to reverse this superiority. Khrushchev did not. And although Brezhnev and Kosygin may not believe in the possibilities of gain from a larger strategic military build-up, they will undoubtedly authorize programs that promise real political or military advantage. They are not likely, however, to be impressed with requests for "requirements" that do not promise specific advantages.

Since the Soviet leaders recognize the limits, as well as the potentialities, of military power, they are prepared to manipulate or bargain to improve their position or to avoid investing in military fields that do not yield a dividend. In short, they are not a priori averse to arms control or disarmament.

Agreements reached so far have been peripheral, but important. By agreeing not to place nuclear weapons or other weapons of mass destruction in outer space, the Soviet leaders have cooperated in preventing a costly, though strategically indecisive, additional burden to the arms race—and to international tension. Soviet military literature indicates there was lobbying for deployment of large-yield thermonuclear weapons in space from the spring of 1962 until Khrushchev's sudden decision in the early fall of 1963 to agree to a ban on deploying such weapons. (There is, however, no restraint against *developing* such weapons, and the U.S.S.R. has paraded an "orbital missile.")

The nuclear-test-ban agreement is the prime example of an arms control agreement having major political as well as military significance. The Soviet leaders had probably begun their campaign for a nuclear test ban in 1956 with an eye to propaganda benefits. When they realized that the experts meeting in Geneva—including Soviet scientists—had concluded that verification would require inspection of the U.S.S.R., they quickly backed down from the negotiations. An informal moratorium on nuclear testing was accepted by both sides, from the fall of 1958 until the Russians resumed their massive test series in the fall of 1961. But after the Cuban missile crisis, Khrushchev—despite the stiff opposition of some of his colleagues[9]— declared Soviet willingness to accept two or three on-site annual inspections. It appears that he believed that the United States would accept this compromise of the previous Soviet stand that no inspections were necessary. The United States position, however, required a minimum number of inspections keyed to the number of unidentified events which might be clandestine tests.

A few months after the failure to agree on a comprehensive test ban, Khrushchev picked up an old Western "fall-back" test-ban proposal, limited to atmospheric, underwater, and outer space testing, which did not call for the on-site inspections necessary to check on possible clandestine underground tests. On August 5, 1963, the partial nuclear-weapons test ban was signed by the United States, the United Kingdom, and the Soviet Union, and subsequently by more than a hundred other nations.

The United States and the U.S.S.R. had on June 20, 1963, agreed to establish a direct communications link between Washington and Moscow (the "hot line"), which, in an emergency, could be used to ward off "accidental" outbreak of war. On October 17, 1963, agreement between the United States and the U.S.S.R. led to the United Nations resolution against placing nuclear weapons and other weapons of mass destruction in outer space. To date, these are the only arms control agreements other than unilateral declarations of reductions in military budgets and in production of fissionable materials for weapons purposes. Other possible measures will be individually judged by military, political, economic, and propaganda criteria. And it should be noted that "stabilized deterrence" (that is, agreement to freeze a state of mutual deterrent strength) would not, to the Soviet leaders, mean a stabilization of the over-all "relation of forces."

There is a vast difference between limited arms control—or even circumscribed arms limitation and reduction—on the one hand, and "general and complete disarmament," on the other. It is one thing to weigh the particular military, political, and other considerations involved in a limited measure; it is something else to face the unknowable consequences of total disarmament.

Since 1959, the Russians have championed general and complete disarmament. Is this what they really want? They have at least had to think seriously about the matter—if only because of the Sino-Soviet ideological polemic.

The exchanges between the Soviet and Chinese Communist parties and governments, indirectly since 1960 and openly since 1963, are instructive. The essence of the Chinese charge is that the Russians are deceiving themselves and others in claiming that complete disarmament is possible in a world of coexisting Communist and capitalist states. As the Chinese Government statement of September 1, 1963, put it: "General and complete disarmament can be realized only after imperialism, capitalism, and all systems of exploitation have been eliminated."[10] It went on to say that the contrary Soviet view was "a total betrayal of Marxism-Leninism." Marshal Lo Jui-ching embellished this statement, often reiterated by the Chinese, in May, 1965, when he said: "The modern revisionists [i.e., the Soviet leaders] have woven a fancy fairy tale in a perverse attempt to make people believe that imperialism and socialism can advance hand in hand toward what they call 'a world without weapons, without armies, without war.' How can Communists spout such contemptible lies and nonsense?"[11]

The Soviet reply is that this line will gain popular world support.[12] The Chinese accept the tactical use of disarmament as a slogan, but they have argued that the Russians have come to believe their own propaganda! Thus, for example, as early as mid-1960, a Chinese spokesman declared:

It is, of course, inconceivable that imperialism will accept proposals for general and complete disarmament. The purpose of putting forward such proposals is to arouse the peoples throughout the world to unite and oppose the imperialistic scheme for an arms drive as war preparations, to unmask the aggressive and bellicose nature of imperialism before the people of the world. . . . But there are people [i.e., the Soviet leaders] who believe that such proposals can be realized when imperialism still exists. . . . This is an unrealistic illusion—only when the socialist revolution is victorious throughout the world can there be a world free from war, a world without arms. Such a world is inconceivable while imperialism still exists.[13]

The Russians could have rebutted or evaded the Chinese charge, or they could have shifted their stand. Instead, they have insisted on it. The Open Letter of the CPSU to the CCP of July 14, 1963, flatly states: "Our struggle for disarmament is *not* a tactical expedient. We sincerely want disarmament. And here, too, we stand foursquare on Marxist-Leninist positions."[14]

Ambassador Valerian Zorin has related the Soviet stand on complete disarmament to the Soviet arms build-up, as an alternative means to provide security. "*Along with* strengthening its defensive might by first-rate nuclear weapons, which are a reliable shield for all socialist states and peace-loving peoples, the Soviet Union has expounded a broad program for general and complete disarmament as a realistic method of safeguarding and strengthening universal peace and the security of peoples."[15]

It appears that the Russians do not realistically regard complete disarmament, or, indeed, any significant disarmament, as urgent, necessary, or likely. However, if mutually acceptable terms could be arranged, the Soviet leaders would consider disarmament worthwhile—even at the very real costs of contributing to alienation of the Chinese and of further dividing the world Communist movement.

Because capitalism more than Communism is considered to be dependent on military instrumentalities, it seems desirable to try to eliminate military supports of capitalism even if it means the socialist states must give them up. War, a classic way of "disarming" an opponent, is not acceptable in the thermonuclear age, and at best, disarmament is a long-range possibility. Meanwhile, the Russians have recourse to broad political action which contributes to the internal undermining of capitalist societies and their armies.

In one way, Moscow views complete disarmament as a revolutionary political development facilitating the victory of world Communism through political, economic, and subversive means. Moreover, the danger of an accidental or desperate Western attack, which could arrest or seriously alter the course of the historical movement of the world to Communism, would be averted. Further, it would offer substantial inducements to achieve the economic goals of Communist society, and might cause Western societies to suffer economic dislocation and disorientation. At the same time, complete disarmament would cause many disadvantages such as the loss of military power, the political implications of inspection, the creation of an international control structure, the risks of evacuating Eastern Europe, and the reduction of the U.S.S.R.'s influence within the Communist world, especially vis-à-vis China.

Ideological factors persuade the Soviet leaders of certain advantages in general and complete disarmament. By the same token, they also believe that the capitalists will recoil from the proposition, and that they will not in the foreseeable future reach agreement. Moreover, they are aware that in the past it has been arms or the threat of arms that has enabled the Communist Bloc to expand; in a decision, they would probably give some weight to this fact, despite their recognition of the undesirability of war in the nuclear age.

The problems of negotiating disarmament agreements are many— ideological, diplomatic, internal political, and security. Although it would be wrong to consider the Soviet leaders dedicated to disarmament as a goal in itself, it would probably also be wrong to conclude that they regard it only from the standpoint of political action and propaganda opportunity.[16] Arms control and disarmament, while accepted reluctantly—and no doubt suspiciously—by the military leadership, are now a real dimension of Soviet national military policy.

"The objective of military strategy," states a Soviet General Staff organ, "is the creation by military means of those conditions under which politics is in a position to achieve the aims it sets for itself."[17] In keeping with this principle, Soviet military doctrine holds that the coordinated use of military power is necessary. This requires a flexible military establishment enabling selectivity of means, and the rejection of any strategy for military operations based predominantly upon reliance on any particular weapons system—including the ICBM. This approach is deeply ingrained in the Communist precept to avoid "adventuristic gambling" on any single or superficially "easy" means to victory. And under contemporary circumstances, the Russians see no margin for general war.

How has the age of nuclear deterrence affected this doctrine? For one thing, the feasibility of waging war successfully is no longer a certainty, nor is the range of military requirements. The framework of Soviet military policy *was* shaken after 1960 by Khrushchev's insistence on shaping military forces for deterrence rather than for war. It is true that technological improvements caused some forces and weapons to become obsolete or unnecessary, but differing opinions on force requirements threatened the maintenance of forces sufficient for waging war should it come. During the Khrushchev decade, the Soviet armed forces were cut from nearly 6 million men to less than 3 million. The number of combat-ready Army divisions was slashed from about one hundred and seventy-five to less than seventy-five. In 1960 alone, the number of combat aircraft in the Tactical Air Forces was cut by one half, in Naval Aviation by two-thirds.

Deterrence reduced the weight given to requirements for waging war, but introduced others. If uses of military power short of war were expanded, so, too, were some of the criteria and requirements for various forms of military power. Arms assistance and sales to other countries, for example, disposed of some surplus weapons and equipment but also drew on current production. By the mid-1960's, the Soviet leaders probably wished they had some aircraft carriers, not for use in a major war, but in order to be able to establish a military presence at great distances from the U.S.S.R. The Soviet Marine Corps (naval infantry), which had been abolished in the early 1950's, was re-established in the early 1960's, to provide a modest wartime amphibious lift in the Baltic, the Turkish Straits, and the Sea of Japan, and perhaps also to provide an option for rapid establishment of a military presence in distant areas. Finally, the whole question of limited non-nuclear wars raises at least contingent requirements, as Soviet military spokesmen have made ever more clear since 1962, and especially since the fall of Khrushchev.[18]

The official published Soviet military budget is neither complete nor accurate, but does indicate trends in the over-all rate of military expenditure (though nothing at all on the changing priorities of its various components). It shows that there was a dip in the mid-1950's, a lower plateau in the last half of the 1950's, and a fairly sharp rise in 1961–62 to a new rough plateau. Some military expenditures have been buried in other parts of the budget, but judging by the official military budget, the Soviet Union has been spending more in the 1960's though the share of the rising gross national product of the country devoted to military outlays has been decreasing.[19]

Strategic-offensive and defensive weapons systems and forces occupy a larger role than they had, and the traditionally dominant "general purpose forces"—ground armies and supporting air and naval forces —have been cut back. Nonetheless, the ground forces and the strategic defensive forces still receive the greatest shares of resources.

To some extent, these changes reflect technological developments, but they also reflect policy choices.

The structure, shape, and size of the Soviet armed forces are determined by many considerations. Deterrence establishes its claim, and the dynamics of the arms race and of continually developing military technology keeps it from being met by any simple minimum deterrent once provided. Counterdeterrence and political uses of military power to influence others may simply add an additional margin to deterrent requirements, or may also establish new demands. A hedge against the possible contingency of waging war—any of several different kinds and intensities of war, nuclear and non-nuclear—is necessarily included. Some of the keenest conflicts over military force levels and resource allotments arise over divergent assessments of the *extent* of hedging to meet the heavy demands of war-waging strategies. Finally, though not of great direct importance so far, arms control and disarmament considerations may affect the mix (as with nuclear testing limitations).

The importance of various political uses of military power, and their relation to over-all Soviet policy, thus also have direct impact on the character and nature of the military establishment.

III

Military Relations in the Communist World

7. Soviet Military Relations with Eastern Europe, 1943–65

With the turning-point of World War II on the Eastern Front in 1943, Stalin and the Soviet leadership began to plan actively for the role the U.S.S.R. would play in Eastern Europe after the war. In addition to cautiously laying the diplomatic groundwork for exerting maximum influence in Eastern and Central Europe, the Russians also provided support to Communist-led partisan movements and formed miiltary units from personnel in the Soviet Union. In 1943, President Beneš of Czechoslovakia signed the first of a series of bilateral treaties of friendship and nonaggression with the U.S.S.R.

On April 2, 1944, units of the Red Army crossed the 1941 border into Romania, and on July 18, into Poland. Soviet war aims were beginning to shift from liberating the U.S.S.R. from German occupation to liberating the peoples of Eastern Europe both from the Germans *and* from non-Communist rule.* By the end of the war, Soviet armies had occupied Poland, the eastern portions of Germany and Austria, most of Czechoslovakia, Hungary, Romania, Bulgaria, and part of Yugoslavia. The presence of Soviet military forces provided strong leverage over these states, and the opportunity was exploited.

The manner of Soviet pressures leading to Communist rule differed within the various countries of Eastern Europe, but the over-all pattern was consistent and clear. By gradual stages, usually with a minimum of direct Soviet intervention, the most effective anti-Communist and non-Communist leaders were neutralized, and Communist control was extended within coalition governments. We need not

---

* Marshal K. Moskalenko, in an article on the twentieth anniversary of the German defeat in Czechoslovakia ("From the Carpathians to Prague," *Red Star*, April 23, 1965), cited this operation as "brilliant proof of the Soviet people's splendid discharge of their international duty and of the accomplishment of the liberation mission which fell their lot in the years of World War II." He went on to note that Soviet military operations were determined by "military *and* political objectives," which included "liberating Prague and the entire remaining territory of western Czechoslovakia as rapidly as possible." The same was true in other areas that Soviet armies could reach.

review the details of the Communist take-over in Poland, Romania, Bulgaria, Hungary, and Czechoslovakia. In each case, it occurred in stages over the period from 1944 through 1948; in Czechoslovakia, it was not consummated until some time after the withdrawal of Soviet military forces in 1945. In Yugoslavia and Albania, the local national Communist partisan forces had come into power during the war, as soon as the Germans were expelled. In Greece, their attempt was unsuccessful.

The armies of some of these countries became an instrument of the expansion of Communist control; in all these countries, the armies were a primary target of attention. Background differences were significant in their early impact on the new military arms of these Communist "people's democracies," and we shall therefore turn to brief accounts of the early postwar (or even wartime) emergence, and later development, of the new armed forces of these states, before considering their recent and current roles or relations to one another and to the U.S.S.R.

Poland

In April, 1943, the Germans disclosed the murder of more than 10,000 Polish officers in Katyn Forest in 1940. Although the Nazis had been responsible for heinous crimes on an even vaster scale, there can be little doubt that the NKVD had murdered the Polish officers at Stalin's command. In the spring of 1943, the effect of the disclosure was a breaking off of relations between the Soviet Government and the Polish Government-in-Exile in London.

As the result of the Sikorski-Maisky Agreement of July 30, 1941, under which diplomatic relations had been established, General Wladyslaw Anders had been released and permitted to form an army of 75,000 men. During 1942, by mutual agreement, this force left the Soviet Union through Iran for service in the West.

On May 8, 1943, the Council of People's Commissars in Moscow announced agreement to the formation of a new Polish army, initially a division (named the Kosciuszko Division for the great Polish hero) under command of Colonel Zygmunt Berling, a professional Polish officer who had split with General Anders. This nucleus was later expanded to form a Polish People's Army—Communist controlled, but stressing national rather than Communist aims.[1] By August a second division and a First Corps headquarters were formed. By the end of 1943, the Polish units totaled 32,400 men, and some had entered service at the front. In March, 1944, the First Corps was expanded to become the First Army. This Army, under

Brigadier (soon Divisional) General Berling, entered Poland with the Soviet First Byelorussian Front. A separate First Tank Corps, and later also a Second Army, were formed and assigned to the First Ukrainian Front.

On July 22, 1944, a Polish High Command was established, with Colonel General Michal Rola-Zymierski as Commander in Chief, and Major General Berling, Brigadier General Alexander Zawadski, and Colonel Marian Spychalski as his deputies. (Spychalski was named the first Chief of Staff, but General Korczyc soon replaced him.) On August 15, 1944, partial conscription began on Polish soil beyond the 1941 borders, and by the end of 1944, some 100,000 men had been called to service (including 4,054 former officers of the pre-war Polish Army).

In October, 1944, a Third Army was created. Command of the First now went to Korczyc, the Second to Poplawski, and the Third to Swierczewski. An air force was established the same month and eventually was given a total of 1,200 aircraft. Generals Korczyc and Poplawski were career Soviet Red Army officers of Polish origin; General Swierczewski was an old-line Communist known as "General Walter" in the Spanish Civil War. By the end of 1944, the Polish forces totaled 286,000 men, and at the end of the war, the Polish People's Army totaled some 400,000 men, of whom over 150,000 had served in action at the front. (The army had incorporated the 40,000 men of the *Gwardia Ludowa*, the People's Guard, as the Communist partisan units were known.*)

Many veterans of the 1939 Polish Army and General Anders' army returned from abroad after the war, and a number were taken into the new Polish Army. However, its central component remained the army created in Russia in 1943 and 1944. The coalition government formed on June 23, 1945, from the Russian-sponsored "Lublin Government" and the legitimate London Government-in-Exile, nominally met the demands of the Western Powers that had reluctantly been accepted by the U.S.S.R. at Yalta in February of that year. But the Russians had no intention of compromising on full control by their Communist-dominated group, and they aggressively contained and reduced the position of the London (and underground *Armia Krajowa*) elements. In October, 1945, the Peasant Party leader and last

* The Polish Communist Party had been dissolved by Stalin in 1938, but a new Polish Workers' Party was formed in January, 1942, and in May of that year placed its first armed partisan unit in action. The *Gwardia Ludowa* was headed by Marian Spychalski, a prewar Communist and architect.

Prime Minister of the Government-in-Exile, Stanislaw Mikolajczyk, was forced to flee to the West.

The new Polish Army was headed by the "non-Party" professional Marshal Michal Rola-Zymierski as Minister of Defense. Generals Berling, Zawadski, Korczyc, and Swierczewski served as deputy ministers at some time in the first two years of the new postwar army.

It has long been known that both the wartime Polish People's Army and its postwar successor were heavily staffed by former Soviet career officers, particularly those of Polish origin. A Polish journal recently disclosed that 17,000 Soviet officers—fully half of the entire Polish officer corps—served in the postwar Polish Army.[2] The chief significance of this well-trained cadre was its tight tie with Moscow. And this was the situation until 1956.

Shortly after the war, armed anti-Communist resistance broke out in several places. The Ukrainian nationalists in Galicia, who were particularly active, also operated in the adjoining Western Ukraine in the U.S.S.R. The Ukrainian Insurgent Army (UPA—*Ukrayins'ka Povstan'ka Armiya*) engaged in guerrilla warfare for several years. In March, 1947, it ambushed and killed General Swierczewski. Later in 1947, the Polish Army and security forces joined the Soviet and Czechoslovak armies in a major campaign ("Operation Vistula"), and broke the back of the organized resistance by the UPA. By April, 1948, military operations were concluded, and the police cleaned up the remaining dissidence.[3]

During the period from 1949 to 1954, the Polish armed forces were built up and re-equipped with new matériel. This period was also marked by changes reflecting the tightened grip of the pro-Muscovite Polish Communist Party leadership under Bierut. In November, 1949, Marshal Konstantin Rokossovsky, a russified Pole whose career had been in the Red Army, was sent from Moscow as Minister of Defense. In 1950, Wladyslaw Gomulka and other Communist leaders who had been in Poland during the war were purged. Generals Spychalski and Komar and three hundred other officers met the same fate. Other officers from the Anders army and Polish Government-in-Exile army and air force units based in England, Italy, and the Middle East during the war were dismissed, and in some cases imprisoned. At about this time, the Polish Army even began to *look* Russian, with Soviet-style uniforms.

Like the Soviet armed forces and those of all the other Eastern European Communist states, the strength of the Polish armed forces reached its peak in the mid-1950's. Poland cut its armed forces by about 50,000 men each year from 1955 to 1957. Meanwhile, the

Soviet Union provided jet fighters and some jet light bombers, and the small Polish Navy acquired a few Soviet destroyers and submarines. In the late 1950's, Poland served as a transmission channel of such naval vessels from the U.S.S.R. to the United Arab Republic.

The aftermath of de-Stalinization in the Soviet Union brought a significant shift in the Polish Workers' Party. By October, 1956, this fermentation burst into a dramatic change in the Party leadership—against Moscow's wishes.* Wladyslaw Gomulka was swept to power in a wave of nationalism. At this point, we need only note its impact on the Polish armed forces and on Polish-Soviet military relations.

Marshal of Poland Rokossovsky who had been, and was again to become, Marshal of the Soviet Union, General Poplawski, and thirty-one other senior Soviet and dual-national officers were returned to the U.S.S.R. "with the thanks of the Polish people" for their services. The new Minister of Defense was General Marian Spychalski. The only significant Soviet holdover was the Chief of the General Staff, General Jerzy Bordzilowski. Even before the October 17, 1956, confrontation of the Polish and Soviet leaders, there had been plans to "polonize" the armed forces; they were now quickly carried through. Distinctively Polish uniforms, insignia, and flags returned. On November 18, 1956, agreement was reached with the Soviet Union on governing the status of Soviet troops in Poland on the line of communications to the Soviet forces garrisoned in Germany. (At that time there were three, now there are two, Soviet divisions in Poland.)

The armed forces became more truly Polish, but they remained Communist. On May 31, 1957, military councils were introduced in all top echelons. By October, 1963, on the twentieth anniversary of the wartime founding of the Polish People's Army, it was disclosed that 70 per cent of the officers were Party members, and 60 per cent of the enlisted men were members of the Party-affiliated military youth organization. Also on that anniversary, Spychalski was named Marshal of Poland, the retired General Berling was named a full General of the Army (Retired), and senior Vice Minister Z. Duszynski also became a General of the Army. A sentimental visit was paid by General Poplawski and twenty-eight other Soviet generals who had served long in the postwar Polish Army.

The latest development, as of this writing, marks a certain turning of the wheel. Early in 1965, General of the Army Bordzilowski, a Soviet career officer until 1944, became the new senior Vice Min-

* This development, and the dilemma it presented to the Soviet leaders, is traced in Chapter 8.

ister, and his place as Chief of the General Staff was taken by the chief of the Political Administration, General of the Army Wojciech Jaruzelski. General Duszynski, General Sliwinski, and several other old-time officers who spent the war as partisan leaders in Poland have been displaced.

But the wheel has not, and will not, turn all the way back to 1943, or even to 1956.

The Polish armed forces (along with those of Czechoslovakia) are the largest, and best trained and equipped, in Eastern Europe. The Polish Army has about fifteen divisions, with over 200,000 men, including several armored, one airborne, and one marine assault division. The Air Force, with nearly 1,000 aircraft (including a small naval air arm), is the largest in Eastern Europe, and it provides air defense and tactical support. There is a modest Navy, with a few destroyers and submarines.

Romania

On August 23, 1944, King Mihai arrested General Antonescu and switched Romania from the Axis camp to the side of the Allies. The Red Army was already advancing on Romanian soil, and the German Sixth Army there was quickly broken. Along with the Soviet Second and Third Ukrainian Fronts, a Romanian division called the Tudor Vladimirescu Division entered the country. It and a second called the Horia-Closca-Crisan Division had been formed by the Russians from Romanian prisoners of war among the 180,000 in Russian camps. These units were the core of the quickly formed First and Fourth Armies, with a total strength of 355,000 men. In addition, another 500 captured Romanian officers who responded favorably to Soviet indoctrination were returned in 1946, and most of them entered the reconstituted Romanian Army.[4]

Repeated Soviet interventions in the Romanian Government from August, 1944, to December, 1947, culminated in the forced abdication of the King and the formation of a Communist government. Emil Bodnaras, a veteran Communist (who had been compelled to flee Romania in 1930 when, as a lieutenant, he was caught spying for the Russians) became Minister of Defense. In 1948, Romania became a "people's democracy." Over the next several years, the army was reorganized, trained, equipped, and indoctrinated along lines of the Soviet Army. The purging of career officers continued, but by the 1950's the balance among senior officers was about even between "converted" professional officers (especially former POW's from the U.S.S.R.), and old-time Communists. There were virtually no wartime "resistance" leaders, in either category, and no dual-nationality Russians.[5]

Following the Polish leadership upheaval and the Hungarian Revolution, a "status of forces" agreement was signed in April, 1957, covering Soviet forces on Romanian soil. In 1958, however, all Soviet military forces were withdrawn.

Since 1962, a rather remarkable policy of independent action has been conducted by the Romanian leadership. Even in the military field, perhaps the most delicate of all, there have been reverberations. For example, it has been reported that following the joint Warsaw Pact maneuvers in Bulgaria in June, 1963, the Romanian Government refused to proceed with an expected visit to Moscow of the Defense Minister, General of the Army Leontin Salajan, until the Soviet contingents temporarily passing through Romania had withdrawn to Soviet territory.[6] In October, 1964, Romania unilaterally and probably against the wishes of the Warsaw Pact command reduced the basic term of military service to sixteen months. Romania continues to be an active member of the Warsaw Pact, but it now sets its own conditions on the political role of that alliance.*

The Romanian Army, like most of the East European armies, reached its peak size in 1953, and then declined during the period 1955–58. Another reduction was effected in 1963–64. In equipment and training, the Romanian Army generally lagged behind most of the other Warsaw Pact powers, but it improved considerably in the early 1960's. It has about eight motorized and one or two armored divisions, with nearly 200,000 men. There is a modest supporting tactical air force, and a very small navy.

Bulgaria

In September, 1944, the Soviet Third Ukrainian Front swept through northern Bulgaria, as the Germans desperately tried to extricate their forces isolated by the collapse of resistance in Romania. The Russians had declared war on Bulgaria only a few days earlier, and there were no Bulgarian POW's in Russia from which a Soviet-sponsored army could have been formed. Under these circumstances, the "new" Bulgarian People's Army looked suspiciously like the old one with a quick face-lifting.

---

* Romanian reserve toward the Warsaw Pact was evident in the complete absence of reference to the Pact in an unusual personal address by Party Chief Ceausescu to a meeting of the Party *aktiv* in the Armed Forces (see *Scinteia*, June 16, 1965).

A non-Communist, General Damyan Velchev, became Minister of War until 1946. A Communist partisan leader, General Blagoi Ivanov, was named Deputy Minister. In December, 1944, General Ivan Kinov, a Soviet Army career officer of Bulgarian origin, became Chief of the General Staff; General P. Iliev, former Chief of Staff of the "People's Liberation Insurgent Army" (the Communist underground partisans) became Chief of Personnel; and Colonel P. Branchev, the partisan intelligence chief, became Chief of the Intelligence Division. The non-Communist field commander in chief, General Ivan Marinov, was retained. Three Bulgarian Armies, totaling 450,000 men, were in the field. The Bulgarian First Army, with 200,-000 men, was attached to the Soviet Third Ukrainian Front and fought in the campaigns in northeastern Yugoslavia, Hungary, and Austria. There was never a complete Soviet military occupation of Bulgaria, and Soviet forces departed in 1947.[7]

"Sovietization" of the Bulgarian Army began in earnest in 1948, and moved more rapidly than elsewhere. By the early 1950's, the army was sovietized, and had attained reasonable training proficiency and readiness. Many Soviet officers served as advisers in key staff positions during the 1950's, and by the end of the 1950's, virtually all of the pre-1944 officer corps had been replaced by newly prepared Communist officers. At present, over 80 per cent of the officers are members of the Communist Party.

General of the Army Dobri Dzhurov, the incumbent Minister of Defense, had been a political officer in the Bulgarian partisan movement. The Bulgarian Army was held in readiness during the period of support to the Greek Communist insurgents (from 1944 to 1948), and later, during the confrontation with Tito's Yugoslavia (from 1948 to 1955). Over the past decade, the Bulgarian Army has been modernized, but has been relatively unaffected by either internal or international developments. Nonetheless, political currents stir even Bulgaria, and in the spring of 1965, the commandant of the Sofia garrison General Tsvetko Anev and (by Bulgarian admission) at least five other officers, including two senior officers in the political administration of the armed forces, were involved with several Party officials in a conspiracy to lead Bulgaria down a more independent national path.[8]

The Bulgarian Army comprises about twelve divisions, of which two or three are armored, with more than 100,000 men. The Air Force provides air defense and tactical air support. The Navy is not significant.

Hungary

On December 22, 1944, a Soviet-sponsored provisional government of Hungary was formed. It was headed by Colonel General Béla Miklos, the former Commander of the First Army, who had negotiated an armistice with the Russians in October, 1944. It immediately declared war against the former ally, Nazi Germany. Some units were dissolved, but the First and Sixth Infantry Divisions were retained.[9]

The Russians imposed political ("orientation") and security officers, but in the initial postwar period wide use was made, even at the top levels, of professional Hungarian officers. General Miklos' provisional government remained in office until November, 1945. The former Chief of the Hungarian General Staff, Colonel General Janos Vörös (who had also gone over to the Russians in 1944), served as Minister of Defense until January, 1946. Both Miklos and Vörös were removed by early 1946. The succeeding prime ministers—until late 1948— were members of the Smallholders Party, and so were several successive ministers of defense: General Jenö Tombor; after his death, General Albert Bartha; then the Smallholder Lajos Dinnyes; and, finally, the National Peasant leader Peter Veres.

Communist subversion continued during the three years of rapidly changing non-Communist governments and ministers of national defense. In the summer of 1946, Lieutenant General Sviridov of the Soviet Army, the acting head of the Allied Control Commission, secretly transferred most of the Army units to the Border Guards, which were under control of the Communist General G. Palffy-Oesterreicher.[10] The Minister of Defense, like the Prime Minister, became more and more of a figurehead. In addition to General Palffy, Generals L. Solyom and G. Illy were leading "sovietizers" during this period. In February, 1947, at the same time that the peasant Smallholders Party was crushed by the arrest of Béla Kovacs and other leaders on grounds of espionage, military counterintelligence (headed by a Communist) arrested ninety-three officers, and Communist penetration of key positions rapidly expanded. In 1948, the Communists seized power, and General Mihaly Farkas, a Communist, was made Minister of Defense. From then on, Communist control was open and thorough. (Incidentally, the "first echelon" of pro-Soviet officers, like Palffy, Solyom, and Illy, were executed in connection with the purge of the alleged Titoist Laszló Rajk.)

Under the administration of General Farkas from 1948 to 1953, and then under General Istvan Bata from 1953 to 1956, the Hungarian Army became more fully sovietized and also increased in combat capability. Beginning in the late 1940's, massive Soviet military arms and equipment were shipped to Hungary; numerous Soviet military advisers were sent, too, reaching a peak number in 1953. In 1950, Soviet military regulations were adopted wholesale, and in 1951, a Russian-style uniform was introduced.

General Farkas had served in the Czechoslovak Army in the early 1930's, and in the Spanish Civil War. Subsequently, he served as an officer in the Red Army, but he was regarded as a nonmilitary man. A member of the Hungarian Politburo, he was commissioned a colonel general after becoming Minister of Defense. Most of his top associates also were long-time Communists, semicivilians, with long records of Soviet service—or at least residence. General Istvan Bata, Farkas' successor in 1953, was a Soviet Army career officer of Hungarian origin. Meanwhile, newly commissioned officers rapidly replaced the former non-Communist professionals of the 1944 army. The number of new officers rose from 5.5 per cent in January, 1949, to 80.7 per cent by January, 1951.[11] From 1948, Hungarian officers were selected to study in Soviet military schools; after 1954, some were sent to the Soviet General Staff Academy.

By the early 1950's, the Hungarian Army had increased to three times the 65,000-man limit imposed by the Peace Treaty in 1947. By 1956, it was "sovietized" and considered reliable, equipped with Soviet matériel, and staffed with many Soviet military advisers.

The Hungarian Revolution of October, 1956, showed the brittleness and shallowness of this Communist veneer. By and large, the Army collapsed during the Revolution. Some units went over to the rebels, others declined to act against them, and still others disintegrated.

On October 24, 1956, at the outset of the revolt, Soviet advisers ordered Hungarian divisions dispersed, and some moved. But Soviet advisers in the Ministry and in the Corps Headquarters soon found they had no authority, and after October 27 they had no role whatsoever. Even so, they spied for the Russians and obstructed pro-Revolution Hungarian officers from effectively rallying the Army to the side of the Freedom Fighters.[12]

After the Revolution was suppressed (by seven divisions of the Soviet Army), it took several years to establish a new Hungarian Army. It is not so large as it was before the Revolution, but it is a new army. In 1957, a distinctively Hungarian uniform was introduced, and Soviet advisers are now less in evidence. A post-1956 officer corps is being developed. The present Minister of Defense, Colonel General Lajos Czinege, is a young postwar Communist officer.

On May 27, 1957, a "status of forces" agreement was signed by the Hungarian and Soviet governments regulating the Soviet forces garrisoned in the country (now four divisions, and tactical air units), which remain discreetly away from the major population centers. The Hungarian Army has six divisions, four motorized infantry and two armored, with about 100,000 men. The air defense and tactical support Air Force is small, but has modern aircraft.

Czechoslovakia

In 1941, an agreement was signed between the U.S.S.R. and the Czechoslovak Government-in-Exile in London to provide for the formation of Czech military units in the Soviet Union. Lieutenant Colonel Ludvík Svoboda and about a hundred other Czech officers and noncommissioned officers were its nucleus. (Overrun by the Red Army in eastern Poland, where they had gone to assist the Poles against the Germans, they were already in the Soviet Union.) A battalion was sent to the front in January, 1943, and this unit was later expanded into the First Czechoslovak Brigade under the promoted Colonel, now General, Svoboda. General Svoboda did not openly become a Communist until 1948; but he was a willing associate of the Russians from the beginning. As Slovak troops mobilized by the Germans were captured by Russians, the brigade gained recruits and became the First Czechoslovak Corps, numbering 18,000 men by the time it entered Slovakia in September, 1944. By the end of the war, it was 60,000 strong, and it became the core of the new postwar Czechoslovak Army.[13]

Meanwhile, other Czech units had been formed, and were serving in the West. A substantial number of Czech airmen served in Great Britain, and a tank brigade later came into Czechoslovakia with the U.S. Third Army in May, 1945. A third element in the postwar Czechoslovak Army was formed of Slovak partisans who had fought in the underground. But the chief element remained the army created in the Soviet Union.

President Eduard Beneš had intended to name Generals S. Ingr and A. Liska as Commander in Chief and Chief of Staff of the new army in 1945. Moscow, however, strongly disapproved, and Beneš capitulated and named General Svoboda Minister of Defense, and General B. Bocek-Chodsky, also from the Soviet-sponsored army, Chief of Staff. The Communists in Czechoslovakia stirred up charges against General Ingr and several other top officers from the London

Government-in-Exile, and succeeded in blackballing some of them. However, a number of London Government generals did hold responsible military positions during the period 1945–48.[14]

As early as April 5, 1945, the Kozice Government Program stipulated that the new Czechoslovak Army would be organized and trained on the pattern of the Red Army. On May 20, 1945, General Svoboda announced that the new army would follow Soviet military regulations and use Soviet equipment. After the *coup d'état* of February, 1948, almost all of the London officers were purged. Many of the officers who had served in the Czech Army in the Soviet Union were prewar career officers and had not previously been Communists. Nonetheless, most of them remained in important positions until several years after the 1948 coup. In 1950, General Svoboda was replaced by Alexei Cepicka. Cepicka, a prewar Communist, and son-in-law of the Communist Party Chief, President Klement Gottwald, had no prior military service. A few months after becoming Minister of National Defense, he received the rank of General of the Army. Also in 1950, General Jaroslav Prochazka, who had fought in the Czechslovak Legion in Russia in World War I, and had become a Communist in 1919, was named Chief of Staff. Prochazka had lived in the Soviet Union from 1924 to 1945, but had not served as a military man, except as a political officer in the latter half of World War II. In 1952, however, he was replaced, and in 1956 General Cepicka was purged. The present Minister of Defense is General of the Army Bohumir Lomsky. General Lomsky spent World War II in the Soviet Union, and was one of the cofounders of the Czechoslovak forces in the U.S.S.R. during the war, but he had not been a professional career officer.

The Czech Army had been permitted to decline in military preparedness during the late 1940's. In 1951, an extensive reorganization and revitalization program was begun. Soviet military equipment was received in quantity, large numbers of Soviet military advisers were brought in, and combat units were reorganized along Soviet lines. Military production gradually assumed some importance, chiefly of Soviet ordnance but including some items of local design.

In the mid-1960's, the Czech Army has shown signs of a more nationalistic tendency—notably with the adoption of a distinctively Czech military uniform in 1964. At present, the Czechoslovak Army is one of the best equipped and best trained in Eastern Europe. The Army has fourteen divisions (of which four or five are armored), with about 200,000 men. The Air Force is second in size only to that of Poland; it provides air defense and tactical air support.

East Germany

There is little direct relationship between the East German Army today and the German Army of World War II. Some officers in the East German Army were drawn from wartime prisoners of war indoctrinated in the Soviet Union. In particular, a number of Stalingrad veterans were recruited during the war by a Soviet-sponsored Free Germany Committee. The East German Army was not created until several years after the war, however, and the main elements in its officer corps have been prewar Communists or newly trained post-war officers.

Since the so-called German Democratic Republic (G.D.R.) was not created until 1949, the case of the East German armed forces is quite different from that of all the other Communist regimes in Eastern Europe. The origins of the East German Army can be traced to the transfer of about 7,500 men from the regular police force into special Alert Units (*Bereitschaften*) in 1948. Many of these men had been prisoners of war in the Soviet Union. By late 1950, this force had grown to a strength of more than 50,000 men, and was organized and trained in basic military units. At that time, Sea Police and Air Police components also were created. This force was renamed the Garrisoned People's Police (*Kasernierte Volkspolize*—KVP), in 1952, comprising ground, sea, and air forces; and by 1953 these units were reorganized into seven infantry divisions, with a total strength of about 100,000 men.

On January 18, 1956, following the establishment of an army in the German Federal Republic and its entrance into NATO, an East German Ministry of National Defense was created, and the KVP was redesignated the National People's Army. Willi Stoph, a long-time Communist and a former Minister of the Interior, was named Defense Minister. Soon after, in 1956, East Germany was formally admitted to the Warsaw Pact, which had been created a year earlier.

The East German Army is a well-equipped and well-organized force. It has often received new items of equipment sooner than any of the other East European Communist armies. Until January, 1962, East Germany was the only state in the Soviet Bloc not to have universal conscription. Volunteer enlistment, however, was not adequate, and conscription was introduced.

It is difficult to judge the reliability of the East German armed forces. The present Minister of Defense is General of the Army Heinz Hoffmann, like his predecessor, a long-time Communist who spent World War II in the Soviet Union. Hoffmann's earlier military service had been as a commissar in the Spanish Civil War. By March, 1962, 90 per cent of the officers were members of the ruling Socialist Unity Party—the same proportion of Party members as in the Soviet Army. But about 30,000 members of the East German armed forces and Frontier Guards—the equivalent in numbers of three entire divisions—have defected to the West. In prospect, then, as well as in origin, the East German Army is quite different from other Eastern European Communist forces, primarily since the G.D.R. lacks the fundamental national status of the other Bloc countries.

In addition to the East German Army, now possessing six modern divisions (four motorized infantry and two armored), the Group of Soviet Forces in Germany comprises ten tank and ten motorized infantry divisions. The modern East German Air Force supplements the sizable Soviet tactical air force in East Germany. There is a small defensive East German naval force in the Baltic.

Yugoslavia

The Yugoslav partisan movement under Marshal Iosip Broz-Tito was primarily responsible for the liberation of Yugoslavia, despite the important support of the Soviet Third Ukrainian Front in liberating the northeastern portion of the country, including Belgrade. By September, 1944, the National Liberation Army totaled 400,000 men. More than any other in Eastern Europe, the postwar army has had a clear lineage from a single cohesive wartime origin. From 1945 to 1948, Yugoslav officers were sent to the Soviet Union for advanced military schooling, and Soviet military advisers were dispatched to Yugoslavia. A substantial beginning was made in reorganizing the Yugoslav Army into a regular Soviet-like force. The Yugoslav Army's basic unity, however, was little affected by the drastic deterioration in Soviet-Yugoslav relations in 1948.

The secret sharp Party letters exchanged between Moscow and Belgrade from March to June, 1948, reveal a great deal about the status of Soviet military advisers in Yugoslavia and, generally, in Eastern Europe.[15] The Russians had provided such advisers at the request of the Yugoslav Government, but the Yugoslavs had to pay for their services at rates three to four times those of a Yugoslav general or cabinet minister. Sometimes the Soviet advisers spoke insultingly of the Tito regime. Moreover, they recruited for the Soviet intelligence services. In March, 1948, the Soviet Government suddenly withdrew all its military advisers—after the Yugoslavs had protested their actions.

After the break between Yugoslavia and the U.S.S.R., the Yugoslav armed forces received considerable military equipment and assistance from the United States. In addition, organization and doctrine were developed on the basis of incorporating elements of Soviet and United States thinking into a primarily Yugoslav base. Since the *rapprochement* between Yugoslavia and the Soviet Union in 1955, and especially since 1962, the Yugoslavs have again been receiving some weapons and equipment from the Soviet Union, as do a number of other countries not allied with the U.S.S.R.

Brief mention has been made of the special circumstances surrounding the early postwar period of Soviet-Yugoslav military cooperation. Real independence was achieved by Tito's Yugoslavia chiefly because Yugoslavia was liberated by an internal force, the partisan movement was cohesive and national though Communist, and there was no postwar Soviet military occupation of the country. Thus Yugoslavia, not subjected to the circumstances which played such an important role in the other East European countries, is a noteworthy contrast.

Albania

Albania alone among the new Communist countries of Eastern Europe had no Soviet troops on its territory during the war. As in Yugoslavia, the Communist partisans took power with little difficulty, and without requiring a period of coalition government with non-Communist elements. The Albanian partisan movement had close ties with Tito's Yugoslav partisans, and these ties continued in the early postwar period. However, when the Soviets broke with Tito in 1948, Enver Hoxha purged his rivals and adopted a bitterly anti-Yugoslav stand.

The Albanian Army, small and ill-equipped, played no significant role in these developments. From 1948 to 1955, the Russians provided modest military assistance to Albania, and in the mid-1950's developed a submarine base at Saseno, in Valona Bay, for joint use by the small Albanian Navy and a Soviet submarine flotilla. Within the Albanian People's Army, in addition to the ground forces, there is a Coastal Defense Command, which includes the few naval units, and a small and ineffective air force component.

Relations between the Soviet Union and Albania began to deteriorate after the 1955 Soviet-Yugoslav *rapprochement*. In 1961, the eight Soviet submarines based in Albania and the entire Soviet military advisory mission were withdrawn. Since that time, the Albanians have had no outside military assistance, except possibly for some equipment supplied by Communist China. Although Albania is still nominally a member of the Warsaw Pact, it has not participated in meetings or other activities of that group since 1961, and for all practical purposes is no longer allied with the Warsaw Pact powers.

The Albanian Army has several infantry brigades, and totals about 25,000 men. Albania still has four submarines, but it is doubtful if they are operational. Its air force is insignificant.

The First Decade: 1945–55

In surveying the establishment and consolidation of Communist rule and the development of the armed forces of the East European states, we see a common pattern. From 1945 to 1948, with the exceptions of Yugoslavia and Albania, Communist rule was only gradually established through a transitional period of coalition governments. In staffing the postwar armies during that period, it was necessary to rely chiefly on professional officers who had served under previous regimes, and the Communists emphasized neutralization and elimination of anti-Communist elements, while they themselves infiltrated. Officers who had been captured and indoctrinated in the Soviet Union during the war played an important role. In Poland, and to a lesser extent in Bulgaria and Hungary, key officers were introduced who had emigrated to the Soviet Union many years before and had served in the Red Army.

Although Soviet troops were withdrawn from Bulgaria, Yugoslavia, and Czechoslovakia soon after the war, Communist subversion and assumption of power in the whole area were facilitated by the shadow of the massive Soviet military presence in Eastern and Central Europe. As Stalin admitted in the secret correspondence with the Yugoslav Party leaders shortly before the 1948 break:

> Even though the French and Italian Communist parties have so far achieved less success than the Communist Party of Yugoslavia, this is not due to any special qualities of the Communist Party of Yugoslavia, but mainly because . . . the Soviet Army came to the aid of the Yugoslav people, crushed the German invader, liberated Belgrade, and in this way created the conditions which were necessary for the Communist Party of Yugoslavia to achieve power. Unfortunately, the Soviet Army did not and could not render such assistance to the French and Italian Communist Parties.[16]

This statement underrates the role of the Yugoslav partisans in expelling the Germans from the country, but it does acknowledge the importance of the Soviet military presence to Communist advances.

From 1944 to 1948, the Greek Communists conducted an aggressive guerrilla campaign to seize power. Until the Soviet Bloc break with Yugoslavia, support was provided through Bulgaria and Yugo-slavia, but Stalin held back from any more direct commitment or support. Thus the Greek case also underlines the crucial role of Soviet military power in determining the outcome of Communist efforts to gain power by guerrilla warfare.

The case of Finland paralleled to some extent—but only to a crucial point—that of Czechoslovakia. Soviet forces did not occupy Finland after the armistice of late 1944, but the Finnish Communists obtained an important role in a new coalition government. In Finland, as in Czechoslovakia, plans were made for a *coup d'état* in 1948, and probably would have succeeded—except that the Communist Minister of the Interior, Ÿrjo Leino, disclosed the plot to the anti-Communist Chief of the General Staff, General A. Sihvo, who alerted the Army. The coup was aborted.[17]

Between 1948 and 1953, the new Communist regimes purged their armies of non-Communist and "Titoist" elements. At the same time, Soviet military assistance was provided on a massive scale, and the armies were built up to a peak of 1,500,000 men by 1953.

After 1953, new officers drawn from the ranks of the Party or in-doctrinated after the war, became the major element of the officer corps in all of the East European Communist states.[18] Only in Poland did a significant share of the officer corps continue, until 1956, to be drawn from russified Poles who had made a career in the prewar Red Army.

The Warsaw Pact: 1955–65

On May 14, 1955, the Warsaw Pact was signed. For the first time, a formal alliance bound the Communist states of Eastern Europe. Previously, there had been an interlocking network of fourteen bilateral pacts among these countries. The Warsaw Pact was signed less than two months after the Federal Republic of Germany entered NATO, and was explicitly designed to counter that development. The Pact itself was formally modeled on the NATO treaty, although it did not establish institutions comparable to those of the North Atlantic Alliance. Albania was among the original signatories; Yugoslavia of course was not. It was explicitly noted that the relationship of the G.D.R. was "to be examined later." The Pact provided for a joint command, a political consultative committee, and such auxiliary organs as might be needed. The members undertook to "abstain from threats of violence in their international relations," to consult on international problems, and not to enter any coalition or agreement contrary to the Warsaw treaty.

The first meeting of the Political Consultative Committee was held in Prague in January, 1956. At that time, a Joint Secretariat was established, and a "Permanent Commission" was created to recommend positions on foreign policy questions. The Political Consultative Committee is to meet a minimum of twice a year; actually, it met only seven times during the Pact's first decade of existence. All meetings for the nine years from January, 1956, until January, 1965, were held in Moscow. The January, 1965, meeting—the seventh—was again held in Warsaw. With the exception of the founding session and the meeting in January, 1965, all the other sessions lasted for only one or two days and served merely to grant rubber-stamp approval to standard Soviet positions on current military-political issues.

The first Commander in Chief of Warsaw Pact forces was Marshal Ivan S. Konev, simultaneously First Deputy Minister of Defense of the U.S.S.R. In June, 1960, he was replaced in both capacities by Marshal Andrei A. Grechko. General of the Army Alexei I. Antonov, Deputy Chief of the Soviet General Staff, was the first Chief of Staff for the Pact. Following Antonov's death in June, 1962, General of the Army Pavel I. Batov replaced him in both his Soviet and Warsaw positions. Nominally, each of the Ministers of Defense of the participating countries is a Deputy Commander in Chief of the Warsaw Pact forces; there are senior liaison officers from each of those countries in Moscow. The planning and coordinating center for the Pact forces is served by a special branch of the Soviet General Staff.

One of the ancillary purposes of the Warsaw Pact was to provide a framework for the continuing presence of Soviet troops in several countries. The Russians signed the State Treaty with Austria on the day following the signing of the Warsaw treaty. The Pact provided new justification for the continued presence of Soviet forces in Hungary and Romania; formerly they had been stationed on the lines of communications to Austria. Following the October and November, 1956, developments in Poland and Hungary, the Soviet Union signed new "status of forces" agreements with Poland, Hungary, Romania, and East Germany in late 1956 and early 1957. In 1958, the Soviet forces were withdrawn from Romania, and in 1961, from Albania.*

Since 1955, the Russians have provided considerable military assistance to Warsaw Pact countries. In addition, Czechoslovakia and Poland further developed local munitions and equipment production, including assembly of Soviet jet aircraft and production of tanks and

---

* In 1955, the Soviet Union also withdrew its forces from the bases at Porkkala-Udd in Finland, which it had been granted for fifty years in the 1947 Peace Treaty, and at Port Arthur in Manchuria.

artillery. Hungary, Romania, and Bulgaria also developed modest small arms and munitions production of Soviet models. Czechoslovakia has contributed new designs of some items of ordnance, including a jet trainer now adopted for use by other members of the Pact including the Soviet Union itself. (In East Germany, an overly ambitious attempt to create a local aircraft industry was scrapped in 1961.)

In this manner, the Warsaw Pact armies were fully equipped with modern Soviet-type equipment and weapons, partly of local manufacture, but in larger measure provided by the Soviet Union. While this process of modernization was under way, from 1955 to 1960, the size of the East European Communist armies was reduced by nearly a third. Since 1960, there have been some variations (a build-up in 1961 during the Berlin crisis, with modest reductions in 1962 and 1963), but the general size of the East European armed forces has remained fairly stable at about 1 million men, organized into slightly over sixty divisions (of which about half are combat strength, with the remainder at low strength levels), with tactical air support, and air defenses.[19]

During the first half of the 1960's, the East European Communist armies substantially replaced their T-34 medium tanks with the more modern T-54 and T-55 tanks, and began receiving modern interceptors and fighter bombers such as the MiG-21 and Su-7, and short-range tactical rockets and missiles of up to about 150 n.m. range. These tactical missiles are capable of carrying nuclear warheads, as well as conventional high-explosive or chemical charges, but represent the first-generation tactical missile gradually eliminated from Soviet units. There is no indication that the Russians have provided nuclear warheads to any of the East European armies, and it is very unlikely that they would do so. The Polish, East German, and Czech armed forces have created airborne units; Poland has an airborne division. These airborne units, and also the Polish and Soviet marines, are "elite" forces, and have distinctive uniforms and berets.

By providing advanced air defense radars, surface-to-air missiles, and fighter interceptors to the East European forces, the Russians also extend the air defenses of the Soviet Union itself. But they have not provided strategic offensive weapons—either medium bombers or medium-range missiles—to their allies. Nor have they found it necessary to station such forces of their own in other countries.

Air defense arrangements have become more closely integrated with those of the Soviet Union. In 1964, Chief Marshal of Aviation

Vladimir Sudets, Commander in Chief of Air Defense in the U.S.S.R., was publicly referred to as Commander in Chief of Air Defense of the Warsaw Pact.

The Warsaw Pact armies did not conduct joint military exercises until the autumn of 1961. At that time, coincident with heightened tension over Berlin, Soviet, Polish, Czech, and East German forces participated in a major field exercise. In April, 1962, Soviet, Hungarian, and Romanian troops took part in a joint exercise in Hungary. In the fall of 1962, the Romanian, Hungarian, and Czech armies engaged in a joint maneuver, and Soviet, Polish, and East German troops engaged in another. In June, 1963, Romanian and Soviet forces participated with Bulgarian troops in Bulgaria. Large Warsaw Pact exercises involving East German, Czech, and Polish troops in September, 1963, were for the first time conducted under the command of a non-Soviet general, Heinz Hoffmann of East Germany. And, in 1964, the Czech General Lomsky was in charge of a combined East German, Czech, and Soviet exercise. Joint maneuvers were again held in Bulgaria in the fall of 1964. An unusual conclave of military commanders of the Warsaw Pact countries met in the Transcarpathian Military District of the U.S.S.R. in May, 1965, for a demonstration of new weapons, equipment, and tactics, as well as for consultation. Large-scale maneuvers of Soviet, Czech, Polish, and East German troops were held again in October, 1965.

In time of war, East European ground force divisions, or even field armies, would probably be incorporated into Soviet Fronts (army groups). The volume *Military Strategy*, written by Marshal Sokolovsky and a group of other Soviet officers, explicitly states:

> Operational units of the armed forces of different socialist states can be created to conduct joint operations in military theaters. The command of these units can be assigned to the Supreme High Command of the Soviet armed forces. . . . In some military theaters, operational units of the allied countries will be under their own supreme high commands.[20]

During 1965, there were several press references to Warsaw Pact countries of the "first echelon": East Germany, Czechoslovakia, and Poland. It would appear that the Soviet Union was establishing a closer tie with these three northwestern members of the Pact, both because of their strategic location vis-à-vis NATO's central front, and in view of the modified political-military relationship between the Soviet Union and Romania.

Soviet Interests in Eastern Europe

The Soviet Union's policy on the development of military power in Eastern Europe has been guided by five considerations. First, the entire area is seen as a defensive buffer against an invasion from the West. This is of serious concern to the Russians, for their traditional fears are buttressed both by the memory of 1941 and by concern over the growing political, economic, and military power of Germany, and of Western Europe generally. Second, the area is seen as an extension of the air defenses of the U.S.S.R., important despite the existence of long-range missiles. Third, the alliance provides an offensive glacis against NATO. This offensive element is important whether or not the Russians have ever planned to launch a deliberate attack on the West. If general war should occur, along with the strategic nuclear confrontation, the Russians would launch a major land campaign to occupy Western Europe. The presence of ninety Soviet and other East European divisions (not all of them combat-ready) west of the Soviet frontier is a powerful hedge against requirements for meeting the contingency of general war. Fourth, the Soviet leaders regard these indoctrinated armies as an instrument for maintaining Communist control within the countries of Eastern Europe. The performance of the Hungarian Army in 1956 greatly shocked the Soviet leaders and remains a lingering concern. Nonetheless, they support the continued modernization of large armies. The Soviet forces in East Germany, and to a lesser extent in Hungary, can serve to deal with any uprisings that may occur. Fifth, the Soviet leaders view the Warsaw Pact as an instrument for maintaining discipline and political unity among the Communist states of Eastern Europe. This was probably a minor consideration in 1955; by 1965, it had become a major one. The Warsaw Pact has become critically important as a corrective since the sharp decrease in discipline in the Communist movement (as seen in the relative independence of the Romanians) and the failure of the Council for Mutual Economic Assistance to serve as a unifying political instrument. The Pact provides for common military organization, joint planning, unified doctrine, and standardized equipment, but today its role in supporting political cohesion is of greatest significance.

The countries of Eastern Europe have somewhat different objectives. They all continue to share, though in differing degrees, a common political and ideological alignment. They all regard their armed forces, and presumably the Warsaw Pact, as a means of enhancing their own security. Prestige and tradition also contribute to the maintenance of their armed forces. Finally, the armed forces do provide an important channel for domestic political education, and to some extent for technical education. It would be difficult to imagine that any of the present members of the Warsaw Pact—except Albania—would succeed in withdrawing from it, even if it wished. The Hungarian attempt to do so in 1956 was the last straw, and persuaded the Soviet leaders to intervene and depose the Nagy Government.*

The Warsaw Pact is evolving into a conventional alliance. It continues to bind its members together, but it is no longer merely an administrative arrangement for coordinating its constituent armies under Moscow's control. No doubt the Soviet Union will continue to dominate military planning under the Pact, but the Soviet leaders can no longer be sure that the other member countries will permit Moscow to commit them to particular courses of action. Romania has led the way in reasserting its national prerogative in several fields related to the military alliance, and in time others will follow. The Warsaw Pact remains, indeed has increasingly become, the chief instrument for coordination of the East European coalition, but as such it cannot help but reflect changing political relations among its members.

* See Chapter 8.

8. The Military Factor in the Soviet Decisions on Poland and Hungary in October, 1956

In the wake of de-Stalinization in the autumn of 1956, the Soviet leaders were suddenly confronted with two sharp challenges to their authority in Eastern Europe. The crises in Warsaw and Budapest, and the differing Soviet responses, offer a unique parallel "case study" on the limits to which the Russians would tolerate setbacks in their own camp without intervening militarily. It is, therefore, particularly useful to survey the Polish and Hungarian crises of October, 1956, from this point of view.

Poland in Crisis: Abortive Coup d'État and Intervention

Wladyslaw Gomulka's rise to power in Poland in 1956, was attended by a sudden dramatic conflict. The Polish Communist (Workers') Party elected a slate headed by Gomulka, against the express wishes of the Soviet Party leadership—and despite a surprise visit to Warsaw by Khrushchev and other Soviet leaders. The Russians were thus faced with a direct challenge to their right to determine, or at least to veto, the leadership of a satellite regime. Yet they did tolerate it; and a month later, Gomulka's visit to Moscow was proof of Soviet reconciliation to the situation. But Gomulka's victory was neither inevitable nor easy. In fact, a pro-Soviet and antiliberal Polish group had made a desperate and unsuccessful pre-emptive bid to seize power in Poland on the eve of Gomulka's triumph, *prior* to Khruschchev's visit. Further direct Soviet intervention was considered after that attempt had failed. This discussion outlines the abortive pro-Soviet Polish *coup d'état* of October 18, 1956, the preparations for a further possible *putsch* on October 19 and 20, and the Soviet decision not to intervene with military force.

Throughout most of 1956, a silent struggle had been waged between "liberal," "center," and "Stalinist" elements of the Polish leadership. After the Poznan uprising and Tito's visit to Moscow, the liberal and center groups consolidated and there was heightened counteractivity by the Stalinists. The liberal group, headed by Premier Jozef Cyrankiewicz, and the centrists, headed by First Secretary Edward Ochab, rallied behind Wladyslaw Gomulka, the formerly imprisoned "Titoist." The right wing, antinationalist "Natolin group" (so called after the locale of their meetings) nonetheless held a precarious majority in the Politburo until October—despite defections and despite the popular support for each limited measure of the liberal wing. The Natolin group's trump card was the support of the "Soviet Polish" Marshal Rokossovsky, and ultimately of Moscow.

Gradually, the liberal-center wing prepared the way for Gomulka's return and the purge of the Natolinists. On October 9, Hilary Minc was ousted as First Deputy Premier and Politburo member. That July and August, Gomulka had declined a Politburo seat unless sweeping changes were made in the leadership. Clearly, he was winning the fight. On October 8, word "leaked" that he would be restored to the Politburo. On the same day, the date of convening the Eighth Plenum of the Central Committee was advanced from November to mid-October. The resolution incorporating Gomulka's program of national independence was drafted by October 17, and the proposed new Politburo list was agreed upon by the dominant liberal-centrists. The days of the Natolin group were not only numbered—their number was by now very small.

Sometime in mid-October (probably October 17), the Natolin group decided on a last-minute military *coup d'état* to prevent Gomulka's imminent victory. Was this plan suggested or approved by Moscow—and if so, by the Soviet leadership as a whole or by only a faction within it? We do not know. But there is substantial information from Poland that a planned coup was foiled, and inconclusive evidence that some or all of the Soviet leaders, if they had not endorsed the original plans, at least were prepared to support a *putsch*. When the Polish leadership showed itself to be united and prepared to resist, the Soviet leaders canceled the plan. Marshal Rokossovsky and other Soviet officers with the Polish armed forces were involved; they probably would have been dismissed in any case, but this development insured their removal by the Polish leadership.

On October 18, the night before the Plenum of the Central Committee, liberal Communists intercepted a list of some 700 persons, including Gomulka and his associates, who were to be arrested by the Army that night. Warned in time, the liberal Communists evaded arrest by not going to their homes. Polish security forces, loyal to the Gomulka group, occupied key points. In certain cases, army officers refused to acknowledge and obey orders for troop movements. A critical incident occurred when Polish Army forces marching on Warsaw were stopped at Sochaczew, only thirty miles from Warsaw, by internal security troops commanded by Brigadier General Waclaw Komar (a former Deputy Minister of Defense, imprisoned in 1951 with Gomulka as a Titoist). After the ultimatum that they would be fired upon if they crossed an indicated line, the Army forces halted their advance and later withdrew to their base. Liberal Polish Communists alerted Central Committee members all over Poland about those troop movements that did occur. The first moment of crisis passed; the military *coup d'état* failed.

The Central Committee met on October 19. Gomulka, Lieutenant General Marian Spychalski (former First Deputy Minister of Defense, imprisoned as a Titoist), and Colonel Ignacy Loga-Sowinsky (a former trade-union official similarly imprisoned) were elected to the Central Committee. The old Politburo resigned, as was customary, and a new Politburo list was presented, removing Rokossovsky and other Natolinists and adding followers of Gomulka. Suddenly the Polish delegates were told of the arrival by air of a Soviet delegation headed by Khrushchev, Mikoyan, Molotov, Kaganovich, and Warsaw Pact chief Marshal Konev, and the Plenum meeting was adjourned to permit the old Politburo members—and Gomulka—to meet and confer with the Soviet leaders.

Khrushchev, refusing to shake Gomulka's hand, called him a traitor and demanded that the old Politburo be restored—with Rokossovsky. When his demand was rejected, Khrushchev reportedly exclaimed: "I'm going to show you what the road to socialism looks like! If you don't obey us, we will crush you. We are going to use force to kill all sorts of uprisings in this country." Edward Ochab, the Polish Party Chief, replied: "Don't think you can keep us here and start a *putsch* outside. The Party and our workers have been warned and are ready." When he learned that Soviet troops were moving on Warsaw, Ochab told Khrushchev: "If you don't halt your troops immediately, we will walk out of here and break off all contact." Khrushchev capitulated and ordered the troops stopped. Soviet troops that had entered Poland from the U.S.S.R. and had advanced to Siedlice halted, and withdrew the next day.

The discussion between the Polish and Soviet leaders lasted until the early morning of October 20, and the Russians departed at 6:45 A.M. Troop movements in and near Poland continued during the day. A Soviet regiment attempted to enter Poland from East Germany near Szczecin (Stettin), was fired upon by Polish internal security forces loyal to Gomulka, and withdrew to Germany. Soviet troops led by Colonel General Galitsky moved to Lodz, but stopped there.

Ochab's warning—that the Party and workers were ready—was no idle claim. The workers of the giant Zeran Auto Works had been armed on the 19th; they remained at the factory with their arms ready during the night of the conference and the following day.

On October 20, the Polish leaders debated their next move. Aleksander Zawadski, President of Poland and a former Natolinist, proposed adding Rokossovsky's name to the new Politburo. But Gomulka and the others stood firm. The new Politburo was elected on October 21, as originally proposed. Gomulka, Ochab, Cyrankiewicz, Rapacki, Loga-Sowinski, Morawski, and Jedrychowski each received from 73 to 75 votes of the total 75. The two former Natolinists who were retained, Zawadski and Zambrowski, got 56 and 54 votes respectively. Rokossovsky obtained only 26, and he and seven other Natolinists were dropped.[1] Gomulka was unanimously elected First Secretary.

The Central Committee questioned Rokossovsky about the Polish troop movements of the previous day. He stated that they were routine and that the units were coming back from maneuvers. According to Staszewski, Secretary of the Warsaw Party Committee, this answer produced "great laughter in the Central Committee." The committee rebuked Rokossovsky for moving the troops from Lodz and Poznan toward Warsaw, and ordered an investigation by a special committee.

Troops returned to their bases. Lieutenant General Spychalski replaced the prominent Natolinist, Lieutenant General Kazmierz Witaszewski, as Deputy Minister of Defense and Chief of the Political Administration on October 23. On the 22nd and 23rd of October, the army, air force, air defense forces, internal security troops, and security police publicly pledged their loyalty to Gomulka. Rokossovsky left on the 28th for several days "on leave" in the U.S.S.R. On the 30th, five other leading Soviet generals were replaced: the Deputy Chief of the General Staff, the Acting Commander in Chief of the Air Forces, the Chief of the Personnel Administration, and the Commander of the Warsaw Military District. Six days later, Poles replaced thirty-two Soviet generals—including the commanders of the Pomeranian and Silesian Military Districts, and the chiefs of artillery, the armored forces, and the supply services. On November 13, General Spychalski replaced Rokossovsky, who returned permanently to the Soviet Union. All danger of internal threat had disappeared.

The victory of Gomulka and national Communism in Poland coincided with the combined recruitment and crushing of the old Natolin group. But one prominent member, Wiktor Klosiewicz (head of the trade unions) made a bold effort to "cover up" the attempted coup of October 18. In a discussion of the Five-Year Plan in the Polish Sejm, on November 9, he said:

> In connection with the diversionary news broadcast by foreign radio stations on the alleged preparations in Poland of a *coup d'état* during the debates of the Eighth Plenum of the PZPR Central Committee and on the alleged preparation of a list of some 700 persons to be arrested, including Comrade Gomulka and other leading personalities, as well as in connection with the rumors on this subject spreading throughout the country and stimulating uneasiness, division, and disorientation among broad sections of public opinion, I should like, taking into account the fact that my name is also on the list of those who allegedly were to prepare the *coup d'état*, to ask the Chairman of the Council of Ministers whether the Government does not deem it correct and indispensable in the interest of the public good to announce officially, as quickly as possible, its attitude in this matter. At the same time, guided by the desire to serve the interests of the country, I ask the Premier to be kind enough to define clearly from this rostrum the attitude of the Government toward all those who are spreading such rumors throughout the country.[2]

By this daring move, Klosiewicz hoped to force the Polish leadership into a dilemma. If they admitted the coup, they must implicate and prosecute the Natolin group, including Marshal Rokossovsky (then still Minister of Defense), and probably implicate the Russians as well. In view of the situation in Hungary, reports of Soviet troop concentrations near Poland, and the imminent visit of Gomulka to Moscow, Klosiewicz hoped the Poles would be compelled to deny the coup. Their denial would discredit the rumors, exonerate the Natolin group, and force the Gomulka regime into a deceit which could perhaps be used to force certain concessions.

The reactions to Klosiewicz's statement were immediate. Other deputies and the press condemned him for raising the question. None commented on the truth of the "rumors." The Politburo issued a statement on November 13 declaring that his action was "irresponsible, bringing harm to the Party . . . when the Party is making effective efforts to insure among the community an atmosphere of solidarity."[3] Consequently, "the Politburo hereby resolves to move at the next Plenum of the Central Committee that Comrade Klosiewicz be excluded from the Central Committee of the Party." Premier Cyrankiewicz declared that the move had been "calculated to embarrass the Government." While he and others noted the harm of rumors (although the Politburo declaration did not mention the word), there was no comment on the substance of the issue and no denial that a military coup had been planned. The attempted coup was an incident better left in silence.

Before Klosiewicz made his statement and reference to the coup was banned, several semi-official Polish sources had revealed that a coup had been attempted. On October 22, a workers' resolution broadcast on the Szczecin Regional Radio had demanded "a full disclosure of the matter of the preparations for a military coup and the punishment of those responsible." Reporting on actions of the People's Council of Szczecin, the same station had commented on the second attempted *putsch*: "A cable was also sent to the Sejm demanding that measures be taken against those responsible for the concentration of the Army around Warsaw at the moment when the historic session of the Eighth Plenum was being held in the city." A speaker on Szczecin Regional Radio on October 23 had asked that "an immediate investigation be made of the foiled military *putsch*, establishing the identity of those guilty." Finally, on October 26, the Gdansk and Szczecin stations had broadcast a report on the meeting of the Gdansk Provincial Party Committee of that day, noting in a discussion of the Natolin group that: "In the period of the fight for full sovereignty . . . that group [Natolin] attempted to carry out a military *coup d'état*." The same stations followed with an account based on reports from the Party units in the Zeran Auto Works in Warsaw. This account spelled out with extraordinary frankness the details of the coup and its failure. The key passage is given below.

Thursday night [October 18] the comrades from the Zeran Works intercepted a list from which it was apparent that the Natolin group had decided to arrest in Warsaw members of the Central Committee, progressive ministers, and comrades from the Zeran Works—a group of 700 persons. It was to be carried out by the Army. It would have been a matter of one hour, and our entire progressive cadre would be non-existent. The Natolinists would have been at the helm. With the speed of lightning, all comrades were warned and not one of them stayed at home. They also prepared pamphlets urging the Army to cooperate, and so forth. These events were followed by the dramatic days of the Eighth Plenum.

The security office in Warsaw, as one man, supported the side of progress. [Applause] The Internal Security Corps also took the side of progress. [Applause] . . . Suspicious troop movements started. And again the Zeran workers, who have many cars at their disposal, distributed comrades practically throughout Poland so that our progressive forces in the Central Committee knew all about these troop movements. The attitude the troops adopted you all know. When orders were issued to staff and political officers [by Soviet officers in the higher command positions], they answered simply that these orders would be ignored. They said they were with the people, and that they would defend the working class. [Applause]

This may be all we shall ever know about the abortive *coup d'état* of October 18 and *putsch* of October 19 and 20. The role of Soviet leaders in the plans for the coup remains the major unanswered question. But the assumption is that the plan was approved, if not instigated, by at least some of them. Rokossovsky and Witaszewski were not likely to take the responsibility for such a move, although the initiative may have come from someone in the Natolin group.

Some "ex-Natolinists," notably Alexander Zawadski, continued to occupy prominent posts. But the group as such was quietly stripped of any power. Jacob Berman had lost his posts as early as May 6, 1956, and Hilary Minc had lost his on October 9. Zenon Nowak, a key figure, was dropped from the Politburo on October 21, as were Rokossovsky, Franciszek Joswiak-Witold, Roman Nowak, and Franciszek Mazur. Lieutenant General Witaszewski was dropped from the Army on October 23, and Marshal Rokossovsky on November 13. Klosiewicz was ousted as trade union head on November 16; and Popiel and Baranowski as ministers on November 13.

Gomulka's "national Communism" evidently won its victory despite serious Soviet opposition. The Russians apparently sanctioned an abortive coup, and then by intimidation tried to prevent Gomulka's full victory. But they capitulated when the popularly supported Polish leader insisted on eliminating the Natolin group (including even Marshal Rokossovsky) and embarking on an independent course, though still within the Soviet alliance system. They were compelled either to acquiesce or to undertake a major military intervention and occupation. The fact that Gomulka, a national Communist, controlled the situation in Poland made it possible—even desirable—to permit his "independence." Gomulka endorsed the alliance with the Soviet Union for (as Gomulka has frequently noted) only the U.S.S.R. guaranteed the future of the German-Polish frontier. For the same reason, Gomulka did not try to obtain the withdrawal of Soviet troops, but sought only a status of forces agreement and Poland's right to agree in advance on Soviet troop movements and stationing on Polish territory. Gomulka's firmness and success in restraining popular Polish demands for withdrawal of Soviet troops and for opposing the Russians showed the Soviet leaders the strength of his position. It also proved his dedication to Communist rule.

Soviet acceptance of the Gomulka regime was in marked contrast to the Soviet military intervention in Hungary. Until it became essentially non-Communist and tried to withdraw entirely from the Soviet Bloc, the Nagy regime in Hungary was also reluctantly accepted by the Russians. But the differences between the two countries were very great. The main distinction was that the revolution in Hungary was not *controlled* by the relatively liberal "national Communists," whereas in Poland it was. Moreover, at the critical moment in Poland, all the people—including both the Army and security forces—stood firm with Gomulka in refusing Soviet demands. The Poles had no Kádár, probably because there was no anti-Communist terror such as occurred in the last days of Nagy's regime. Finally, the Poles did not attempt to break away from the Soviet Bloc. Bulganin had warned in Warsaw, on July 21, 1956, that while "every country should go its own way to socialism, . . . we cannot permit this to be used to break up the solidarity of the camp of peace [the Soviet Bloc]." The Polish leaders realized that the Russians fully meant the limit they had set; the Hungarian leaders unfortunately felt pushed to go beyond it. Crushing the Hungarian Revolution proved to all that Moscow would not tolerate any attempt to break away from the Soviet Bloc and establish neutrality.

Hungary in Crisis: The Soviet Decision to Intervene

The Soviet decision to intervene with military force and crush the 1956 Revolution in Hungary climaxed a story of tragedy. The repression might not have occurred. Initially, the Revolution had not only succeeded in Hungary, it had been accepted in Moscow as an unwanted but hard fact by October 29. By then, however, violent popular feelings in Hungary demanded complete independence from Communism's yoke. On October 30–31, the Hungarian people and their leaders drove beyond the point of possible Soviet acceptance, and Moscow decided upon a course of military intervention and repression.

The immediate background of the Hungarian Revolution may be traced to the public rehabilitation of Laszló Rajk, who had been executed as a Titoist in 1949. Rajk's name was quietly restored to grace on March 29, 1956, shortly after Khrushchev denounced Stalin. The Hungarian "little Stalin," Mátyás Rákosi, was openly criticized in the press in May, and on July 18 he was replaced as Party chief by Ernö Gerö. Probably influenced by the endorsement of "different roads to socialism" in the Tito-Khrushchev communiqué of June 20, Gerö called for reconciliation with Tito.

While Khrushchev and Zhukov went to Warsaw, however, Mikoyan visited Budapest on July 21, to promulgate the new and harder Soviet "post-Poznan" line. (This had been reflected in the CPSU Central Committee's June 30 resolution on tighter discipline among foreign Communists, and had been expressed by *Pravda* on July 16 in an attack on the concept of "national Communism.") Moscow sent a secret directive to the satellite leaders in September, stating plainly that the U.S.S.R., not Yugoslavia, was to be the model for satellite development. That directive led to Yugoslav reactions culminating in Khrushchev's visit to Belgrade and Tito's to the Crimea in September. Gerö also went to the Crimea on September 30 to join the talks.

The precise course of these discussions is not known, but it is significant that Hungary, like Poland (but unlike all the other satellites), continued to de-Stalinize and de-Sovietize. Rajk's body was disinterred on October 6 and some 200,000 Hungarians attended his public funeral. Expelled from the Party as a Titoist in November, 1955, and reinstated only on October 4, 1956, Imre Nagy ("the Hungarian Malenkov," who had served as premier from July, 1953, to April, 1955) publicly embraced "Rajkism" by kissing Rajk's widow. A Budapest broadcast of October 10 praised Tito for his fight against "Stalinist tyranny." Nagy was reinstated in the Party on October 13. That same day, the regime announced the arrest of former Minister of Defense Mihaly Farkas, Rákosi's secret policy chief, who had been expelled from the Party a few days after Rákosi's fall. Three thousand students of the University of Szeged broke with the Communist youth organization on October 20, and the Party organ *Szabad Nép* declared the need for a "Hungarian way to socialism." Nagy was restored to the Academy of Sciences. Radio Budapest "welcomed" the readmission of Gomulka to the Polish Politburo, and praised the

Polish Communists for not being "afraid to draw the absolutely necessary consequences" of their march forward.

On October 21, students of the universities of Szeged and Pecs and the Budapest University of Technology formulated "demands" for greater personal and national freedom. By the next day, more precise demands were circulated among the population. In Györ, popular demonstrations called for the release of Cardinal Mindszenty and, more significantly, for the withdrawal of all Soviet troops from Hungary. This new demand was issued in Budapest by crowds that also called for the return of Nagy. Radio Budapest philosophized on Hungary's following the example of Poland, which had just witnessed Wladyslaw Gomulka's successful bid to set an "independent" Communist course.

Under pressure from the student demonstrators, the Ministry of the Interior formally lifted the ban on public assembly on October 23. Without interference by the uniformed police, the demonstrators became more vociferous in repeating demands for withdrawal of Soviet troops and reinstatement of Nagy. Only after the AVH (secret police) fired on unarmed crowds (reportedly including Hungarian Army officers) did the Budapest demonstrations become violent and uncontrollable. Individual soldiers and officers joined the demonstrators. At this juncture, Gerö, Premier Andras Hegedus, and Party Secretary János Kádár returned from a week's visit to Belgrade.

Thus the Hungarian search for greater freedom led to armed conflict. Meeting in an all-night session October 23–24, the Hungarian Central Committee reached its first major, fateful decision: Gerö called Moscow, painted a picture of disastrous rioting and imminent danger, and asked for Soviet military assistance. The Soviet leaders responded by sending orders to the Russian forces in Hungary. Hegedus resigned and Nagy was named Premier, primarily to soothe the populace. By the early morning of October 24, Hungarian Army forces, with some Soviet troops, were sent to suppress the demonstrators. But some Hungarian Army units went over to the insurgents, and others stood "neutral." The Hungarian regime appealed to the insurgents to lay down their arms, promising amnesty but threatening those who would not surrender. Lacking firm leadership and authority, the rioters turned to rebellion. A virtual prisoner, Nagy broadcast at pistol-point under AVH orders.[4] The crowds demanded that Gerö go.

A second major development occurred on October 25, when Mikoyan and Suslov flew into Budapest, ousted Gerö as Party chief, and acceded to Nagy's assumption of the Premiership in fact as well as in name. An account of the circumstances surrounding these moves was later furnished to a Western correspondent by a high Hungarian official who reportedly had been present at Gerö's meeting with Mikoyan and Suslov; though the account cannot be verified, its details accord with the steps taken on that day.[5] According to the source, Mikoyan berated Gerö for having "stampeded" Moscow into an ill-advised commitment of Soviet troops through his "exaggerated and distorted" picture of the situation. Suslov "suggested" that Gerö resign at once. When Gerö protested, citing Moscow's earlier statement that he was needed to hold the Party together, Mikoyan replied angrily, "the Party already has fallen apart, thanks to your incredible blunders." The Soviet leaders then summoned János Kádár, purged under Rákosi and Gerö, and informed him that he would succeed Gerö as First Secretary of the Party. The no-longer-useful Gerö was taken away in protective custody. Next, Mikoyan and Suslov agreed that Nagy should announce a series of "concessions," especially those promising withdrawal of Soviet troops from Budapest and a review of Soviet-Hungarian treaties. By then the rebellion had become nationwide revolt.

On October 26, Nagy publicly recognized the justice of some of the insurgents' demands. He attributed the conditions leading to these demands to "mistakes and crimes" of the previous ten years. Finally, he promised eventual but complete Soviet military withdrawal from Hungary. Appeals for cease-fire and surrender continued. By this time, most of the Hungarian Army was either neutral or on the side of the insurgents.

A new coalition government formed and made public on October 27 included the non-Communist leaders Zoltán Tildy and Béla Kovacs as Minister of State Affairs and Minister of Agriculture. The next day, Sunday the 28th, Radio Budapest announced to the rebels: "You have won!" Nagy reiterated that he would seek complete withdrawal of Soviet troops from Hungary (now no longer "eventual" withdrawal). A "new" army and police were recognized. The Kossuth coat of arms was officially sanctioned to replace the Communist ear of corn on the flag and the red star on uniforms. The AVH (secret police) was abolished, and the Russians began to withdraw from Budapest on October 29. But complete withdrawal from the city was tied to a rebel cease-fire.

After a week of popular uprising—from nonviolent demonstration to national revolt—the Revolution was virtually consummated. Nagy announced on the 30th that free elections, with all the parties of 1945, would be held. He publicly declared that he had not approved the call for intervention of Soviet troops, and demanded their immediate withdrawal from Budapest. The withdrawal began on a substantial scale in the afternoon. Flushed with victory, the Hungarian Air Force Command published an "ultimatum" giving the Soviet troops twelve hours to leave Budapest or be attacked. Fighting died down everywhere.

The Soviet press and radio had been cautious in reporting events in Hungary. The reports of October 24–28 described merely the liquidation of a counterrevolutionary revolt by the Hungarians "with the assistance of units of the Soviet Army." The United States was said to have "fomented" the revolt. Each day it was said that the situation had now cleared up. On the 28th, *Pravda* featured an article on "The Liquidation of a Counterrevolutionary Adventure in Hungary," but that same day, Radio Moscow reported that "workers' councils (soviets)" had been set up and cited Nagy on the "just demands" of the people. On October 30 it was revealed that Hungary had established a "coalition of democratic parties" and restored the Smallholders' and Social Democratic parties. The Soviet press and radio asserted on October 31 that the rebellion was "not an uprising against socialism," that "Soviet troops have been withdrawn from Budapest," and that "life in the town has begun to revive." These were hardly the terms to describe to the Soviet people a situation in which Soviet troops would intervene anew in force. By October 30, the Russians had decided to make their peace with the Revolution. Soviet withdrawal from Budapest was by then virtually completed. The extent of the Hungarians' victory was evident with the appointment of Major General Pal Maleter as First Deputy Defense Minister. A popular hero of the Revolution, Maleter, as a colonel, had been among the first to defect to the people's side with his men and tanks, and had led the defense of the Kilian Barracks against the Russians.

On the 30th also, the Soviet Government drafted a remarkable statement—hinting at a review of the policy of stationing Soviet troops in the satellites and implying that they would be withdrawn from all East European countries except East Germany. The pronouncement (*Pravda*, October 31, 1956) included the following passage on the situation in Hungary:

> Since it considers that the further presence of Soviet army units in Hungary can serve as a cause for an even greater deterioration of the situation, the Soviet Government has instructed its military command to withdraw Soviet Army units from Budapest . . . [and] is ready to

enter into negotiations with the Hungarian People's Republic and other participants of the Warsaw Treaty on the question of the presence of Soviet troops on the territory of Hungary.

The very issuance of this statement suggested a Soviet readiness to withdraw once order had been re-established and after due formalization by a joint decision of the Warsaw Pact members.

On October 31, however, Mikoyan and Suslov reappeared in Budapest for secret meetings with Nagy and Tildy. They had evidently been dispatched to size up the situation and to stabilize the new coalition government—short of granting additional major concessions, especially relating to Soviet-Hungarian relations. Mikoyan offered immediately to withdraw from Hungary all Soviet troops other than the contingents previously stationed under the Warsaw Pact agreement. Withdrawal of those stationed under the Pact provisions was to be negotiated by the Pact powers. But Tildy *rejected* this offer and demanded withdrawal of all troops *at once*; moreover, he told Mikoyan that Hungary would definitely "repudiate the Warsaw Pact *in any case*."[6] The Hungarians proposed a joint commission to discuss the Soviet withdrawal; the Russians agreed, and Mikoyan and Suslov departed.

Mikoyan and Suslov may have been empowered to decide whether Soviet military intervention was necessary. But probably the Soviet leaders did not anticipate that the situation would entail such a decision—the Government declaration of the previous day, Soviet military inaction, and Moscow home-service radio reportage strongly suggest that they did not. But the shock of Tildy's repudiation of the Warsaw Pact "in any case," and Nagy's and Tildy's defiant insistence on immediate withdrawal must have led Mikoyan and Suslov—probably in consultation with Moscow—to decide on the need for intervention. Early the next morning (November 1), Mikoyan and Suslov met with Kádár and probably then laid the basis for a new, separate government that would call for Soviet military intervention. Then they returned to Moscow.

The Soviet decision of October 31 to intervene with force was a reluctant one.[7] Obviously it would clash with the newly cultivated Soviet foreign policy of peaceful coexistence and anticolonialism. But the imminent danger of a pro-Western, anti-Communist "neutral" Hungary bordering the U.S.S.R. was more than the Soviet leaders could tolerate. The danger of igniting the flames of revolt in the entire satellite empire was too great.

The decision to intervene and the consequences of intervention were serious setbacks to the liberalization of Soviet-satellite relations, but they did not foreshadow either general reversal to a "hard" Stalinist line or victory of a pro-Stalinist faction in the Soviet leadership. They did indicate that even the Soviet leadership's moderate faction agreed that Hungary had gone too far. Bulganin had clearly stated the limits of permissibility in Warsaw in July: "Every country should go its own way to socialism, but we cannot permit this to be used to break up the solidarity of the camp of peace [i.e., the Soviet Bloc]."[8]

The Soviet decision to intervene was facilitated, although by no means determined, by the diversion of world opinion to events in the Middle East. The Anglo-French ultimatum of October 30 had made clear the intention of those states to intervene with force in Egypt. The Soviet leaders therefore could be sure that the shock caused by the use of brutal force in Hungary would be substantially mitigated throughout the world.

Nagy formally told Soviet Ambassador Andropov on November 1 that Hungary was withdrawing immediately from the Warsaw Pact, declaring its neutrality, and seeking U.N. and Big Four guarantees of this neutrality. Later in the day, Soviet troops surrounded Hungarian Air Force bases and occupied the Budapest airport "to safeguard evacuation" of Soviet forces. For three days, substantial additional Soviet forces moved into Hungary (raising the total to seven divisions), sealed most of the Austrian border, and cut off all the highways leading out of Budapest. Hungarian troops, previously ordered by the Government to "refrain from any hostile acts" toward the Soviet forces, were powerless to prevent these so-called "peaceful" regroupings.[9] Nagy protested to the Soviet Ambassador, to no avail.

Radio Moscow propagandized the Soviet declaration of October 30; it announced the withdrawal of Soviet troops from Budapest and reported the trip of Social Democrat Anna Kethly to Vienna for a meeting of the Second International. But by November 2, it noted "a new menacing stage" in Hungary.

On Saturday, November 3, Nagy announced an "encouraging start" in withdrawal negotiations. But answering a correspondent's question on Soviet guarantees not to initiate hostilities, Tildy stated that "The Soviet reply given so far was not satisfactory."[10] Major General Pal Maleter was named Minister of Defense, and he and the new Chief of Staff, Lieutenant General Istvan Kovacs, began discussions with the Soviet military delegation led by General of the Army Mikhail Malinin, Deputy Chief of the General Staff.[11]

At dawn on November 4, Soviet forces launched a general offensive against Budapest and against other strongholds of the Hungarian Army and the Freedom Fighters. The news of the formation of a "Hungarian Revolutionary Workers' and Peasants'" government was broadcast on a provincial radio station at 4:00 A.M. by its new Minister of Armed Forces and Public Security, Ferenc Muennich (who had served in the Nagy cabinet until a few days earlier). Muennich revealed that the regime had been set up November 1 (presumably in secret and at the demand of Mikoyan and Suslov); this step, he explained, was necessary because Nagy had become "impotent" under reactionary pressure. An hour later, the new Kádár government program and appeal were broadcast, followed by a speech by Kádár. That same morning Radio Moscow broadcast Kádár's program, with its appeal for Soviet military assistance. Also broadcast were a *Pravda* editorial entitled "Chaos is Reigning in Hungary" and an attack on Nagy for being "in direct connivance with reactionaries." Soviet troops were "helping to curb the dire forces of reaction."

The Hungarian Army and Air Force, effectively neutralized by the Soviet military reinforcement and deployment of November 1–4, were unable to resist. Nagy had been maneuvered into such a position that when the Soviet attack was launched, he had to call desperately over the radio for his Minister of Defense and Chief of Staff to "return to their posts." Only then did he learn that they were already Soviet prisoners at the "secret meeting place" for "negotiation."[12] Isolated Army units and armed civilian insurgents fought on for ten heroic but hopeless days.

However brutal the Soviet suppression of the Revolution, the Kádár regime did not attempt to return to Gerö's position of October 15, much less to Rákosi and Stalinism. Kádár's initial statement, broadcast by the Balaton Szabadi Provincial Radio on November 4, declared:

> On October 23 *a mass movement* began in our country, whose *noble purpose* was to make good the anti-Party and antinational mistakes committed by Rákosi and his accomplices [elsewhere referred to as "the Rákosi-Gerö clique"] and to defend the national independence and sovereignty of Hungary. [Italics added.]

Kádár offered full amnesty to the population and promised to improve living standards. Coalition popular-front government also was promised: "we shall definitely invite representatives of other parties" to assume ministries. He also pledged that after the restoration of order, the regime would negotiate with the other Warsaw Pact states "on the question" of the stationing of Soviet troops in

Hungary; other broadcasts specifically promised negotiation "for withdrawal." Free elections were not mentioned, however, and there was no hint of neutrality or of withdrawal from the Warsaw Pact.

In several speeches, Kádár explained his motives and those of his colleagues for leaving the Nagy regime, establishing a new government, and requesting Soviet assistance. In a speech broadcast on November 11, he pinpointed the timing of the decision:

> It became clear as early [sic] as the middle of last week [October 31] that there were only two ways leading out of the grave situation. One way was to continue on the road to collapse which was followed by the Imre Nagy government . . . The alternative road was to stop the counterrevolutionary wave with every force, including the help of Soviet forces . . . [or, as he put it a few days later, "*even* with the help of the Soviet Army."]

In that speech and in several others, Kádár stated:

> after order has been restored, we should start negotiations with member states of the Warsaw Pact concerning the withdrawal of Soviet troops from Hungarian territory. Only in this way is it possible . . . to assure our complete national independence and sovereignty.

The official organ *Népszabadság* continued to stress the need for Soviet withdrawal; thus on November 18:

> If anyone tries to prevent the bringing about of Hungarian independence, he will find himself confronted with the resistance of an entire united nation. Against a resistance of this kind, 10,000 tanks and masses of guns and airplanes would be of no use. The Hungarian people's desire for independence is so great now that there exists no force which could quell it.

On November 15, a delegation of workers asked Kádár why Soviet troops did not leave Hungary. He replied that his government wanted them to leave but that the Russians *declined to do so* until order was restored! Moreover, he went beyond his initial program and declared (as reported the same day on Radio Budapest): "We want a multiparty system and free honest elections," with all parties participating which "stand for socialist principles and serve the interests of the workers." He stated that "Nagy never has been an enemy of our system, and I see no reason why he should not resume a position in public life." That day, Gerö, Hegedus, Colonel General Istvan Bata ("the Rokossovsky of Hungary," a long-time Soviet Army officer of Hungarian ethnic origin, and later Hungarian Defense Minister) and other Stalinists were barred "forever" from public and Party activity.

Over a period of a few weeks, the Kádár regime paid lip service to all the major measures of the Nagy Government. No doubt, many of the official statements were prompted by desperation over the continuing heroic resistance of the population. Eventually, some of the promises were honored. The Revolution was not a complete failure.

As early as November 12, Mikoyan and Suslov (possibly with Khrushchev) returned to Budapest and immediately thereafter Kádár sought, unsuccessfully, Imre Nagy's aid in forming a new, more popular government.[13] Kádár, and at least part of the Soviet leadership, had expected the massive Soviet intervention of November 4 to stun the nation and stamp out all resistance quickly, permitting a show of "magnanimity in victory" by Kádár. The ten days of resistance and the continuing general strike made this course impossible.

What has emerged over the years since 1956 is a Soviet-permitted national Communist government. From the very beginning, Kádár's program attempted to create the basis for this, even though he had been branded a Russian puppet for conspiring in and justifying the Soviet intervention and by permitting himself to be a "front" for Soviet deportations, revenge repressions, and military occupation.

In retrospect, the tragedy of the Hungarian Revolution was its inability to stand on the achievements of October 30. By precipitously withdrawing from the Warsaw Pact, it threatened (in Soviet eyes) to place a Western base on the very borders of the Soviet Union and to dynamite the entire satellite empire. The actions of Nagy and Tildy on October 31—under the tremendous pressure of the populace and the provincial "revolutionary councils" (especially at Györ)—compelled the Russians to intervene.

The timing of the Soviet decision to intervene indicates that there was—prior to October 30–31—a readiness to permit, under pressure, a substantial departure from traditional satellite status *without* intervention. If Nagy had held to the gains of October 30 and had been able to restore order, the Russians might have withdrawn their forces from Hungary (and from Romania and possibly even from Poland) in the relatively near future. Becoming more Titoist than Tito, Nagy might have been permitted to exercise the substantial degree of independence implied by that position.

During the course of intensified polemics between the Soviet and Chinese Communist parties in 1963, the Chinese publicly claimed credit for supporting the Poles against the Russians in October, 1956, and charged that the Soviet leaders "committed the error of great power chauvinism . . . by moving up troops in an attempt to subdue the Polish comrades by force."[14] At the same time, the Chinese also confirmed the fact that the Soviet leaders had "intended for a time to adopt a policy of capitulation abandoning socialist Hungary to the counterrevolution."[15] Contemporary accounts of 1956 and 1957 indicate that the Chinese did, in fact, advise the Russians not to use force against another Communist Party, but to use force only when Communist rule was threatened. However, there is no evidence or reason to believe that the Soviet leaders needed such advice—or heeded it. They reached these decisions themselves.

The Soviet decisions of October-November, 1956, helped to clarify the military factors and calculations that would underlie Soviet decisions on whether to resort to force to preserve an existing element of the Communist Bloc. Such considerations would include the stakes, the nature of the prospective loss in prestige, the geostrategic gains, and the general balance of power in the world.

9. Sino-Soviet Military Relations, 1945–65

The Soviet Union and Communist China are both drawn together and divided by ideology, national interest, military alliance and collaboration. The military is only one strand in a complex pattern of relationships. Military frictions have aggravated the serious rift between the two powers; even more significantly, the military has been the victim of political and ideological conflicts.

Chinese Communist-Soviet military relations have passed through four more or less equal periods. First is the background period from the Soviet occupation of Manchuria in August, 1945, through the Chinese Civil War to the establishment of Communist rule in Mainland China and the signing of the Sino-Soviet treaty of alliance in February, 1950. The second period can be traced from that date through the Korean War until late 1954, following the visit of Khrushchev and Bulganin to Peking. Their subsequent succession to power in Moscow in February, 1955, marks the beginning of a period of growing but strained cooperation. The current period began in mid-1960 with the sudden cut-off of Soviet military and other assistance. This phase has been distinguished by the virtual absence of military relations in any form. Each of these periods is sufficiently distinctive, and sufficiently significant, to merit close attention.

Cautious and Limited Cooperation: 1945–50

The full story of Soviet relations with the Chinese Communists during the postwar phase of the Chinese Civil War is not yet clear, but the features relevant to our present inquiry are known. Stalin cautiously reinsured Soviet influence by his "correct" diplomatic dealings with the Nationalist Government, while he gave some assistance to the Communists. The Soviet policy of double-dealing may be explained by Stalin's uncertainty as to the outcome of the Civil War, but it is also entirely possible that he wanted China to remain divided for a long period, and therefore chose to aid both sides in different ways.

During the critical years from 1945 through 1948, Soviet assistance to China was limited. Military assistance consisted in allowing the Chinese Communists to gain strategic footholds and to acquire captured Japanese ordnance in Manchuria; political assistance was initially given to the Nationalist Government by the 1945 Treaty of Friendship by clearly recognizing it as the government of all China; and economic "assistance" was limited to stripping Manchuria of its industrial assets at the expense of both Chinese rivals.

The chief Soviet objectives in declaring war on Japan and in occupying Manchuria were: (1) to acquire a voice in the future of the Northern Pacific, including Japan; (2) to seize and incorporate into the U.S.S.R. southern Sakhalin and the Kurils; (3) to eliminate Japanese and pre-empt Western presence on the North Asian continent; and (4) to re-establish former Russian influence and also rail and base rights in Manchuria, and to consolidate the status of their Mongolian satrap. There is no good evidence that assistance to the Chinese Communists entered into this decision, but there is a wealth of evidence that Stalin expected that the Nationalist Government—though weak and ineffective—would remain in control even in Manchuria. For this reason, he negotiated the 1945 Treaty which, at some cost to local Communist pretensions, assisted in meeting the above objectives. The Soviet looting of Manchurian "reparations" is inconsistent with the contention that the Russians handed Manchuria over to the Chinese Communists so that they could have a base to defeat the Nationalists. If that were the case, why destroy the major part of the great Mukden arsenals which could have given the Chinese Communists the wherewithal to fight? Finally, there is evidence that in 1945 and 1946 Stalin urged the Chinese Communists to form a coalition with the Nationalists.[1] Mao did not do so, not only because he may have been more aware of the opportunities than Stalin, but because his one objective was to seize complete power and build a strong Communist China. The Soviet objective was to win concessions and influence for the U.S.S.R. from a weak China, and to keep China weak through a nominal Nationalist rule in which the Russians had powerful leverage through the Communists (and through other elements such as dissidents in Sinkiang, and various war lords).

The Russians therefore permitted the Chinese Communist Eighth Route Army to enter Manchuria, harassed (but did not prevent) the arrival of Chinese Nationalist troops, and allowed the Communists to "seize" captured Japanese military equipment and supplies in raids on lightly "guarded" stocks. In all, the Russians captured from the

Japanese about 300,000 rifles, nearly 5,000 machine guns, 1,226 artillery pieces, 369 tanks, and 925 aircraft. Much of the artillery and small arms, and a few of the tanks and aircraft, were then acquired by the Chinese Communist forces in the spring of 1946. This equipment included their first tanks and combat aircraft in the whole Civil War. The Russians also released the ex-Manchukuo Army personnel, a number of whom were recruited by the Communists. In May, 1946, the Russians withdrew from Manchuria, leaving the Chinese Nationalists in nominal control—but the Communists in effective control of the northeastern two-thirds of the region.[2]

There is no evidence of further Soviet military assistance to the Chinese Communists during the four years of Civil War. The Chinese Communist forces were equipped with a conglomeration of U.S.- and Japanese-produced weapons, most of them captured from the Nationalist forces. Chinese Communist claims for *gross* capture during the whole period from mid-1946 to 1950 were 3,160,000 rifles, 320,000 machine guns, 55,000 artillery pieces, 622 tanks and 389 armored cars, 189 military aircraft, and 200 small warships.[3] Assuming these figures are correct, it is evident that the Russians permitted the Chinese Communists to seize only small amounts of tanks and aircraft in Manchuria. The Chinese Nationalists took much larger quantities of captured Japanese ordnance in 1945–46 than the Russians did—twice as many rifles, six times as many machine guns, and ten times as many artillery pieces.[4] The items the Communists seized from the Nationalists, including the U.S. matériel originally supplied to the Nationalist armies, and not Soviet-supplied weapons, provided the Chinese Communist forces with the implements for winning the Civil War.

By the end of the Civil War in 1950, the People's Liberation Army (as it had been renamed in 1946) was a poorly equipped and ill-balanced infantry force of about 5 million men (many from the Nationalist or war-lord armies) formed loosely into four "field armies" with a total of 215 "divisions."[5] Air, naval, armored, and technical units were few and miscellaneous. When, in 1949, the retreating Nationalists stood their ground at Quemoy, the Chinese Communists were not even able to take that modestly defended offshore island.

Building an Alliance: 1950–54

A Treaty of Friendship, Alliance, and Mutual Assistance between the U.S.S.R. and the C.P.R. was signed in Moscow on February 14, 1950. An economic development loan of $300 million from the Soviet

Union was included in the agreements.[6] Protocol for military assistance were not known or published, but it is clear that arrangements
were made for the Soviet Union to supply matériel and training.
Under these arrangements, a Soviet military mission was established
in Peking and an estimated 3,000 Soviet military advisers were sent
to China.[7] Some Chinese military men may also have been sent to
the U.S.S.R. for specialized training.[8] Hundreds of obsolescent Soviet
La-9 and La-11 piston fighters and Tu-2 twin piston-engine light
bombers appeared in China. Thus a program of military aid was
begun.

In his exhaustive analysis of Chinese policy on the eve of the
Korean War, Dr. Allen Whiting finds no signs of Chinese Communist participation in planning that conflict, nor, until the summer of
1950, any preparation for possible participation in it.[9] The Russians
alone had been involved in building up the North Korean Army and
in unleashing it. However, the unexpected U.S. intervention in support of the defenders, and the unexpected U.S. success in crushing
the North Korean forces (autumn, 1950), led to what General Mac-
Arthur termed, with some justice, "an entirely new war." The Chinese
entered the contest.

The Sino-Soviet military relationship also entered a new phase, for
the Chinese had to be entrusted with waging a war begun without
them. It is likely that the Russians had been planning that the
Chinese acquire jet fighters—apart from the Korean War. But under
the exigencies of the war, MiG fighters appeared in Manchuria in late
October, and entered combat against U.S. aircraft along the Yalu on
November 1, 1950.[10] By December, 1951, the Chinese Communists
had about 700 MiG-15 fighters and 200 Tu-2 piston light bombers,
mostly concentrated in North China, and claimed a total air strength
of 2,400 aircraft of all types.[11] By 1952, they had Il-28 jet light bombers, though these were not used in combat.[12] Later, at about the end
of the war, a token number of Tu-4's (B-29-type piston medium
bombers) were transferred to Communist China.

Military expenditures represented 48 per cent of the Chinese budget by 1951.[13] The Soviet military-aid program became and remained
extensive, but it also was expensive. The Chinese were compelled to
purchase all this matériel, and they incurred heavy debts in the
process. From 1950 to 1957, the value of such aid approximated $2
billion of which perhaps half was covered by Soviet credits.[14] Even
school children were canvassed for funds to be spent on Soviet tanks
and aircraft in 1953.[15] Early in 1957, during a period of relative freedom of expression in China, General Lung Yun, a former dissident

Nationalist, but then a member of the Revolutionary Military Committee of the C.P.R. and a vice chairman of the National Defense Committee, publicly declared that it was "totally unfair for the People's Republic of China to bear all the expenses of the Korean War."[16] He noted that the United States had forgiven Allied debts in World Wars I and II, while the Soviet Union had not done so for Communist China. Finally, he recalled that the Soviet Army had dismantled and taken away Manchurian industry in 1946.

Soviet assistance was essential to China; the Chinese had no choice but to accept Soviet terms. Modernization and mechanization of the Chinese military establishment required production, logistics, and communications systems which would have been impossible to obtain otherwise.

While building Chinese military power, Stalin kept it fully dependent on the Soviet Union. Weapons were supplied, but not assistance in creating military production. China was held on a short leash for a few years: The MiG's and Ilyushins, and a few obsolescent Soviet submarines and destroyers, would need to be replaced in a few years, and their replacements could come only from the U.S.S.R. The Russians could not directly prevent the Chinese Communists from building their own military industry, but they could withhold their assistance while arguing that it was more economical to buy Soviet-produced weapons. And, by saddling them with outlays as heavy as they could bear, the Russians further held back the Chinese from building an independent military establishment.

Stalin used the occasion of the Korean War to sell more modern weapons to China; he also pressed the Chinese in other ways. In September, 1952, he forced a modification of the 1950 Treaty extending indefinitely the Soviet occupation of Port Arthur on the Yellow Sea by deferring withdrawal until after a Japanese peace treaty was signed.[17]

The death of Stalin profoundly—though not immediately—affected Sino-Soviet relations. Soviet and Chinese interests converged in finishing the Korean War, but beyond this, both countries recognized the need for redefining their relationship. Accordingly, a high-level Soviet delegation visited Peking in October, 1954.

Progress and Strain in the Alliance: 1954–60

Symbolically, it was important that the review of Sino-Soviet relations took place in Peking rather than in Moscow. Khrushchev, Bulganin, Mikoyan, and Shvernik headed the delegation, reflecting the combined political, Party, economic, and military interests involved.

Agreements were signed on October 11, 1954. One reversed the Stalin *diktat* of only two years earlier; the U.S.S.R. agreed to withdraw from Port Arthur by May 31, 1955, and turn over the Soviet installations there without compensation. A scientific-technical agreement was also signed. The provision of the 1950 treaty for joint exploitation of uranium resources in Sinkiang was revoked,[18] with full control reverting to China on January 1, 1955. No new military agreements were announced or, apparently, reached.

In May, 1955, Marshal P'eng Teh-huai, the Chinese Communist Minister of Defense, was invited to the ceremony founding the War-saw Pact, and then spent June in Moscow in discussions with Soviet military representatives. But China did not become a member of the Warsaw Pact.

In 1955, the Russians withdrew from Port Arthur as promised, leaving the aircraft belonging to their units there to extend the impression of generosity. An additional agreement on cooperation in the peaceful applications of atomic energy was reached in 1955. The following year, China joined other Communist states in entering the cooperative "socialist" nonmilitary atomic research center at Dubna near Moscow (where the Russians, incidentally, could siphon off the work of the best East European and Chinese nuclear physicists). Chinese specialists at Dubna were finally all withdrawn in 1965.

The flow of Soviet modern weapons diminished during the late 1950's, not because the Russians decided to choke it off but because the short-term air force and naval strength levels had been reached. In retrospect, it seems clear that the Chinese demand that modern defense industry be built up in China was gaining acceptance. Progress had been made by the Chinese in conventional basic land armaments such as small arms and artillery; but now, with Soviet help, a beginning was also made in the partial construction and assembly of jet fighters, complete construction of light piston aircraft, and construction of tanks, submarines, and small patrol craft. By September, 1956, the first jet fighters of Chinese "manufacture" were flown—with some fanfare.[19] By the end of the 1950's, the Chinese Communist Air Force had hundreds of MiG-17's and some MiG-19's, as well as many older MiG-15's.

The Chinese Communist Army, by the late 1950's, had been substantially modernized into a force of reasonably well-equipped light infantry divisions.[20] Soviet training activities had been largely completed and phased out in the mid- and late-1950's, and the military mission in Peking turned to problems of production facilities in more modern armaments and to coordination of military activities.

It should be noted that throughout both the Stalin and post-Stalin periods, there has been no indication of coordinated training exercises or maneuvers between the Soviet and Chinese Communist armies, navies, or air forces. Apart from the very limited direct Soviet support to the Chinese during the Korean War, there has been no real coordination of their military operations or training. In the Far East there has been no bilateral equivalent of the Warsaw Pact to integrate air defenses and naval operations. Why? Political factors must have put a damper on the exercising of alliance privileges that would bring such military benefit. Political charges between the Soviet and Chinese Communist parties later revealed that a Soviet-proposed joint naval command in the Pacific foundered because of Chinese refusal to accept a subordinate role.[21] Chinese sensitivity over equality of roles probably also was responsible for failure to integrate an air defense system.

Ultimately, the growing political estrangement between the Russian and Chinese Communists more sharply affected military relationships, but even when the political surface was placid and harmonious, there were severe limits on the nature and extent of military relationships.

During the period after 1954, there were important developments in military doctrine in the Soviet Union and Communist China. Both countries belatedly recognized the implications of nuclear war, though the implications for each were very different. The Russians had to adjust their concepts to weapons they had or were acquiring, while the Chinese military leaders were faced with the frustration of recognizing the decisive importance of weapons they did not possess.

In 1955, a number of Chinese military men began to stress the importance of nuclear weapons and of new military technology in general, and to state specifically that China needed and would acquire "a sufficient quantity of the most modern matériel to arm the Chinese People's Liberation Army."[22] However, some military leaders (especially in the General Staff) placed most emphasis on the immediate need for modern weapons, while those in the Ministry of Defense (and the political officers) continued to emphasize the basic political-morale factors of a people's army, in the Maoist tradition.[23] This divergence was in part over doctrine and in part over policy: Should Communist China acquire her own nuclear weapons or rely on the Soviet Union? By either approach, China would depend heavily on the U.S.S.R.—either for Soviet nuclear protection and support, or for Soviet assistance in developing Chinese capabilities.[24] In 1955, also, the Russians began to assist in the development of a modern Chinese military industry and a nonmilitary nuclear program.

On October 15, 1957, an important agreement with respect to "new technology for national defense" was concluded between the U.S.S.R. and Communist China. This agreement was secret, and was disclosed by the Chinese only in 1963, in protest over alleged Soviet perfidy in unilaterally "tearing it up" in June, 1959.[25] The Russians have not explicitly discussed the agreement, but they have implicitly acknowledged its existence by criticizing the Chinese for revealing joint defense secrets. The precise terms of the agreement are still not known, but it is likely that they were vague and general. The Chinese disclosure of the agreement did not specify its content, but stated that in June, 1959, the Russians "tore up the agreement, *and* refused to supply a sample atomic bomb and technical data concerning its manufacture"; they did not state that the supply of a sample nuclear weapon and technical data was promised in the agreement, which is extremely unlikely, but they implied that liberal interpretation of the spirit of the agreement *should* have extended to supplying detailed data on nuclear weapons.

On the fortieth anniversary of the Russian Revolution, November, 1957, Mao Tse-tung and a delegation of Chinese military leaders visited Moscow. The successful Soviet testing of an ICBM and launching of the first artificial earth satellite encouraged the Chinese almost more than it did the Russians, but it also underlined the gap between Chinese and Soviet capabilities. Later indications suggest that Mao sought a greater role for China in the Communist camp, and that he may have requested nuclear weapons for China and other far-reaching concrete actions not specified in the new agreement.[26] Among Mao's colleagues visiting Moscow were Minister of Defense Marshal P'eng Teh-huai and the two leading Army "modernizers," Marshal Yeh Chien-ying and General Su Yu, the Chief of the General Staff.[27] Presumably the military mission was concerned with implementing the October agreement. It is, however, possible that additional assistance on nuclear weapons was requested —and denied. It is thus possible that the nuclear issue became associated with the ideological-political disagreements over the 1957 multi-Party declaration.

During the period from late 1957 until mid-1960, the Russians continued to aid the Chinese in developing their own missiles and aircraft, and probably in working toward construction of their own fissionable materials production. But it is quite clear that at some point between November, 1957, and May, 1958, the Russians disclosed the "strings" that they placed on any disposition of nuclear warheads: Soviet control in a joint enterprise. The Chinese have since declared: "In 1958 the leadership of the CPSU put forward unreasonable demands designed to bring China under Soviet military control. These unreasonable demands were rightly and firmly rejected by the Chinese Government."[28] The Russian proposals were for a joint Sino-Soviet naval command in the Far East, for more closely integrated air defenses, and possibly also concerned deployments of offensive Soviet nuclear weapons systems. The Secretary General of the Sino-Japanese Friendship Association, Chang An-po, has said that these Soviet proposals were made in April, 1958.[29]

At some point (or points) between October, 1957, and June, 1959, the Chinese pressed to get actual nuclear weapons. The Russians themselves have acknowledged that they refused even to consider Chinese requests for nuclear weapons. As Radio Moscow has stated: "The Chinese leaders have been at great pains to obtain possession of nuclear weapons. They strenuously tried—this is no secret—to get the Soviet Union to give them the atomic bomb. The CPSU and the Soviet Government naturally could not consider this, since it might have led to the most serious consequences."[30]

As the facts of nuclear-missile warfare, and the implications of Soviet refusal to provide nuclear weapons to China, sank more deeply into the Chinese consciousness in 1958, significant policy disputes led to new decisions. During the spring and summer of 1958, a debate over military doctrine erupted. The unreconstructed "modernizers" who stressed the urgent need for nuclear weapons and other advanced military technology were pitted against the "conservatives" who stressed the importance of the basic political factors and massive military manpower and relied on eventual Chinese development of its own weapons needs.

As early as January, Marshal P'eng declared that the Chinese must "on the basis of *our national* industrialization systematically arm our army with new technical equipment. In the light of *our* industrial capacity, we can do so only gradually."[31] In May, Foreign Minister Marshal Chen Yi remarked in an interview that "At the moment China does not own atomic weapons, but we shall have them in the future."[32] And also in May, Air Force General Liu Ya-lou emphasized the need first to press priority economic build-up of the country, and then, on that basis, "*China's* working class and scientists will certainly be able to make the most up-to-date aircraft and atomic bombs in the not distant future."[33]

This new line combined the importance of nuclear weapons with a major *Chinese* effort to design and construct them (Chinese scientists, as well as workers and engineers, were referred to). But, faced with the Soviet refusal to supply nuclear weapons, the new line did not last long. It placed too much emphasis on the need for early Chinese acquisition of nuclear weapons—an impossibility, despite vigorous efforts. Doctrinal confusion over balancing the decisive importance of something that they did not have with assertions of *current* Chinese strength was too great. The military leaders may also have pressed Mao too hard. For these reasons, a major conference called by the Military Committee of the Party's Central Committee met from May 27 until July 22—two whole months of debate. Party leaders (including Mao) addressed the conference, which reportedly was attended by a thousand Chinese military officers. By the end of July, a new line had been adopted. Marshal Chu Teh spoke on July 31 of "defects" resulting from "tendencies toward an exclusive military viewpoint."[34] He said that the Chinese should study Soviet military experience, but by a "selective and creative" approach. The *Liberation Army Daily* on the next day explained that "a very few comrades" had "one-sidedly stressed the role of atomic weapons and modern military technology, and neglected the role of man."[35] Also on August 1, Marshal Ho Lung warned in *People's Daily* against relying on "outside aid" in solving China's military problems.[36] Yu Chao-li, in *Red Flag* on August 16, quoted Mao that "the atomic bomb is a paper tiger," a theme quickly picked up by others.[37] Finally, on September 6, 1958, the Central Committee of the Party adopted a resolution to mobilize the entire male population into a "people's militia," a development explicitly tied to Mao Tse-tung's "strategic thinking on the people's war."[38] In October, General Su Yu was removed as Chief of the General Staff.

The Chinese thus were forced gradually to build up advanced weapons capabilities with minimal Soviet assistance, while playing down the significance of those weapons which they did not yet have. There were ample signs of undercurrents of military dissatisfaction with this solution.[39]

The impotence of the Chinese, and Soviet refusal to back them in any risky situation of Chinese interest, was evident in the Quemoy crisis of August–September, 1958.[40] It is not clear to what extent the Russians approved Chinese plans to stir up a crisis in the Taiwan Straits by heavy artillery bombardment of Quemoy. Khrushchev met Mao in Peking at the end of July, 1958, probably to discuss both the recent Middle Eastern crisis and the Chinese plans with respect to

Quemoy. In meeting the Middle Eastern crisis, which had been touched off by the revolution in Iraq on July 13, Khrushchev veered from one line to another, and the Chinese were probably troubled by his shift from bellicosity to proposing either a meeting of U.N. Security Council or of the Big Five (with India)—either of which would have involved settlement of an Asian crisis with Communist China conspicuously absent and either the Republic of China or India involved. Thus by the time of Mao's meeting with Khrushchev, the Chinese leaders had doubts about the consistency of Soviet support.

Subsequent Soviet action in the course of the Quemoy crisis was hardly reassuring. Only when the Russians were sure that the Chinese would enter negotiations and not press the confrontation to the extent of a direct challenge to the United States did Khrushchev on September 7 give a public pledge of Soviet assistance, and then only if China itself were attacked by the United States. Thus the Russians attempted to deter the United States from expanding the crisis, but also did not lend real support to Mao's offensive move against the offshore islands.

At the time of Khrushchev's meeting with Mao, Marshals Malinovsky and P'eng Teh-huai were also present. Soon thereafter, "leaks" in Warsaw allegedly disclosed Soviet-Chinese accords on increased economic and military assistance. These reports suggested that the Russians had even agreed to supply the Chinese with nuclear warheads.[41] On the basis of later information, it is clear that nuclear warheads were neither promised nor supplied, and neither the Russians nor the Chinese have ever referred to such an agreement.

During 1958 and 1959, the Chinese continued to stress their determination to get nuclear weapons. At first, in 1958, the Chinese supported the idea of a nuclear-free zone in the Far East, but when Khrushchev proposed this in a speech on January 27, 1959, Chinese reaction was cool.[42] Rather, the Chinese seized an East German statement of January 26 that if West Germany got nuclear missiles they too would "request" them from *their* allies. The Chinese (alone of the other Communist states) commented this would be "not only fully justified, but also *necessary*."[43] On January 21, 1960, the National People's Congress passed a resolution stressing that China would not be bound by any disarmament agreement except with its express consent, and that it would accept no disarmament agreement unless it had participated in its negotiation. The Russians were not being trusted to look out for Chinese politico-military interests.

Two startling developments in over-all Sino-Soviet relations occurred in mid-1959. From April 24 to June 13, 1959, Minister of Defense P'eng Teh-huai visited Eastern Europe, and was in Albania at the time of Khrushchev's visit. Marshal P'eng had not been one of the ardent "modernizers" in the mid-1950's, but he was well aware of the crucial importance of modern weapons. If he again asked for increased Soviet assistance, there is no evidence that he achieved anything. (In June, W. Averell Harriman was told by Khrushchev that the Soviet Union had sent missiles—he did not say with nuclear warheads—to protect Communist China against Taiwan, but this may have been an overstatement.)[44]

Suddenly, on September 17, 1959, the dismissal of Marshal P'eng Teh-huai and four vice-ministers was announced. P'eng was charged with heading an "anti-Party group." And, indeed, he *had* directly challenged Mao at the Lushan Central Committee plenum in August, 1959.[45] Moreover, P'eng had apparently written a letter to the Soviet Communist Party attacking Chinese Communist policies. (In an unpublished speech at Bucharest in June, 1960, Khrushchev criticized the Chinese Communist removal of P'eng for having communicated his views to the CPSU.)[46] P'eng may have been disturbed that the growing breach with the U.S.S.R. jeopardized Soviet arms aid. Meanwhile, another sign of the growing estrangement between the two Communist powers was the rehabilitation in April, 1959, of former General Lung Yun who, in 1957, had openly criticized Soviet military assistance.[47]

Details are not known of the Russians' alleged repudiation of the 1957 agreement on June 20, 1959, and of their refusal to supply data on nuclear weapons technology. Perhaps Chinese Defense Minister P'eng Teh-huai had requested such aid during his visit to Moscow, and a Soviet reply on June 20 canceled the 1957 arrangements. If so, the Russians may have contributed to P'eng's downfall on his return to China. Be that as it may, such a Soviet move in June, 1959, fits both the trend of the deteriorating relationship between the two countries and the pattern of *détente* being built between the U.S.S.R. and the United States at that time.

The deterioration of Sino-Soviet relations over the next year was rapid, and finally erupted in April, 1960, with the publication by the Chinese of an ideological attack on the Russians. In July and August, 1960, the Russians withdrew their 1,300 economic and military advisers and technicians. This action was drastic, sudden, and virtually complete.

The Relationship Ruptured: 1960 to the Present

Since the sudden virtual cessation of Soviet military and economic assistance, there has been almost no Sino-Soviet military relationship. The effects, even in the short run, have been significant for the Chinese. Continued, though declining, Soviet export of petroleum products to China has been the chief form of indirect aid. On the other hand, clashes on the Sinkiang border have been reported.

Since 1960, the Chinese Communist armed forces have *decreased* in net capability. In the few years immediately ahead, the Chinese will undoubtedly develop their own capacity to build some jet fighters, defensive surface-to-air missiles, radar, small warships, and short-range rockets. It is also expected that they will develop their nuclear devices into deliverable bombs and warheads, and will probably develop medium-range missiles. But all these developments are being hindered by the sharp slow-down of Soviet military and economic assistance of mid-1960, its complete cessation by 1963, and declining over-all trade since that time. For several years, the Chinese had to postpone their production of jet fighters and submarines; also postponed were whatever plans they may have had for producing jet medium bombers. The numbers, and still more the proficiency, of the air forces have declined from attrition of matériel and from shortage of fuel for proficiency training. The ground forces have been much less affected, but they, too, are short of modern heavy ordnance.

At present, the Chinese Communist Army numbers about 2.5 million men, with about 110 infantry, two to four armored, and one or two airborne, divisions.[48] The Air Forces total about 2,500 aircraft of all types, including about 2,000 combat aircraft, mainly jet fighters (nearly all older model MiG-15's and MiG-17's, with some MiG-19's and a few MiG-21's), and 200 to 300 Il-28 jet light bombers. Apart from a few Tu-4 piston medium bombers, not new when given to the Chinese in the mid-1950's, and one Tu-16 medium jet bomber, the Chinese have no long-range air forces.[49] The Navy has four destroyers, four destroyer escorts, about thirty conventional attack submarines, and a modest number of patrol craft. Probably not even all of these units are operational. In 1965, the Chinese were probably beginning to produce their own modern aircraft and submarines, and reportedly they had one missile-launching submarine.[50]

The end of Soviet aid—apart from its material effects on the Chinese—placed the military alliance commitment in question. Soviet spokesman Titarenko, in a celebrated article in August, 1960, mentioned China directly regarding the economic and military vulnerability of a socialist state which had strayed outside the socialist camp, was "isolated," and no longer engaged in "mutual cooperation." By the same token, he implied that Soviet support to China in case of war was conditional.[51] Marshal Malinovsky, in January, 1962, noted that Soviet strength would defend only "those socialist states *friendly* to us"—a very blunt warning indeed.[52] *Pravda*, in January, 1963, bitterly remarked that those who criticized the U.S.S.R. for the Cuban venture couldn't hold off the imperialists without the U.S.S.R.[53]

The Soviet Government statement of September 21, 1963, carried further the earlier indications of a more careful and controlled Soviet interpretation of alliance commitments to China. On the one hand, the statement nullified any Chinese Communist requirement for nuclear weapons of its own by pledging the protection of the Soviet nuclear deterrent to the whole socialist camp; but on the other hand, it criticized Chinese Communist pursuit of "special aims and interests" which go *beyond* the legitimate interests of the socialist camp and "which *cannot* be supported by the military power of the socialist camp."[54] Thus it made clear that Soviet alliance commitments do *not* extend to such situations and that Moscow will make the ultimate decision on what it regards as the legitimate interests of China (or Cuba, or any other socialist state), and therefore on its own course of action if China becomes embroiled with the United States.

The Chinese, in turn, have had to recognize (as Li Fu-Ch'un put it—coincidentally on the same day Titarenko's article was published in August, 1960) that China must "mainly rely on our own efforts" in the future.[55] And again, when Malinovsky was threatening the Chinese in 1962, Marshal Chen Yi was saying that all the Chinese problems including "*national* defense" could be solved by self-reliance.[56]

Unfettered by considerations of the Chinese reaction, the Russians opened new military assistance programs with more modern armament to Indonesia and the Middle East. Thanks to the U.S.S.R., Indonesia had a cruiser, Tu-16 jet medium bombers, and air-defense and short-range missiles by 1965, while the Chinese did not. Tu-16's were provided to several other neutrals. In a move particularly galling to the Chinese, the Russians promised to provide India with a factory to produce MiG-21's. The Russians have apparently tried, with some success, to bribe the North Koreans to their side in the dispute within the Communist Bloc with modern military aid. (Both the U.S.S.R. and China signed separate military defense pacts with

North Korea in July, 1961.) Some Chinese military men may hanker for military cooperation with the U.S.S.R., but they probably exert no influence on the political controversy.

The Future

One or two paramount features of the decline in Sino-Soviet military relations may help in understanding, if not in predicting, future developments.

As the Soviet Union became increasingly concerned with avoiding risks of a nuclear war, and saw advantage in cultivating a *détente* with the United States, the Chinese Communists became increasingly assertive in urging more active confrontation of the imperialists.

The Russians have not wished to lessen fundamental Chinese dependence on the U.S.S.R., to give the Chinese Communists a fulcrum for bargaining power vis-à-vis the Russians, to raise Chinese prestige in the Communist movement or the world at large, or to increase the risks they themselves would run if the Chinese had capabilities which might tempt them to risk a conflict with the West. The Russians recognize the dilemma they would then face of supporting China at unacceptable costs to the Soviet Union, or of seeing Communist China destroyed at irreparable cost to Communism. Intensifying these concerns is the Chinese Communist pressure for stronger support of revolutionary activity by Communists elsewhere, as well as for more vigorous support of immediate Chinese aims. The Soviets define their policy in terms of their own interests.

Consequently, it is not surprising that in pursuing *their* objectives the Chinese have been dissatisfied with Soviet policy. The Russians may want a nuclear-free zone in the Far East to disarm both the United States and Communist China; the Chinese are unwilling to give up their aspirations to nuclear-great power status, even if their "security" were otherwise ensured. The Soviet efforts in the mid-1950's to give up the most imperialistic of Stalin's extortions vis-à-vis China, such as the Port Arthur base, were not sufficient; neither was the grudging support given from 1957 to mid-1960 to the production of aircraft and the development of missiles.

Lobbying *within* the opposing countries is another point of interest in respect to the present and future. Chinese leaders, by indirection discussing Soviet internal affairs, made a fairly open bid to the Soviet *military* to oppose Khrushchev. In his interview with foreign reporters on October 28, 1963, Foreign Minister Chen Yi stated: "the CPSU, the Soviet people, *and the Red Army* will not readily give up their friendship toward China," despite the Khrushchev policies.[57] With equal pointedness, the Chinese, on November 19, 1963, declared that while the Red Army remains "a great force safe-guarding world peace . . . Khrushchev's whole set of military theories runs completely counter to Marxist-Leninist teachings on war and the army. To follow his wrong theories will necessarily involve dis-integrating the Army."[58] The situation has not basically changed in the post-Khrushchev period.

The broader political causes of the Sino-Soviet dispute, and the widening split since 1959, have intensified further military disassocia-tion from the never-intimate relationship of the 1950's. These devel-opments burden and delay, but do not completely foreclose, Chinese military modernization.

If the conflict continues to deepen, and either side feels vitally threatened by the other, even the possibility of Sino-Soviet military hostilities cannot be entirely excluded from the consideration of both parties. From secret Chinese Communist People's Liberation Army papers released by the U.S. Department of State, we now know of a Military Affairs Committee directive of early 1961 on the need to preserve security of the Southwest and *Northwest* (i.e., Sino-Soviet) frontiers of China.[59] There have been reports since 1963 of tightening the Soviet frontier defenses and Border Guard units along the Sino-Soviet frontiers. Soviet military exercises in the Far East have involved mock repulse of a Chinese attack into the Maritime Province.[60]

Complete reconciliation, with broad and deep alliance ties in all aspects of military preparation and planning—which would go far beyond anything achieved in the 1950's—seems at least as remote and unlikely as open conflict. The outlook is for a continuation of rela-tive mutual military isolation and conditional alliance commitments. The course of Sino-Soviet military relations will depend upon the political relations of the two powers.

IV

War and the Communist Revolution

10. War, Peace, and Revolution in Soviet Policy

World Communism is the ultimate goal of the Soviet leaders, in the sense of their aspiration. This aim is based on expectations derived from the Marxist-Leninist view of history; it also nourishes a striving for power. Nonetheless, while seeking to expand their influence and power into the non-Communist world, the Soviet leaders give primary attention to maintaining the security of the Soviet state. They also maintain goals of internal national development and progress not exclusively directed toward amassing power in the world. The Soviet leaders attempt to advance the power of the U.S.S.R. in whatever ways are most expedient, so long as Soviet survival is not endangered.

The Soviet leaders recognize full well that over the span of the forseeable future general war would certainly not be in their interest. "Peaceful coexistence" means that the Russians will continue to pursue a vigorous policy of expansion of influence and power by means short of major war.

While ideological considerations importantly affect the outlook of Soviet leaders, there is no divergence or discrepancy on the basic issue of war or peace.* Both Communist ideology and power-political considerations place the criterion of calculated risk, cost, and gain at the foundation of any strategic initiative. Communist doctrine *does* inject unusually strong hostility and suspicion into Soviet policy-making, but Marxism-Leninism does *not* propel the Soviet Union blindly toward war or the witting assumption of great risks. Why should the Soviet leaders, confident that they are moving with the sweep of history, court disaster by a premature gamble?

Mutual deterrence has already resulted from the acquisition of global thermonuclear striking power by the United States and now by the Soviet Union. Mutual deterrence has been described as a "delicate balance of terror." But while this balance should not be

---

* For more detailed consideration, see the discussion in Chapter 4.

taken for granted, it is not fragile. The Soviet leaders recognize the risks and consequences of a global thermonuclear holocaust, and they strive to avoid any "adventurist" gamble. The importance of the over-all balance of power—the "relation of forces in the world arena," as they call it—militates against Soviet preoccupation with purely military solutions. The Soviet leaders are not poised to unleash the terrible might of their—and our—military power even on the basis of a theoretical probability of military victory. In the Communist view, history cannot be made hostage to the mathematical computations of some "Communivac."

Nuclear war, then, is a highly unlikely tool for the Soviet Union to use in trying to advance its position. Of course, an irrational decision is always conceivable. But more dangerous, because more probable, is the possibility of a war by miscalculation. There are a number of ways in which an unintended general nuclear war could occur. A very important one, often noted, is the possibility that local hostilities might be expanded in a vortex of actions and reactions into a general nuclear war. No less dangerous would be the miscalculation arising from one side's incorrectly believing the enemy to be about to launch a surprise attack, and therefore launching a pre-emptive blow in a desperate last-minute effort to blunt surprise, seize the initiative, and get in the first strike.

Are there circumstances under which the Soviets might *deliberately* choose to initiate general war? Such a decision could be based only on calculations of the assured probability of destroying U.S. retaliatory military power without suffering unacceptable losses—and such a decision is unlikely in the extreme. No theoretical computation can be assured, and the dangers to the Soviet state would be both incalculable and ominous. To be an attractive objective, a first strike must not only assure a high probability of success, it must also virtually eliminate the possibility of disaster. The Soviet leaders expect the eventual victory of Communism in the world without this cost and risk. Finally, self-preservation is accorded an even higher priority in Soviet policy than expansion of Communist control.

What, then, about the victory of Communism?

Soviet expectations of the ultimate victory of Communism throughout the world are deeply rooted in Marxist belief in a dialectic of history, in which progressive socio-economic forces will sweep away the old political, economic, and social order by Revolution. War between states, or even between systems of states, was never the instrument relied on, though Stalinist pragmatism realistically trusted only the elements of Soviet state control and power—including military power. Communism was imposed on Eastern Europe only in the wake of Soviet military victory, and under the shadow of Soviet military power. But the implications of nuclear war have led Stalin's successors (Malenkov prematurely, in open discourse) to recognize something they all have shared: awareness that general nuclear war in the age of multimegaton warheads and intercontinental ballistic missiles is simply not a feasible, rational instrument for extending state or class authority.

The Chinese Communists either fail to realize this or, more likely, pretend not to; they press the Soviet Union to assume policies that might risk such war, and then castigate them for failure to do so. Of course, the Soviet leaders recognize and practice various techniques of the political use of nuclear military strength, ranging from passive deterrence to active counterdeterrence and ballistic blackmail.* But they do not see nuclear war as the means to achieve world victory of Communism.

In this extremely significant respect, Khrushchev—and his successors—returned to early Leninism, relying on the forces of internal revolution rather than on the military power of the U.S.S.R., as the means to the eventual victory of Communism in the world. In the nuclear age, as war has become utterly inexpedient as an instrument of extending either Russian control or Communist rule, it has been relegated to the ultimate defensive recourse of the Soviet state. And Soviet expectations, in turn, become identified with indigenous revolution or even peaceful transition to Communist rule, with peoples influenced by the powerful example of successful, productive Soviet society.

In the Stalinist postwar era, attention was frequently drawn to the fact that the socialist revolution in Russia had been born in the ashes of World War I and the extension of socialist rule into Eastern Europe and East Asia had issued from World War II. Soviet spokesmen predicted that as a consequence of a third world war, the entire globe would become socialist. By 1956, the Soviet leaders at the Twentieth Congress of the CPSU specifically rejected the inevitability of war, and by 1960 they also rejected the implication that a third world war would be desirable because it would lead to the end of capitalism.

Thus the old definition of the relationship between war and revo-

* See Chapter 6.

lution has been significantly revised to accord with the power realities of the age. An authoritative statement in *Kommunist*, the theoretical organ of the Communist Party, expresses this new doctrinal position:

> After World War I, our country fell away from the imperialist system, and so did China and other people's democracies after World War II. But do these facts indicate some internal law in the maturing of socialist revolutions? No. Marxist-Leninist theory has never held that war constitutes a source or prerequisite necessary for the emergence of revolutions. . . . But the question of the relation of war and the revolution has assumed a different character in our times. . . . The creation of modern weapons of mass destruction, of atomic and hydrogen weapons and the means of their delivery to any point on the globe, has fundamentally altered the nature of war, making it many times more destructive. . . . [A world war] would cause the complete destruction of the main centers of civilization and the annihilation of whole peoples. It would bring untold suffering to all mankind. Only madmen could want such a catastrophe to happen. . . . The working class does not think of creating a Communist civilization on the ruins of the centers of world culture, on desolated territories contaminated by thermonuclear fallout, which would be the inevitable consequences of such a war. . . . It is therefore obvious that a contemporary nuclear war, however one looks at it, can in no way be a factor that would accelerate the revolution and bring nearer the victory of socialism. On the contrary, such a war would throw mankind, the revolutionary workers' movement throughout the world, and the construction of socialism and Communism back for many decades.[1]

The question of war has been posed sharply in the polemics between the Soviet and Chinese Communist parties. While the Russians intentionally exaggerate Chinese readiness to contemplate with equanimity the prospect of a global nuclear holocaust, they make very clear their own rejection of war in the nuclear age as a means of advancing Communism—or for any other aim. Probably the most authoritative Soviet statement is that made by Party Secretary and Presidium member Mikhail Suslov in his report to the CPSU Central Committee Plenum on February 14, 1964 (not made public until April 3 of that year). This report continues to be circulated in the post-Khrushchev period as a fundamental statement of the Soviet position. It is therefore instructive to read the key passage:

> The task of averting war has become especially urgent because the most destructive weapons in the history of mankind have been created, and stocks of them have been accumulated which could bring incalculable disaster upon all peoples.

All this the Chinese leaders do not want to take into account. Displaying their recklessness with bravado, they give assurances that the nuclear bomb is a paper tiger and that it makes no new contribution to the problem of war and peace. In conformity with such logic, which is contrary to elementary common sense, at the Moscow Conference of 1957, Mao Tse-tung tried to prove that the cause of the struggle for socialism would even gain as a result of a thermonuclear world war. "Could one estimate the number of human victims to result from a future war?" he asked. "Perhaps there would be one-third of the 2.7 billion people of the whole world, only 900 million people. I had an argument with Nehru on the subject; he is more pessimistic in this respect than I am. I told him: 'If half of mankind is destroyed, the other half will remain, while imperialism will be completely destroyed, and only socialism will remain in the whole world. And in half a century, or a whole century, the population will again increase by even more than half.' "

A similar concept is still more clearly put in the collective work *Long Live Leninism!*, approved and popularized by the CCP Central Committee. The victorious people, it says, with utmost speed will establish on the ruins of the defunct imperialism a thousand times more beautiful future. This is an example of ultrarevolutionary phrasemongering, of utter political irresponsibility, which is especially dangerous because it is shown by people at the helm of a large socialist state.

It is known that as early as 1918 Vladimir Ilich Lenin pointed out that world war, in which mighty gains in technology are applied with such energy to the mass destruction of millions of human lives, is not only one of the greatest crimes but can also lead to undermining the very conditions of human existence. In our time, with the creation and development of rocket-nuclear weapons, this danger has grown even more. How can people, and especially supporters of Communist teaching, ignore this fact? World war is not needed by the countries of socialism; it is not needed by the working people; it cannot serve the cause of the triumph of socialism. . . .

One can say frankly that if a world thermonuclear conflict arose, it would be a most terrible tragedy for mankind and would, of course, be a heavy loss to the cause of Communism.

Not a single party to which the interests of the people are really dear can fail to recognize its responsibility in the struggle to prevent a new world war. But the Chinese leaders, as we have seen, even boast about being prepared, as if for the sake of revolution, to agree to the annihilation of half of mankind. They are not in the least disturbed by the fact that the losses in countries with a great population density which are in the center of military action would be so great that for entire nations the questions of the victory of socialism would no longer arise at all since they would disappear from the face of the earth.[2]

The Chinese have not actually favored a general nuclear war. And in their own policies they have cautiously avoided a direct confrontation with the United States. Nonetheless, their theoretical strategic position is decidedly in favor of strong support by the socialist states for active Communist subversion, guerrilla warfare, and revolutions. Revolution should be waged, even if it threatens to provoke war. Moreover, the Chinese directly oppose the Soviet contention that the increased destructiveness of nuclear weapons affects questions of the role of war or peace in respect to the "world revolution." Thus, the Chinese Communists charge:

> In asserting that rocket-nuclear weapons have changed the former notion about war, the CPSU leaders say nothing about the class character of war, completely evade the fundamental question whether war is righteous or not righteous, and hold that "it would suffice to say one thing," that is, "the explosive power of a powerful thermonuclear bomb will exceed the explosive power of all the firearms used in all the past wars including World War I and World War II." They and their followers have repeatedly declared in a mass of articles, speeches, statements, and resolutions that the consequence of nuclear war will be "universal destruction" of mankind and will be "the end of any kind of politics." We need not speak of how absurd the theory of "destruction of mankind" is and how it grossly violates the spirit of the common documents of the international Communist movement. This viewpoint of dwelling and commenting on the character of war from the angle of the scope and destructiveness of war is precisely not a Marxist-Leninist viewpoint but a bourgeois viewpoint. All the imperialists and opportunists substitute the publicizing of the horrors, destructiveness and disasters of war for class analysis, and gloss over the real root and class substance of war.[3]

This judgment, noted in a lengthy article in the Chinese theoretical journal *Red Flag*, also appeared in the official Chinese Government statement of September 1, 1963:

> In short, in the opinion of the Soviet leaders, the emergence of nuclear weapons has changed everything; it has changed both the nature of imperialism and the nature of our epoch. Our epoch is no longer one of revolution as defined in the Moscow statement, but a nuclear epoch, a nuclear century. In the July 14 [1963] Open Letter of the Central Committee of the CPSU, the Soviet leaders said, "The nuclear rocket weapons that were created in the middle of our century changed old notions about wars." In reality, this means that after the emergence of nuclear weapons war is no longer the continuation of politics, there is no longer any difference between unjust and just wars, imperialism is

no longer the source of war, and the people of various countries should no longer wage just wars against imperialist armed aggression and armed suppression by the reactionary regime for such just wars cannot possibly be won but will only bring about the annihilation of mankind. . . .

But there is a limit to everything, and once the limit is exceeded, the thing is reduced to absurdity. It is a pity that in their attitude toward the Soviet Union's possession of nuclear weapons the Soviet leaders have exceeded the limit. The Soviet leaders insist on exaggerating the role of nuclear weapons and trust blindly in them, despise the masses, and have forgotten that the masses are the makers of history, and so they have degenerated into worshippers of nuclear weapons.[4]

In direct rebuttal, the Russians continue not only to emphasize the practical policy implications of the prospects of nuclear devastation. As *Kommunist* stated: "Fundamental changes in the means of waging contemporary war require Communists to have a realistic understanding and analysis, based on scientific data, of the potential consequences of war. This data must not be concealed from the people; they must be told the whole truth."[5]

The basic issue with respect to contemporary Communist attitudes toward war as an instrument of policy has of course focused on total nuclear war. But the question is much broader. The Soviet Government statement of September 20, 1963, states flatly: "We are most resolutely opposed to world war, and *we are opposed to wars between states in general.*"[6]

In a speech in January, 1961, reporting on the Moscow Conference of Eighty-one Communist Parties, Khrushchev listed three categories of wars: "world wars, local wars, and liberation wars and popular uprisings." He reiterated the familiar description of the disastrous and completely unacceptable consequences of a general or world war, and went on to stress the great dangers of direct Communist-Western confrontation in local wars, since they could escalate into a world nuclear war. The third category of wars, as he defined it, was "national liberation wars" of oppressed peoples—inevitable, just, and supported by Communists.*

*Khrushchev's distinction of wars into these three categories by scale was openly criticized because such a distinction blurred over the political "class" nature of wars, and hence the concept of "just wars." (See Colonel I. Sidel'nikov, "V. I. Lenin on the Class Approach to the Definition of the Character of Wars," *Krasnaya zvezda*, September 22, 1965.) However, there has been no challenge to the underlying unspoken reliance on expediency restraining actual Soviet involvement in any kind of war.

The purposes of the Soviet attempt to differentiate national liberation wars from local wars are quite clear—to justify Soviet abstention from direct involvement in local wars, and to inhibit Western involvement in such wars, while preserving an ideologically correct position of "support" for internal revolutionary liberation wars and uprisings.

Throughout this period, Soviet military doctrine has strongly criticized limited and local wars, alleging that the "imperialists" now wish to start such wars for aggressive purposes since general war is no longer attractive. The Russians do accept as a fundamental principle that war, as an instrument of policy, may assume various forms.

Limited conflicts represent the classic form of Communist military action, waged for limited objectives, at limited risk. In recent years, *Military Strategy* and other publications have noted that socialist countries need to study the requirements for such wars. But there are no indications that the Russians are likely to swerve from their general line of political competition and extension of their influence without resort to interstate war. Notably, the Russians have been much more concerned over possible Western initiation of limited wars, and over the dangers of their escalation, than they have been attracted to the notion that they might be able to gain from such wars.

All in all, the Soviet leaders have a clear appreciation of the dangers of nuclear war, and genuinely strive to avoid any—even limited—direct Soviet-Western armed hostilities, because of the risks. The Russians have been very selective in giving overt political commitments or military support to anyone. They do not eschew violence in "internal" revolutions—though there, too, they are selective in providing real assistance.* They are also very cautious about the risks taken in projecting their military power in nonwar situations. The consequences of the main exception—missiles to Cuba—have probably reinforced this caution for the future.

The Chinese Communists strongly criticize the Russians for "betraying the Communist stand of supporting just wars" especially by their concern for the danger of local wars and their efforts to "put out the sparks that may set off the flames of war."[7] And in fact the Soviet Government statement to which the Chinese refer declares: "The CPSU and the other Marxist-Leninist parties deem it necessary to display maximum vigilance toward all local wars and conflicts. . . . It is all the more important that *local wars might be the spark that would ignite the flames of world war*."[8] In rebuttal, the

* See Chapter 11.

Russians exaggerate: "The Chinese leaders make a serious error in contending that under no conditions would local conflicts lead to a universal thermonuclear war."[9] The Chinese do not go so far as to say that escalation is not possible. But the Soviets are nearer the mark in their criticism of the Chinese, and very clear on their own stand, when they continue: "The logic of this reasoning leads to recognition of local wars as an acceptable and expedient political method for the socialist countries as well, in particular for the 'export' of revolution." The Chinese are accused of "directly linking the victory of revolutions with wars."[10] Against this view, the Russians now claim:

> When developing the theory of the socialist revolution, V. I. Lenin never was an advocate of unleashing a war to push or to accelerate the revolutionary process . . . the "theory" that revolution is inevitable only in connection with a war, that is, only with an aggravation of the external contradictions between nations and states, is alien and hostile to Marxism-Leninism.[11]

Revolution and war, war and revolution—their relationship is a key to determining the foreign policy of any socialist state whose leaders seek the victory of Communism in the world.

Since Lenin first faced the issue in early 1918 at Brest-Litovsk, successive Soviet leaders have consistently placed the security of the Soviet state (whether rationalized as "the base of the Revolution" is immaterial) above considerations of aiding "the Revolution" elsewhere. But only since about 1960 have these considerations been fully spelled out, together with theoretical justification. The reason is that apart from Trotsky's efforts in the 1930's, it was not until the Chinese Communists began their open theoretical assaults on the Soviet position in 1960 that authoritative theoretical rationalization and rebuttal became necessary.

The Soviet position has been elaborated to cover a series of inter-related points:

(1) *Peace* is necessary to preserve millions of lives and the achievements of world civilization, and to ensure "the successful building of socialism and Communism."[12]

(2) *Peaceful coexistence* between *states* with different social systems is necessary to preserve peace, but this does not mean cessation of the struggle of ideologies, and does not mean cessation or even inhibition of the national liberation movement and indigenous revolutions.

(3) *Peaceful competition* between the socialist and capitalist systems will be facilitated by absence of war, and the superiorities of the socialist system will be demonstrated, leading other peoples to choose socialism.

(4) *Peaceful transition* from the capitalist to the socialist system is preferable to the use of force, and is made more feasible by global peaceful coexistence and competition. The Russians continue to recognize and support the possibility of violent revolution but they regard it as appropriate only when the *bourgeoisie* and colonialists compel them to resort to force. But they stress both preference and increased prospects for "nonviolent revolution."

The Declaration of the Eighty-one Communist Parties in Moscow in November, 1960, endorsed peaceful coexistence and the struggle for peace, but that document was a compromise of sharply differing Soviet and Chinese views, and the differences have persisted. The Suslov report of February, 1964, placed the Soviet emphasis on the virtues of peace itself, and on peace for the construction of socialism and Communism: "Marxist-Leninist parties regard a consistent struggle for peace not only as a fulfillment of their historic mission to mankind to avert wars of extermination, to avert the extermination of people in a thermonuclear war, but also as one of the most important conditions for the successful building of socialism and Communism. . . ."[13] The Soviet Government statement of September 20, 1963, described peace as "The *prime* condition for consolidating and expanding the positions of socialism in the world arena. Socialism does not need war. Under conditions of peace, the socialist system has the best chance to display its superiority to capitalism, to achieve successes in economic development. . . ."[14] From this, the Russians have moved on to say: "The question of peace has been and remains *the cardinal issue of all contemporary life.*"[15]

The Russians do not interpret this position as a transient one. A recent booklet on *Socialist Foreign Policy* states:

It stands to reason that the fundamental bases, the principles of socialist foreign policy, its *main aim*, its *general line*—the struggle for peace and peaceful coexistence, for the creation of favorable foreign policy conditions for the construction of socialism and Communism—remain and will remain unshakeable, constitute and will constitute the inalterable foundations of the international actions of the Soviet state in all stages and *under all circumstances.*"[16]

In fact, the Russians have moved from stressing that Communism did not *need* war in order to triumph in the world, to asserting that

"in order to guarantee the final preponderance of the forces of socialism over the forces of capitalism, to win victory in peaceful competition, *peace is essential.*"[17] This line of thinking, apart from the
tautology in the last two clauses, is indicative of the Soviet conversion in the nuclear age to "peaceful competition," that is, to avoiding any interstate war that would threaten the Soviet state itself.

The Chinese, and the Albanians, charge that placing peace *above*
revolution is treason to true Marxism-Leninism.[18] The Russians reject
and attempt to rebut this charge, of course, but in doing so they
reaffirm the primacy they accord to peace. Thus they argue:

> Soberly appraising the entire seriousness of the danger of a thermo-
> nuclear war, Marxist-Leninists consider that at the present time *no
> question of social progress can be solved apart from the struggle for
> peace.* Naturally, it does not follow that they have put off their supreme
> goal—the struggle for the triumph of Communism. But they realize
> that preventing a nuclear catastrophe can best facilitate its accomplish-
> ment.[19]

We have referred earlier to the Soviet argument that, in the words
of Suslov's report, "*the socialist countries exert their main influence
on the development of world revolution by their economic successes.*"[20] *Kommunist* even describes the economic success of socialism as "*the main thing that decides the success of the cause of
Communism.*"[21]

Indeed, the Russians increasingly stress persuasion by example of
the success of socialism, which should lead to the peaceful transition
to socialism in other countries, as the method for replacing capitalism
by socialism. They had managed to get their point recognized in the
1960 Declaration of the Eighty-one Communist Parties, but they
spelled it out much more fully and consistently (without the need
for compromise) in the extremely important *Program of the Communist Party of the Soviet Union.* Adopted at the Twenty-first Party
Congress in October, 1961, and replacing the Party Program of 1919,
it endorsed not only peaceful coexistence and peaceful competition
but also peaceful transition to Communism.[22]

The Russians strongly attack the Chinese Communists' concept
that "revolutionary wars" are the necessary path to socialism. Here
is a key passage from the Soviet Government statement of September 20, 1963:

> Revising the teaching of Marxism-Leninism, revising the general line
> of the Communist movement, the Chinese leaders are trying to impose
> on the international working class and the national liberation move-

ment the theory of accelerating revolution by means of "revolutionary wars." They believe that only in this way can the socialist countries promote the cause of revolution in the capitalist countries. Here we are dealing with violation of the Leninist thesis that revolution is the internal affair of the working people of each country and that revolution cannot be imported from abroad. Having adopted a policy of accelerating revolution, the C.P.R. leaders irresponsibly proceed from the assumption that revolutions are possible always, everywhere, and under all conditions. They ignore the real balance of class forces, ignore the matter of the revolutionary situation in each particular country, and disregard the international situation.

Chinese theoreticians deliberately make a hodgepodge of a multitude of different issues: world war, local wars, national liberation and civil wars—popular uprisings, peaceful and nonpeaceful ways of revolution. They need this to distort the position of the C.P.S.U. and other fraternal parties, to present matters in such a way as if the Communist movement, by having adopted a policy of defending peace, is by this very fact opposing revolution. . . .

Not the C.P.S.U., or the Communist movement, but the Chinese leaders, are departing from these theses. They directly link the victory of the revolution with wars. Mao Tse-tung says outright that "the world can be reorganized only with the help of a rifle," that "war can be destroyed only through war." War, to quote Mao Tse-tung, is the bridge over which "mankind will pass to the new historic epoch."[23]

The Russians charge Mao Tse-tung with confusing and merging the concepts of "war" and "revolution" in an un-Marxist way.[24] They note that when applied to the socialist states this amounts to "pushing the Revolution along with the help of wars," and thus leads the Chinese "to maintain that war constitutes an acceptable—and in essence the sole—means of solving the contradiction between capitalism and socialism."[25] Moreover, it results in a "theory of violence" which is adventuristic, militaristic, and chauvinistic.[26] The Russians believe that violence may have a role in *internal* revolution, but they reject "the use of *military* means to force revolutions in other countries, for the 'export of revolution' by means of *military* intervention."[27] They argue: "This conception of 'world revolution' coincides with the views expressed by Trotsky and his supporters. . . ."[28]

Thus the Russians are led to re-emphasize, in the words of their *Party Program*: "The proletarian revolution in every country, being part of the world socialist revolution, is carried out by the working class, by the masses *of the given country*. Revolution cannot be ordered. It cannot be imposed on a people from outside."[29] More explicitly, the Russians say that: "It is not possible to define from outside, from far away, for instance from Moscow, Peking or some other center, when and how the working class of one country or another must accomplish the socialist revolution."[30] They dryly ask the Chinese to name any countries where revolution is already ripe and is being deterred by the local Communist Party.[31]

The Chinese and Albanian Communists have vigorously attacked the whole Soviet position on war, peace, and revolution. The Chinese argue that the Soviet leaders are being taken in by their own propaganda on peaceful coexistence! The Chinese defend Lenin's and Stalin's concept of peaceful coexistence because it *was* limited to a tactical policy of expediency; it did not become the "general line." Thus, the Chinese declare:

Lenin's policy of peaceful coexistence constitutes one aspect of the international policy of the proletariat in power, whereas Khrushchev stretches peaceful coexistence into the general line of foreign policy for the socialist countries and even further into the general line for all Communist parties. . . .

Lenin's policy of peaceful coexistence proceeds from the historical mission of the international proletariat and therefore requires the socialist countries to give firm support to the revolutionary struggles of all the oppressed peoples and nations while pursuing this policy, whereas Khrushchev's peaceful coexistence seeks to replace the proletarian world revolution with pacifism and thus renounces proletarian internationalism. . . .

In contrast with Lenin and Stalin, Khrushchev makes peaceful coexistence the general line of foreign policy for socialist countries, and in so doing excludes from this policy the proletarian internationalist task of helping the revolutionary struggles of the oppressed peoples and nations. So, far from being a "creative development" of the policy of peaceful coexistence, this is a betrayal of proletarian internationalism on the pretext of peaceful coexistence. . . .

We should like to ask the leaders of the C.P.S.U.: Since the policy of peaceful coexistence constitutes only one aspect of the foreign policy of socialist countries, why have you asserted recently that it represents "the strategic line for the whole period of transition from capitalism to socialism on a world scale"? In requiring the Communist parties of all the capitalist countries and of the oppressed nations to make peaceful coexistence their general line, are you not aiming at replacing the revolutionary line of the Communist parties with your policy of "peaceful coexistence" and willfully applying the policy of peaceful coexistence to the relations between oppressed and oppressor classes and between oppressed and oppressor nations? . . .

We should further like to ask the leaders of the C.P.S.U.: Economic successes in socialist countries and the victories they score in economic competition with capitalist countries undoubtedly play an exemplary role and are an inspiration to oppressed peoples and nations. But how can it be said that socialism will triumph on a world-wide scale through peaceful coexistence and peaceful competition instead of through the revolutionary struggles of the peoples?

The leaders of the C.P.S.U. advertise reliance on peaceful coexistence and peaceful competition as being enough to "deliver a crushing blow to the entire system of capitalist relationships" and bring about world-wide peaceful transition to socialism. This is equivalent to saying that the oppressed peoples and nations have no need to wage struggles, make revolution, and overthrow the reactionary rule of imperialism and colonialism and their lackeys, and that they should just wait quietly until the production levels and living standards of the Soviet Union outstrip those of the most developed capitalist countries, when the oppressed and exploited slaves throughout the world are able to enter Communism together with their oppressors and exploiters. Is this not an attempt on the part of the leaders of the C.P.S.U. to substitute what they call peaceful coexistence for the revolutionary struggle of the peoples and to liquidate such struggle?[32]

The Chinese accuse the Soviet leaders of pushing peaceful coexistence to the point of "opposing revolution in the name of safeguarding peace."[33] The Soviet leadership is said to "fear that revolutions by the oppressed classes and nations create trouble for it and implicate it."[34]

The Albanians are even more outspoken in attacking the Soviet leaders. They, too, distinguish between Lenin's and Stalin's attitude toward peaceful coexistence, peaceful transition, and revolution, and that of Khrushchev and his successors. And they accuse the Soviet leaders of "abandoning their support for the revolutionary movement in other countries,"[35] having

embarked on the path to treason, treason to the Revolution, and it tries by its views and actions to divert the peoples from the struggle against capitalism and imperialism, paralyze their revolutionary energies, and sow in them fear and panic of the horrors of thermonuclear war. . . . They have renounced revolution. . . . The revisionists have proclaimed their final aim is to preserve peace at any price. According to them, everything must be sacrificed for the sake of peace, including the Revolution and the struggle against imperialism.[36]

The Albanians accuse the Soviet leaders not only of abandoning the revolution in the name of peace, but of taking away "the revolutionary spirit" of Marxism-Leninism: the Russians have *"repudiated violent revolution as the general rule for proletarian revolution,* and have put forward the peaceful way as a strategic world principle."[37] On the occasion of this long Albanian diatribe (the Ninety-fifth anniversary of Lenin's birth, April 22, 1965), the main Soviet address, by Party Secretary Pëtr Demichev, made little reference to revolution, and dealt mainly with the internal "construction of Communism" in the U.S.S.R. When Demichev did speak of rendering "active support to the international workers' and national liberation movement," he sandwiched it between references to building socialism and Communism, "defending the principles of peaceful coexistence of states with different social systems," and "consistently defending universal peace."[38] The Chinese Communists also commemorated the Ninety-fifth anniversary of Lenin's birth, and with it the fifth anniversary of their article "Long Live Leninism!," which had precipitated the open Sino-Soviet ideological confrontation. They argued: "Like Khrushchev, the new leadership of the C.P.S.U. in the name of 'peaceful coexistence' is plainly substituting class collaboration for class struggle in the international sphere. This 'peaceful coexistence' of theirs can only be capitulationist coexistence."[39] As for the Soviet claim that the socialist states aid the revolution by the power of example of their progress, the Chinese reply: "Whether or not a country which has won victory dares to serve as a base area for the world revolution and to support and aid the people's revolution in other countries is the touchstone of whether it is really for revolution and whether it really opposes imperialism."[40]

The Chinese view of the Soviet position was summed up in mid-1965 in the following indictment:

The question of how to deal with U.S. imperialism is a question of whether the two-thirds of the world's population still living under the imperialist-capitalist system need to make revolution and the remaining one-third already on the path of socialism need to carry their revolution through to the end. The question is one that affects the destiny of the whole of mankind. It is a touchstone for everyone in the world. Everyone must make a choice and thereby show himself as revolutionary, nonrevolutionary, or counterrevolutionary. It is on this momentous question that the Marxist-Leninists and the Khrushchev revisionists are following two diametrically opposed lines.

The Khrushchev revisionists, cowed by the U.S. imperialist war blackmail, have succumbed to U.S. imperialist pressure. Thus they are afflicted with incurable spinelessness. They are scared of revolution, shirk at sacrifice, dare not engage in a retaliatory struggle with U.S. imperialism, and even oppose the revolutionary cause of the people of all countries. They go out of their way to publicize the terrors of war and counterpose world revolution against the cause of safeguarding world peace. They complain that there are certain people who "assert that world revolution is more important than the preservation of peace." In order to beg for peace, they turn traitor to the revolution; instead of preferring death to slavery, they are willing to become slaves just to save their own skins. This is the renegade philosophy of Khrushchev revisionists.[41]

The Chinese and Albanians are wrong when they accuse the Soviet leadership of collaborating with the capitalist powers to smother revolution, but they are right when they say that the Soviet leaders place the security of the U.S.S.R.—and therefore avoidance of nuclear war or actions seriously risking it—ahead of stimulation of, or support for "the world revolution." By stressing the indigenous nature of revolutions, the Russians *have* gone a long way toward burying "the world revolution" in its Leninist conception. But they do not consider this a betrayal of the Revolution. They continue to regard support of revolutions and national liberation movements as right and as incumbent on themselves—so long as such action does not threaten war and, with it, the destruction of the foundations of Communism built over the past half century.

11. Internal Revolutionary Warfare in Communist Strategy

"Class" war—internal, unconventional, irregular—is the hallmark of Marxist-Leninist strategy. Stalin relied on the Red Army and the Soviet intelligence services for forceful intervention in international politics, but post-Stalin strategy reverts more to the old, fundamental Communist reliance on maneuvering and manipulating power on an indigenous political fulcrum.

Internal warfare assumes various forms, depending on the situation, its opportunities, and constraints. Not all activities of Soviet, Chinese, or indigenous Communists are a form of internal war—though the Communist leaders do assign a major role to active civil violence at a certain stage of development of the class conflict. For the advanced Western countries, that stage lies in a vague and distant future.* But in volatile and unstable societies emerging from colonial rule or undergoing modernization without adequate tools for the job, internal war is expected to have a future—if it is not already present. Thus the Communists expect, plan, and wage internal war as the final stage of class struggle leading to the seizure of power. Internal war is above all *revolutionary* war.

Bolshevism originated as a revolutionary movement with international pretensions; it was fundamentally hostile to the existing international order. But after a number of unsuccessful attempts to wage revolutionary war beyond the borders of the old Russian Empire, from 1918 to 1923, the Bolshevik leaders began to recognize the need to be more selective in choosing the time and place to conduct revolutionary war. Also, their energies were increasingly directed to internal matters: Building "socialism in one country" was an extension of the original compromise by which the Soviet Union proposed to coexist with the outside world.

The subordination of all Communist parties to Moscow meant

* See Chapter 12.

that the suitability of local internal wars was determined by the prevailing foreign policy objectives of the Soviet Union. As a consequence, for over two decades, Communist "internal war" boasted few campaigns and no victories. Only in China did an active revolutionary war stay alive, and it did so by liberating itself from Moscow's strategic direction.

Aware that "the Revolution" would not soon be coming to Europe, the Russians looked to the Orient and the Southern Hemisphere during the 1920's. After the Congress of Baku in 1919, Soviet interest and gradual Communist penetration into these areas grew. But neither Soviet nor indigenous Communist contribution to the "national liberation movements" was of great significance in the 1920's, 1930's, and 1940's. Apart from occasional abortive revolts (as in Indonesia in 1927), and propagandizing among displaced intellectuals, little happened. China was the exception.

World War II brought new opportunities for building undergrounds and waging partisan warfare in many countries occupied by an alien invader. Aided by the Allies, local Communists (as well as other resistance elements) established strong forces in several countries. The Russians themselves built up sizable guerrilla forces on their own German-occupied territory. At the close of the war, the Yugoslav and Albanian partisans were able to seize power with little opposition. The Chinese Communists were also immeasurably aided by the course and outcome of the war.

In the early postwar period, the sudden shift in the balance of power in areas on the Soviet periphery led to new opportunities for expanding Communist rule. Where Soviet occupation was prolonged, political and subversive techniques were effectively used to establish Communist puppet regimes. But beyond the shadow of the Soviet Army the story was quite different. A wave of attempts at subversion, rebellion, and revolution erupted in 1948–49. Success in Czechoslovakia by subversive coup was not matched in an attempt in Finland, nor even tried in France and Italy. In China, the Communists—against Stalin's advice—pushed on to take all continental China. But the revolutionary guerrilla campaigns in Greece, Malaya, Burma, South Korea, the Philippines, and Indonesia ended in failure; only in Viet-Nam did such a campaign drag on to an important partial victory in 1954. Causes of failure varied, but one important reason was that the balance of power in the world had become stabilized anew.[1]

The current phase, since about 1960, has seen a new wave of intense Communist guerrilla activity in Laos and especially in South

Viet-Nam, several failures but persistent efforts in the Congo, and a seizure from within its leadership of the successful guerrilla movement in Cuba. Similar efforts to take over other native, non-Communist rebel forces, for example in Angola and Colombia, are under way.

A prerequisite to resorting to revolutionary war, in the Communist view, is the appraisal of the general world situation, as well as of the local situation. And while the strategic balance of terror today increases the dangers of resorting to direct aggression and creating Soviet-Western military confrontations, it reduces the risks involved in indirect, unconventional war.

Communist strategies for waging revolutionary warfare place a high premium on the political aspects of a campaign. Some strategies involve exclusively political action. Others involve infiltration and subversion, in which the political vulnerability of the opponent is of cardinal importance. Subversion (as distinguished from agitation, propaganda, trouble-making, and other overt or underground Communist activities) can be either a substitute for a revolutionary war or a complementary tactic in it. In general, though, it has not proved to be a versatile tool. Subversion is usually directed against existing governments, but it may instead be directed against indigenous revolutionary movements, as in Cuba. Infiltration and subversion, political isolation and manipulation, and economic penetration all should —in the Communist strategy—lay the groundwork for the ultimate seizure of power either by *coup d'état* or by revolutionary war.

The Soviet leaders generally prefer subversion, or other nonviolent means, to guerrilla war, because the seizure of power by indigenous revolutionary forces tends to make local Communist rulers too independent of Moscow's control. The only countries other than Russia where local Communist forces fought and won their own victories are China, Yugoslavia, Albania, North Viet-Nam, and Cuba. *All* today pose serious problems for the Soviet Union.

The Chinese—absorbed by internal problems and struggles with the Russians, smarting at being frustrated over irredentist claims, and "on the make"—do not share the Soviet attitude toward the means of extending Communist power. Maoism as an export item has done well in Indochina; a number of other Communist parties— especially in Asia—are turning to China in the course of the growing division within the Communist movement. The Soviet leaders do not turn their backs on the theory or even the practice of national-liberation revolutionary war, but it seems likely that in the future the Chinese Communists will be the guiding spirit in most Communist revolutionary guerrilla wars.

In Russia, guerrilla warfare was supplementary and distinctly subordinate to the actions of regular armies; it was national rather than class, and defensive rather than offensive in character. Communist revolutionaries today are aware that Soviet experience in 1941–44 (and 1918–20) is not really relevant to the current problems of Communist revolutionary war. As Che Guevara stated, early in his book *La Guerra de Guerrillas*:

> For the proper analysis of guerrilla warfare, it should be noted that there are two different types: first, the guerrillas supplement the effort of a large regular army as in the case of the Ukrainian guerrillas; second, an armed group is fighting against an established government. We are not interested in the first type. We are interested only in the type where an armed group is carrying on a fight against an established colonial (or other) power.[2]

In the 1930's, Mao paid tribute to the Soviet experience and to the theoretical contributions of Lenin and Stalin, but stressed that they could not be transferred to the Chinese scene because, as he put it,

> there are a great number of conditions special to the Chinese revolution and the Chinese Red Army. . . . [The] laws of war and military directives in the Soviet Union embody the special characteristics of the civil war and the Red Army of the Soviet Union; if we copy them and apply them mechanically and allow no change whatsoever, it will also be like whittling down our feet to fit the shoes,* and we shall be defeated.[3]

Mao's leadership of the Chinese Communist Party was won in a bitter contest over the very issue of independence from Moscow. He insisted that the Chinese experience in revolutionary war was unique —having important features and even "laws" of its own.

The Communists correctly foresaw the collapse of colonialism. They incorrectly assumed that the anticolonial revolution could be readily converted into a Communist one. Faced with the emergence of literally dozens of newly independent nations, the Russians concluded that their best opportunities lay in the extension of Soviet influence—through diplomacy, economic assistance, trade, military

---

* Mao's curious figure of speech implies that the Russians couldn't fill the shoes of the Chinese!

assistance, and other means—rather than through Communist leadership or subversion of the national liberation movement.

Wars of national liberation will be waged in very few places. As the area of colonial rule has shrunk, so has the area suitable for wars of national liberation. To be sure, the Russians speak of "neocolonialism," economic dependence on the capitalist West, and in some cases, they see alignment with the West. But it is difficult to claim that the independence of several dozen countries is a complete sham—without antagonizing those countries. The Russians, then, have chosen to accept the new nations as they are, and to seek ways of building their influence with them, rather than to rely upon the Communist movement to push steadily forward against them.

The strident Soviet declarations of support to North Viet-Nam and the Viet-Công, and verbal attacks on the United States role in the Vietnamese conflict, may appear to belie this reasoned and restrained Soviet attitude toward revolutionary and guerrilla war. In fact, there is no inconsistency. The Russians are in a difficult situation. They refrain from direct involvement of any kind that might precipitate war with the United States—even when the United States is bombing a socialist state. But at the same time, indeed especially because their tangible support is so cautious and limited, they feel compelled to voice strong protestations of support for the Vietnamese Communists. Could they do less? Moreover, they are sensitive to their vulnerability within the Communist world to Chinese assaults of their stand, and attempt to blunt these assaults by their strong propaganda position on Viet-Nam.

In ideological terms, the Soviets—unlike their Chinese colleagues—postpone to a later stage their expectations for a second revolutionary wave leading to Communist rule. They have concluded that the hallmark of the present area is a defeat for colonialism, without yet being a victory for socialism.

The Russians, as well as the Chinese, favor internal "wars of national liberation," so long as they are against the West. The difference between them is that the Russians are more cautious than the Chinese in evaluating the risks the Communist powers would incur by overtly supporting revolutionary wars. Khrushchev stated the Soviet position at the Twenty-second Congress of the CPSU by declaring: "Communists are against the export of revolution . . . but we do not recognize anyone's right to export counterrevolution." From Communist practice and from recent Soviet statements, it seems clear that the Russians see the arena of open military conflict as one involving primarily non-Bloc forces, with the Communist powers supporting Communist and other anti-Western factions indirectly by military aid and by exerting pressure to prevent or weaken Western support to pro-Western or neutral opposition. But, unlike the professed views of the Chinese Communists, they do not see this struggle as the main arena.

In what remains the most explicit and authoritative Soviet pronouncement on revolutionary war, Khrushchev declared, in 1961:

> Liberation wars will continue to exist as long as imperialism exists, as long as colonialism exists. These are revolutionary wars. Such wars are not only admissible, but inevitable, since the colonialists do not grant independence voluntarily. Therefore, the peoples can attain their freedom and independence only by struggle, including armed struggle.[4]

But it is clear from Soviet discourse and action that while the Russians favor such wars in principle and do sometimes support them, Soviet support is neither unqualified nor universal. In practice, the Russians are highly selective in granting support, and are cool to stirring up situations in which the West may intervene, risking the prestige or the security of the U.S.S.R. itself. Support for national liberation wars is geared to instances of congruence with both the local objectives and the broad lines of Soviet foreign policy.

It may be useful to consider more fully the role of the "national liberation movement" in Soviet strategy as spelled out during 1963 and 1964 in the bitter controversy with the Chinese Communists. As noted earlier,* the Chinese strongly attack the Russians for failing to aid "revolution" because of Soviet fear of becoming involved in war. Beginning in the fall of 1963, the Chinese went much further and said that "the leaders of the CPSU have been trying by every means to make the people of Asia, Africa, and Latin America abandon their revolutionary struggle, because they themselves are sorely afraid of the revolutionary storm."[5] It is one thing to say the Soviet leaders fear war and are therefore too cautious; it is another to say they fear revolution itself. Similarly, the Chinese say that:

> In contrast to Lenin and Stalin, Khrushchev makes peaceful coexistence the general line of foreign policy for the socialist countries, and in so doing *excludes* from this policy the proletarian internalist task of helping the revolutionary struggles of the oppressed peoples and nations.

* See Chapter 10.

So far from being a "creative development" of the policy of peaceful coexistence, this is a *betrayal* of proletarian internationalism on the pretext of peaceful coexistence [italics added].[6]

Finally, the Chinese conclude that "The modern revisionists [subsequently specifically equated with the present leaders of the CPSU] in fact side with the imperialists and colonialists and *repudiate and oppose* the national liberation movement *in every possible way.*"[7]

The Russians hotly deny that they oppose the national liberation movement or side with the imperialists. Two weeks after the second of the Chinese blasts cited above (and while Chou En-lai was touring Africa), Khrushchev, replying to questions by certain Algerian, Ghanaian, and Burmese newspapers, again pledged Soviet support for the national liberation movement and even claimed that the "decisive" contribution in the struggles for national liberation had come from "the forces of world socialism." "Every nation," he said, "which has fought against the colonialists has felt the firm support of the Soviet Union and other socialist states. Today we again declare for all to hear that the peoples struggling for their liberation can definitely count *on the same support* in the future."[8] The key question is what *kind* of support the Soviet Union has given and will give, but the Russians have always been chary of defining the "support" they would render. In one of the most specific and far-reaching statements, they declared: "The CPSU and the Soviet people consider it their international duty to give all-round political and economic support, *and if necessary, the help of arms too,* to the national liberation struggle of the people. Everyone knows the role played by this support in the struggles of the peoples of the U.A.R., Indonesia, Yemen, and other countries against the colonialists."[9] On the face of it, this statement appears to offer Soviet *military* support; in fact, it does not. In the first place, the Party and the people—not the Soviet state—are duty-bound to give support. In the second place, only political and economic aid is "all-round"; and last, the "help of arms" refers to providing military equipment, rather than to Soviet military intervention.* The very examples cited bear out these sharp

---

* Subsequently Khrushchev declared to a World Youth Forum in Moscow: "The Soviet Union has stated more than once that if the countries struggling against the colonialists need weapons, and *if* [sic] these weapons can be delivered by the Soviet Union, we *can* [not "shall"] provide them." In the same statement, he clearly indicated that Soviet military involvement would be undertaken only "if the aggressors unleash war." (Khrushchev, Speech of September 19, 1964, TASS broadcast, *Radio Moscow,* September 21, 1964.)

limits on actual Soviet assistance.* It is particularly significant that Khrushchev promised only *"the same support* in the future."

The Russians place heavy emphasis on their claim that "the achievements of socialist countries in the economic competition with capitalism increase the attractiveness of the idea of socialism, enhance the influence of socialist countries in the international arena, and create conditions for increasing assistance to the national liberation movement by socialist countries."[10] The Chinese are said to "ignore" this point; in fact, they challenge its relevance and effectiveness.

Peaceful coexistence, the Russians feel, is not only compatible with the national liberation struggle; it assists it in various indirect ways. Moreover, "national liberation and social revolutions are caused by internal factors, such as exploitation. . . . They cannot serve as an obstacle to peaceful coexistence between states with different systems."[11]

The two "offensive" positions the Russians take against the Chinese stand are: first, that the Chinese advocate a blind resort to violence whether or not it is appropriate to the circumstances, and whether or not the time is ripe for revolution; and, second, that the Chinese Communist leaders are interested not in the success of the national liberation movement but in gaining Chinese hegemony over it.

Suslov, in his report to the Central Committee Plenum of February 14, 1964, stressed both these points. With respect to the former, he said:

> The Chinese leaders side-step the essential issue of the present stage of the national liberation revolution, failing to see the differences in the situation in individual countries, and give the peoples of all countries the same prescription—an armed struggle and establishment of the dictatorship of the proletariat. In actual fact, such aims can lead to undermining the national front and strengthening the positions of the colonialists and neocolonialists.[12]

The charge that the Chinese Communist leaders are, as Suslov put it, trying "to isolate the national liberation movement from the international working class"[13] is more complicated. This charge was

___

* A post-Khrushchev discussion extended the list to include Iraq in 1958 and Cuba "in 1961 and 1962" as well as Egypt in 1956 and Yemen in 1962—scarcely a convincing record! (Sergeyev, "The U.S.S.R.—Faithful Friend of Those Engaged in the National Liberation Struggle," *Radio Moscow*, March 1, 1965; and V. V. Rimaliv, "The Economic and Political Cooperation of the Socialist States with the Liberated Countries," *Radio Moscow*, April 1, 1965.)

first leveled in the CPSU Open Letter of July 14, 1963. According to the Russians,

> The Chinese leaders are trying to prove something that cannot be proved, that the leading part in the world revolutionary process is played not by the international revolutionary workers movement, which in our day embraces both the working class in the capitalist countries following the communist parties *and the world socialist system,* but by the national liberation movement.[14]

Suslov's report criticizes the Chinese for having said that "the national liberation movement is now the most important force directly striking at imperialism." "The prime role in the world revolutionary process," corrects Suslov, "belongs to the socialist countries." He goes on to say that in addition to being theoretically in error, the Chinese interpretation "is not in accordance with the actual relation of world forces."[15] The Russians hold that "The national liberation movement is a great force in the world revolutionary process; nevertheless, the areas where it is developing are *not* the main arena of the international class struggle."[16] But what most disturbs and angers the Russians is their concern over Chinese efforts to supplant them as leaders of revolutionary forces in the world. The Chinese position on the main role of the national liberation struggle is, the Soviets insist, "*not* based on concern for the world revolution, or concern for the further upsurge of the national liberation movement. . . . This is nothing but an attempt at acquiring, by means of flattery, a cheap popularity among the Asian, African, and Latin-American peoples, at establishing one's hegemony over them, and exploiting them for one's egotistic great-power purposes."[17] In his report, Suslov argued caustically that the Chinese "slogan about some magic strength of the East Wind is clearly calculated to fan nationalist and even racial feelings among people struggling against colonialism . . . this slogan is nothing more or less than an ideological and political expression of the hegemonic stirrings of the Chinese leaders." Finally, again in Suslov's words, "The scheme of the CCP leadership amounts to an intention to foist their *adventurist* conceptions and methods on to the peoples of Asia, Africa, and Latin America, to set peoples against one another according to racial distinctions, to tear apart the union between the national liberation and workers' [Communist] movements, which in practice would only serve to disorganize and weaken the national liberation movement."[18]

The Chinese are aware that revolution is not feasible everywhere. Nonetheless, they wish to push for a militant, revolutionary posture by the Communist powers, and for stimulation of such a stand by the peoples of Asia, Africa, the Middle East, and Latin America. Moreover, the Chinese leaders tend to view the world through their own experience in protracted guerrilla war.[19] The Chinese view has been spelled out at length in a major statement by the Minister of Defense, Lin Piao, in September, 1965, eulogizing "the people's war." In his article, analogy is made between the Chinese Communist strategy of struggle from the countryside against the bourgeois city strongholds—repeating Mao's unorthodox Marxist stress on the peasantry, rather than the proletariat—and the alleged struggle today between the underdeveloped regions of the world (the world's "countryside") against the advanced capitalist countries (the world's "cities").[20] It is pervaded by emphasis on unremitting struggle by the underdeveloped countries, and by the socialist countries, against "imperialism." This position thus presents a direct challenge to the Soviet general line of peaceful coexistence and competition.

The Russians are attempting to maintain a pose of leadership over the national liberation movement, though they are sharply restricting their actual support and cautiously calculating the expediency of any particular use of violence. At the same time, they must deal with the essentially correct Chinese charges that they place primary emphasis on Soviet rather than internationalist revolutionary interests.

It would be unwise to write off entirely the Soviet interest in and influence on Communist revolutionary war and warfare. The Russians have substantial relevant assets, and they have not forsworn all violence. But they do not have the doctrine, the cadres, or the missionary zeal of the Chinese Communists for revolutionary guerrilla warfare.

Mao Tse-tung is the leading Communist theoretician of guerrilla warfare; the other two most influential writers are General Vo Nguyên Giap of North Viet-Nam and Che Guevara of Cuba. Without summarizing the development of Mao's doctrine on guerrilla warfare, or reviewing in detail the Chinese Communist and Vietnamese experience, we can draw on these sources for our review of Communist doctrine for waging guerrilla warfare.

Almost all Mao's writings on military matters date from 1936–38. But in 1929, in one of his earliest pieces, he succinctly stated the political purpose of irregular, internal war: "When the Red Army fights, it fights not merely for the sake of fighting, but to agitate the masses, to organize them, to arm them, and to help them establish revolutionary political power; apart from such objectives, fighting

loses its meaning and the Red Army the reason for its existence."[21]
One of the best known of Mao's dicta is the statement, "Every Communist must grasp the truth: 'Political power grows out of the barrel of a gun.' "[22] Mao's thought was that in a revolutionary class war it was necessary to implant and cultivate awareness in the masses of the people that they could, with gun in hand, seize power. Naturally, the Communist Party would lead them in this effort and harvest the result. But the idea was not simply that with military might one could take power; it was that the very process of revolutionary mass warfare could give invaluable political impetus to the military effort. The Communists see revolutionary war not only as a means, expedient under some conditions, to *seize* power, but also as a means to *build* political support that will *sustain* power.

General Giap, in *People's War, People's Army*, stresses that guerrilla war is waged for people, not for territory.[23] Space is often traded for time, and time is used for political advance. Most important is popular support, or at least popular nonsupport of the incumbent authority. Mao considered this cardinal. As he put it, "Without a political goal, guerrilla warfare must fail, as it must if its political objectives do not coincide with the aspirations of the people."[24] This is probably true, but with the important qualifications that the political objectives must *appear* to coincide with the aspirations of the people—even if they do not—and that the people compare the revolutionaries with the incumbent regime on the basis of both their own experience and the net image that propaganda and information from all sides convey. Finally, apart from "aspirations," the popular reaction is strongly influenced by expectations of who is winning.

Mao, Giap, and Guevara all stress the importance of exemplary conduct in relations with the population. Mao, especially, warned against excessive or indiscriminate repressive measures. In the mid-1950's, Giap repeated this Maoist doctrine, but also gave attention to a minor-key Maoist theme recommending selective terror against local representatives of the incumbent regime in order to destroy its control. More recently, in South Viet-Nam, the Communist-led Viet-Công has made widespread use of this tactic to intimidate those who could organize opposition to their activities, and to paralyze the existing administration of the countryside at its very base.

The Communists have considerable experience and a basically sound theory on the military tactics of revolutionary guerrilla warfare. In 1942, the Russians prepared a manual on partisan operations, and in 1944 added a chapter on the subject to their regular army *Field Regulations*. But these technical guides on combined and supporting operations for regular war are of little relevance to Communist guerrillas in other countries. (Incidentally, Mao's chief military writings, and Guevara's, have only recently appeared in Russian translation.)

Mao proceeds from the premise that "The principle of preserving oneself and annihilating the enemy is the basis of all military principles."[25] Measures to achieve flexibility and adaptability include dispersion and temporary concentration to achieve local superiority for sharp attacks before shifting to another point of pressure. The enemy is thus forced to disperse and is kept off balance. Guerrilla campaigns must be carefully planned and purposeful in terms of a broad strategic design, and yet susceptible to alteration in order to meet changed conditions. Bases should not be established if their defense involves pitched battles and position warfare. Surprise, speed, secrecy, deception, initiative, and reliable intelligence are all at high premium. Guerrillas, said Mao, should be "as cautious as virgins and as quick as rabbits."[26] Mobility, maneuverability, ability to melt into inaccessible terrain or into the peaceful population are requisite in an effective force. Also important, in addition to morale and rapport with the population, are discipline, ingenuity, Spartan living, ability to live off the land, and substantial reliance on captured arms and equipment.

Mao's concept of "protracted war" is now widely known. Basically, his thesis explains the Chinese situation in the 1930's when neither the government forces nor the guerrillas were strong enough to annihilate the other. A protracted period was necessary to shift the balance to the revolutionaries.[27]

Guerrilla or revolutionary warfare, in Communist strategy, is only a stage in the growth of the revolution in a particular country; usually, it must be succeeded by regular civil war. Mao categorically stated that "guerrilla operations must not be considered as an independent form of warfare."[28] "In the course of the prolonged, ruthless war, guerrilla warfare should not remain its old self but must develop into mobile warfare. Thus the strategic role of guerrilla warfare is twofold: supporting regular warfare and transforming itself into regular warfare."[29] Guevara likewise holds that "guerrilla combat is a phase of warfare that cannot of itself attain complete victory; it is important to remember that guerrilla fighting is only a beginning or preparation for conventional warfare."[30]

The future role of revolutionary guerrilla war in Communist strategy probably depends more on local opportunity than on anything else. The Soviet "line" has swerved from "soft" in 1963 to "hard" in 1965, but there is no reason to expect any drastic change in the ambivalent and cautious Soviet approach. In time, Chinese encouragement of such warfare may attentuate in practice, but for a long period, Chinese—and Castroist—support will be forthcoming. As Zanzibar and the Congo bear witness, this aid can sometimes reach to far and unexpected places. The politico-military premises of Communist—chiefly Chinese—thought on revolutionary warfare are basically sound, as is their tactical doctrine for such operations. The most vulnerable point is in the local societies that may be threatened. This point is a confirmation that there are no short cuts for either side—no basic flaws in the Communist approach, but also no secret weapon in their arsenal.

12. The Revolution and the West

A proletarian revolution in the advanced capitalist countries of Western Europe and North America was at the core of Marx's expectations and of subsequent Marxist thinking until after the consolidation of Bolshevik rule in Russia. The decade beginning in 1914, however, marked a major divide in socialist thinking on the world revolution, as orthodox Marxism underwent three severe shocks. First was the discovery that most socialists persisted in retaining their national consciousness and patriotism in a war among "bourgeois" states. Within the socialist movement, disagreements between revisionists and the old school were, for a time, overlaid by a new split into socialist nationalists and radical internationalists. The second shock was the initial success of the socialist revolution in relatively underdeveloped and autocratic Russia—contrary to all prior Marxist expectations, including Lenin's. Moreover, it was revolution by *coup d'état* rather than by a real proletarian uprising, and was achieved only with the help of the peasantry. The third startling development was the failure of the socialist revolution in the advanced countries, above all in Germany. Not only was the revolution not to have originated in Russia, it was not to have been suspended—even temporarily—because of its success in any single country, least of all in Russia.

Adjustments in Marxist thinking were influenced by a posteriori reasoning: Success in practice facilitates rationalizing and reinterpreting theory; also, a "going concern" develops its own needs and aims, which can deeply affect the actions and viewpoints of the practitioners of any ideology. And ideologies, including Marxism-Leninism, become part of the superstructure of deeper underlying politico-economic realities.

In subsequent decades, the U.S.S.R. has developed into the second most powerful country in the world by placing its interests above the interests of the world Communist revolution whenever and however the two objectives conflicted. (Naturally, when they converge, each reinforces the other.) Soviet policy seems to have been based on the premise, "What's good for the Soviet Union is good for the Communist world revolution."

If World War I left both unexpected victory and unexpected defeats for the Marxists, so did World War II. The postwar "victory" of socialism imposed on underdeveloped Eastern Europe was heralded as a sign of the future; in fact, it was a consolation prize for the Communists who failed to extend their foothold in the advanced Western countries. During the wartime heyday of the Soviet-Western alliance, the Communists were able to achieve a much greater degree of popular support in the advanced countries than they had achieved before, or have since. In France, Belgium, and Italy they seized control of much of the popular resistance movement; in Britain, Canada, and the United States, they infiltrated some elements of society and even of government, and in many ways influenced public opinion.

Following World War II, the Communists hoped to gain political dividends by maintaining the wartime antifascist coalition and moving to a dominant position within it. But from the outset, Stalin knew that the strength of the Western powers as a whole, and the relative weaknesses both of the internal Communist stature in the advanced countries and of the U.S.S.R. vis-à-vis the United States, made it unrealistic to expect Communist seizure of power. Consequently, he never seriously attempted to set off revolution in the two countries where Communist strength was substantial—France and Italy.[1] The high tide of Communist power was reached in 1947, but ebbed within a few years. Stalin's crude and obsessive pursuit of narrowly defined security interests of the U.S.S.R. and his suspicious lowering of the Iron Curtain worked against Russian influence in the West. Thus, from 1945 to 1949, the antifascist coalition disintegrated in the climate of Stalin's "Cold War." Revolution was sacrificed to Soviet policies. During the 1950's, the advanced countries of Western Europe, North America, and the Pacific increased markedly in economic, political, and military strength—both individually and in collective alliances.

Four decades have confirmed the lesson of 1917–23: If, as the Communists believe, the whole world is going to become socialist, the advanced capitalist countries would be the last to fall. The current generation of Communist leaders therefore believe that the advanced countries will be economically, politically, and militarily isolated by a gradual sweep of socialism over the rest of the globe. The "rear" of the capitalist countries—the former colonial and economically underdeveloped areas of Asia, Africa, and Latin America—is seen as the next stage for the advance of Communism.

Another legacy of World War II was the victory of Communism

in China. By the early 1960's, the fruits of victory turned bittersweet; Peking is not only an "ally" of Moscow, it is a rival and competitor. Significantly, one symptom—and cause—of conflict between Moscow and Peking is a divergence of policy with respect to the advanced countries. Soviet recognition of the need to wage any conflict through "peaceful coexistence" has clashed with Chinese desires to prod the "paper tiger" of imperialism.

Chinese and Soviet policy differences regarding the advanced countries parallel disagreements about strategy to be pursued in the rest of the world. While the Russians affirm their interest in the "national liberation movement" in colonial and neocolonial areas, and sometimes provide support, this assistance is selective, given when local objectives mesh with broad Soviet foreign-policy aims. The Chinese argue for more militant and energetic support to such campaigns.

Although Communist hopes for the rapid disintegration of colonial rule have been fulfilled, expectations of Communist advance in the wake of chaos during colonial departure have been frustrated. Chaos in the Congo, temporary alienation of Guinea, uneasy repression in Angola, and radical anti-Westernism in countries such as Ghana, Tanzania, and Indonesia have been exceptions to literally dozens of nations with hundreds of millions of people that made the extraordinary transition from colonial status to independence *without* leaving the "free world." Only Cuba, under maverick Castroism, is in the Communist fold. And although this trend must be sorely disappointing to the Communists, they still expect eventually to extend their authority throughout this area—by power of example, diplomatic influence, and revolution waged by guerrilla campaigns or subversion.

The advanced countries of Western Europe (Great Britain, West Germany, France, Italy, Belgium, the Netherlands, Switzerland, and the Scandinavian countries), North America (the United States and Canada), and the Pacific (Japan, Australia, and New Zealand) represent diverse cultural, political, and economic backgrounds. Nonetheless, in the context of the world as a whole, the generally shared cultural traditions and political development (except for Japan), and economic, political, and military alliances (except for a few small European neutrals) stand out as enormously more significant. The advanced industrial countries are, strategically, the "hard core" of the non-Communist world, despite differences among them.

It has long been a premise of Communist thinking that the capitalist countries are inevitably at one another's throats competing for economic raw materials and markets. The development of the Common Market does not conform to this Communist tenet. As recently as 1952, Stalin was ponderously weighing the likelihood of war among capitalist powers; now the Communists must weigh the prospects of the eventual unity of some of the principal capitalist nations. In contrast, the form and degree of conflict between the *Communist* powers is now more serious.

The advanced countries are obviously growing stronger, individually and as a category. There are, of course, variations. Internal political instability may recur in France or Japan, and there is a large Communist Party and voting minority in Italy. But in none of these cases can the Communists foresee any real prospect of gaining power. Even in France and Italy, the voting strength of the Communist parties—which, particularly in those countries, is no index of revolutionary potential—is respectively about 20 and 25 per cent. Moreover, the trend of Party membership, Party unity, and voting strength is running against the Communists almost everywhere. In all the advanced countries together, except Italy, there are fewer than one-half million Communists, and in Italy less than one and a half million. This represents only about 40 per cent of comparable Communist strength in 1946.[2]

Communist political influence can be brought to bear only indirectly and, even then, usually ineffectually, in the advanced countries. In Italy, the "opening to the left" may isolate the Communists completely. Moreover, the Communist movement in Italy has grown "satisfied," and supports the status quo in those local areas where its strength is generally settled. In France, the Communists' only hope is to provoke a polarization of political forces into Left vs. Right in the uncertainty that is bound to follow de Gaulle, and then to press their influence within the Left coalition. In Great Britain, they spur on pacifist movements. But beyond these limited forms of indirect maneuver, the Communists have practically no political leverage. Their general tactic, therefore, is to support the most "left" elements and hope either to infiltrate or otherwise to influence others. In the rare instances when the Communists do acquire some real influence, the usual outcome is that they have killed the infiltrated movement by their very association with it—as was the case with the Progressive Party in the United States in 1948. And, as so often happens when a small group has no external prospects, there is a tendency to splinter in internal debate and conflict. Until fairly recently, such tendencies were usually limited to personal maneuvering within the leadership; but now, the Sino-Soviet split within the bloc of Communist

powers has provided the Communist movement with alternate outside sources of support and allegiance. As a result, some Communist
parties (including a few in advanced countries such as Belgium) have
divided into rival pro-Moscow and pro-Peking factions. There have
also been recurrent "revisionist" deviations, especially in the small
American and British parties.

In the fall of 1962, a world conference of "Marxist scientists" was
held in Moscow to discuss the decline of capitalism. The conference
was sponsored jointly by the Institute for World Economics and International Relations, the U.S.S.R. Academy of Sciences, and the
journal *Problems of Peace and Socialism* (*World Marxist Review*).
It fell to the lot of this conference to analyze the broad trends in
the advanced capitalist countries, and to square the facts with the
Marxist-Leninist line. The conferees could not totally ignore the
relative prosperity, economic advance, and trend to economic cooperation highlighted by such developments as the success of the European Economic Community. Nonetheless, while citing Lenin on the
continuing advance of capitalism for a limited time, they argued that
basic flaws in the system and contradictions among the capitalist
states would eventually lead to the decline and downfall of the capitalist system. The standard themes of growing monopolies, spreading
unemployment, and increased class stratification and conflict were
aired.[3] A similar account of the class struggle appeared in a collective
volume published after the Conference of Eighty-one Communist
Parties held in Moscow in November, 1961. These same hackneyed
themes were featured, and strikes were defined as the chief form of
class conflict in the capitalist countries at this stage. The book also
offered unusual statistics on the class structure of the advanced countries: the *bourgeoisie* was said to comprise 1 to 4 per cent of the
population, the middle class, 45 to 50 per cent, and the proletariat,
45 to 50 per cent.[4] Other discussions in the same volume stressed that
while the class struggle was accelerating, peaceful transition had now
become "the fundamental form" of achieving socialism in the capitalist countries.[5]

Communist ideologists and economists usually find excuses for the
continuing successes of capitalism, and they elaborately select data to
exaggerate its failings. But Communist policy-makers cannot always
accept a grossly distorted image. They may remain confident of their
future expectations, but they must sometimes recognize the present
realities of prosperity, economic advance, and political cooperation
in the West. As they look ahead into the "long range" of practical
policy-planning—over the next decade or more—they see only mar-

ginal possibilities for direct Communist political action in the advanced countries.

One possible exception is France, where the instability of several successive Republics, and a strong Left current in which the Communists have a certain base for maneuver, offers some hope. There are probably residual assets from the 1930's and 1940's in the form of experienced cadres, and perhaps even matériel for violent action. Another possible exception lies in the semideveloped southern fringes of Europe: Spain, Portugal, Southern Italy, and Greece. If these countries are counted as part of the advanced capitalist camp, they are its least economically developed and least politically stable areas. But these are only marginal possible exceptions to the general situation in the major advanced nations.

The failure of the Communist Party of the U.S.A., though not typical of all the advanced countries, is of particular importance because of the leading role the United States plays in the "capitalist" world. After more than two decades of stormy beginnings and a gradual rise during the Great Depression, sometimes tactically facilitated but strategically blunted and foreclosed by the New Deal, the CPUSA reached its peak in mid-1945. It then had about 80,000 members, two Communist city councilmen in New York, and two American Labor Party fellow-travelers from that city in the national House of Representatives. In July of that year, the "soft" line was dropped (and with it Earl Browder, the Party's wartime leader), and a more assertive position adopted, under pressure from Moscow. By 1948, a policy of stimulating the creation of a third party and then bending it to Communist control succeeded. The embrace of the Progressive Party by the Communists was a kiss of death, and in the process the Communists lost what influence they had in the major parties, and also in the CIO and other trade unions. The Party declined constantly—to 54,000 in 1950, to 25,000 in 1953, and since 1958, to well under 10,000 members.[6] (Even of these, according to a report by a former FBI man, one in six is an FBI informant!)[7]

The CPUSA failed with hard tactics and with soft, with penetration and with agitation, in depression and in prosperity. The Cold War confrontation with the U.S.S.R. also contributed to its isolation and decline. But the basic reason for its total failure was its irrelevance to American political life.

In the advanced industrial capitalist countries of the West, the Left is more gauche than sinister.

The vitality of the advanced countries has not only affected the status of the Communist parties in those countries; it has also challenged the Communist ideology itself. Efforts to express or codify development of Western economic ideology have not been effective, but nonetheless the Communists—even in the U.S.S.R.—have been greatly agitated by such ideas as "people's capitalism," and by the effects of social democracy in power in a number of Western countries. And, of course, the very problem of explaining away Western prosperity and economic advance continues to be difficult.

The advanced countries have moved—in terms of Communist expectations—from being first to last in line for the Revolution. Consequently, they are seen not as the target for current attempts to extend Communist influence, but rather as obstacles to Communist efforts to extend influence and control in *other* parts of the world. Thus, for the present, the Communists seek to neutralize, rather than to overthrow, the advanced states. They attempt to prevent the advanced countries from bringing their great power to bear effectively against erosion of traditional Western influence and against extension of Communist power into the underdeveloped, often politically uncommitted, and sometimes unstable areas of the world.

The Communists realize that even though they believe the strength of the major advanced countries to be on the wane, it is necessary to conduct the internal struggle within the advanced countries cautiously and indirectly. Direct action is focused on two other spheres: building the economic and military power of the U.S.S.R. and of the socialist camp under the leadership of Moscow; and extending Marxist-Leninist influence, and the influence of the U.S.S.R., in the most vulnerable areas of the free world. During the decades ahead, while building their own power, the Russians aim at gradual political and economic isolation of the advanced countries; gradual internal undermining of their political, economic, and moral strengths; and infiltration and gradual building up of Communist and "progressive" forces within them.[8] These courses of action involve military and political threats and pressures, but neither war nor direct political violence. Along with military pressure, complementing but far outweighing it in importance, are campaigns for disarmament, accommodation, and relaxation of tensions. Naturally, by manipulating pressures within the advanced countries (while attempting to control reciprocal pressures in the socialist countries), they seek to use indigenous peace movements and other appropriate vehicles to lessen Western efforts and to bring about concessions.

War between the Communist states and the advanced countries is now ruled out as a course that Soviet leaders would choose.[9]

General nuclear war would devastate the Communist societies, as well as other parts of the world. Limited war would carry unnecessarily great risks of escalating into general nuclear war. Local hostilities might occur due to miscalculation as to the Western reaction, but the Communists would seek to prevent or to put down such occurrences. Because the Communists believe that the contingency of a Western surprise attack is not excluded, they recognize the need to be cautious of premature pressure on vital interests of the advanced countries, as well as the need to build strong Soviet strategic nuclear offensive and defensive capabilities to deter such possible Western resort to arms—or, in the extremity, to lessen its terrible blow. In the long run, the Communists believe they would have to consider the possible desperate attempt of the cornered and dying imperialist "beast" to lash out with its formidable strength, bringing enormous destruction, albeit foredoomed to failure.

Bolshevism had always been based on the concept of Communist victory through internal revolution rather than war between nations. *After* the success of the Revolution in Russia, and in the wake of World War II, postwar Stalinist discourse strongly implied that a third world war was a logical, if not *the* logical, path to the extension of socialism throughout the world. However, in the post-Stalin period, spurred by increasing recognition of the consequences of a global nuclear war, this view has been rejected.[10] Similarly, Leninist doctrine has been solemnly revised, and now rejects the inevitability of war.[11]

The Communist powers believe that their expected gains in other areas, the arena of activity at this historical stage, would not only add to their own relative weight but would also subtract from the strength (and confidence) of the capitalist states. The Communists regard the advanced countries as economically dependent on other areas, and think their own expected economic advances will be persuasive. Thus they believe that the socialist world system will extend its influence at the expense of the advanced countries and that the decline of the old system will contribute directly to the growth of the socialist system. At the same time, despite some temporary continuing economic progress by the capitalist states in the next few decades, a superior Communist system is expected to outstrip them gradually and to attract others—including many within the advanced countries themselves—by the power of successful example.

The final victory of Communism in the world is only dimly seen—not seen, really, but assumed. How do the Communist leaders visualize the final push, the final fall of the powerful advanced countries? They do not. They believe in it, but they do not have a clear image of how or when the advanced countries would fall. Guiding ideological works—including the most authoritative recent work of all, the *Program of the CPSU* adopted in 1961—do not have an answer. All of the old Marxist-Leninist doctrine is there, tailored to meet the current Soviet outlook, but with nothing more than articles of faith on the ultimate victory. The most poignant, if not very concrete, expression of this credo appeared in Khrushchev's 1962 Supreme Soviet election speech when, in an aside from his prepared text, he declared:

> This victory will come. It will, it will. No prayers, alms, or bribes will help the capitalists—and they do offer bribes. It is a question of time. We have patience. One must be patient and wait—and not only be patient and wait. Our work, the construction of Communism, is like yeast used to raise leaven. . . . You and I, our Communist Party, the fraternal Communist parties, and our practical construction of Communism are the yeast of the world for, so to speak, insuring the victory of Communism.[12]

The question of the ultimate victory of Communism intrudes into current Soviet thinking most directly in ideological discussions of the achievement of Communism within the U.S.S.R. itself. Now that the Soviet Union is officially "building Communism," the Russians must, at least in their theoretical "building," deal with awkward questions such as the withering-away of the state. Since the existence of the state is required so long as there exist a number of capitalist states, Communism either cannot come about until there is no longer a capitalist system, or Communism must occur before the state withers away.

That the Communist leaders have not thought about the ultimate stage of the world revolution in operative policy terms is certainly not surprising; it is realistic. But it is not often realized, and it is extremely significant. It contrasts with their attention to and disagreements over the forms and extent of aid to "national liberation movements" in the less advanced countries.

Khrushchev predicted that the ultimate stage of the revolution would occur in the days of his grandchildren—roughly within half a century. It is doubtful that any responsible Communist leader would expect the fall of the advanced countries within the next few decades. The Communists do have a strong expectation of the achievement of a Communist world, but they do not have a timetable, a deadline, or prophecies on timing of victory to reinterpret when they go wrong. It is not unlikely that the hazy distant image of ultimate victory will continue to recede time and again, perhaps until it finally is recognized to be a mirage.

The manner and form of the fall of capitalism (in contrast to its alleged decline) is also not predetermined in Communist doctrine. Soviet writings indicate that in the capitalist citadels, peaceful assumption of power is the principal means now envisaged. The *Fundamentals of Marxism-Leninism* (1959) stresses the possibility of, and the preference for, peaceful transition to socialism:

> Thus, peaceful revolution has become feasible not because the nature of the ruling classes has changed or that they now display an inclination to cede power voluntarily, but because in a number of countries it has now become possible to achieve a preponderance over the reactionary classes that will make them conscious of the futility of resisting, leaving them with no choice but that of capitulating to the revolutionary people. And so, in this case too, the outcome of the revolution is decided by the actual relation of forces.[13]

The distinction between this view and that of despised "reformists" or "revisionists," as explained by the *Fundamentals*, is in reformist denial of the class struggle and of even the possibility of nonpeaceful roads to socialism. But the protestation is a weak one (as the Chinese and Albanian Communists charge). Even when arguing for "striking at the heart of capitalism," the Russians lamely fall back on convincing peoples by the power of example. Thus, for instance, the *World Marxist Review* (which provides guidance to Communist parties under Moscow's direction) has stated:

> A realistic view of things—and the Communists have always been noted for their realism—impels the conclusion that the outcome of the struggle between the two social systems in the world today cannot be decided by blows, however painful, at the periphery; by "nibbling," as Alsop puts it, at the edges of the capitalist world. No, the complete and final victory of socialism throughout the world will come only when it strikes a mortal blow at the very heart of capitalism, that is, by demonstrating its superiority as a social system all along the line, and by convincing the people in the capitalist countries of that superiority. This is how the people will be won for socialism. With capitalism gripped by deepening contradictions, this conviction of the superiority of socialism will generate such a mighty upsurge of revolutionary struggle that imperialism will have to give way, and socialism will win the final victory in the struggle between the two systems.[14]

This is the general line, despite reminders of the need for active, rather than merely passive, exploitation of the superiority claimed for Soviet socialism. Thus an editorial in *World Marxist Review* in early 1960 declared: "It would be a mistake to think that in the capitalist countries profound social changes will take place automatically, merely as a result of the strength and prestige of the socialist countries. . . . Only resolute action by the masses will compel the *bourgeoisie* to make social and political concessions."[15] But even such indications of vague "resolute action" refer to actions *within* the advanced countries. Nor is this mere double-talk or deception. The Russians will surely continue to instigate and support subversion and, as appropriate, other forms of revolutionary activity. But there is every reason in logic and in history to believe in Soviet sincerity when the Russians protest their desire "to ensure a situation in which internal processes in particular countries do *not* lead to *military* clashes of the two opposing systems."[16]

The Soviet leaders' attitude toward outside assistance for revolutions is doubtless based mainly on their policy calculations of feasibility. Their frequently repeated statements that one cannot export revolution (or counterrevolution) is probably valid as a general policy statement, even though such statements reflect prudence and propaganda. We are, after all, interested in operative Communist thinking rather than in scholastic ideology. In *Kommunist*, we find the statement: "The socialist revolution is not a ballistic missile, and cannot be sent across the seas."[17]

Perhaps most revealing of the Soviet leaders' attitudes on transition to Communism in the advanced capitalist countries is Khrushchev's statement commenting on the meaning of his earlier declaration "We shall bury you." Khrushchev expressed what were probably real views when he explained:

We are convinced that Communism will win, as it provides better conditions for the development of the productive forces of society, provides the conditions for the fullest and most harmonious development of the society in general and for every individual in particular. Capitalism fights against Communism, but it is impossible to arrest the process of the development of mankind. Sooner or later, Communism will bury capitalism. This is how my statement should be understood. It is not a question of someone burying someone physically, but of a change in the social system in the course of the historic development of society. When we say that Communism will bury capitalism, this does not mean, of course, that the Soviet people, the Communists of the Soviet Union, will inter capitalists of this or that country. No,

Communism is winning in the Soviet Union, and many other countries are now following the road of Communist development. Communism is growing out of the dedicated labor and struggle of the
peoples of the socialist countries for a new, better, the most just, creative life on earth. Such is the teaching of life, of history: a more
progressive social system inevitably comes to replace a system which is
outliving itself, a progressive system buries a moribund one. This is how
we regard the historic process of the development of society. I have
spoken of this more than once. I spoke of this in the United States,
too, when I visited your country. We do not impose our Communist
convictions by force on anybody. We believe that in America, too,
mighty forces will grow—they already exist there and are growing and
developing all the time. These progressive forces which are growing
within the American people itself will ultimately win. In place of
capitalism, which reigns in America today, the American people will
themselves establish a social system, and this system will be Communism. Thus, it can be said that one system, asserting itself, buries
another system, which is outliving itself. It is not that one people
buries a part of another. This would be monstrous; this would mean
war between states. The question of the victory of one social system
over another is one of class struggle. It is a new class which is developing and gaining in strength now—the working class, the people themselves—that will, so to speak, reign in the world, including the United
States.[18]

According to a Soviet broadcast to China in 1962, "Many Communist parties—including those in Italy, France, the United States,
Japan, Britain, Norway, and other countries—consider peaceful transition to socialism their goal."[19] The CPSU Program adopted at
the Twenty-second Party Congress reiterated that the Communist
preference is to achieve power by peaceful means; it even speculated
that in some cases the capitalists would *sell* the means of production
to the proletariat.[20]

Revolution by insurrection, *coup d'état*, guerrilla warfare, and civil
war is the broad alternative path. Soviet, and much more emphat-
ically, Chinese and Albanian, ideological sources endorse this alternative if it proves necessary. Soviet accounts usually refer to this
alternative delicately as "the nonpeaceful transition to socialism,"
and stress that it occurs only when the imperialists most unreason-
ably compel it by waging civil war against the working classes. The
Russians have interpreted the peaceful path and "parliamentary
means of struggle" broadly enough to include the Czech coup[21]—
which, indeed, is probably the nearest thing on record to a peaceful

and "parliamentary" Communist assumption of power, even if it stretches the liberal conception of parliamentary behavior.

Although other ideological and policy differences and the clash of ambitions have been the leading causes of splits within the Communist world, Communist leaders continue to maintain diverging views on the current and future prospects and means of Communist action against the advanced countries.

Reflecting their greater reliance on violent means for achieving Communist goals, the Chinese and Albanians have assumed a greater, and earlier, role for political violence in the advanced countries than have the Russians or Yugoslavs. In assessing the current situation in the advanced countries, the Albanians have alleged that a revolutionary situation was ripe. Mehmet Shehu declared in mid-1962: "In recent years, crippling strikes have been staged in the United States, West Germany, Britain, France, Italy, Spain, Greece, Japan, Argentina, and elsewhere. Today, we observe with satisfaction a democratic, anti-imperialist, and revolutionary movement in the capitalist world headed by the working class."[22] Another Albanian Politburo member, in speaking of the alleged strike movement, mentioned nearly all the same advanced countries (Belgium was included, and Japan and Greece omitted).[23] Enver Hoxha, in a speech emphasizing revolutionary transition, implied inclusion of North America in his prediction when he said: "The American peoples and the Communist and workers' parties of that continent will undoubtedly follow heroic Cuba's example in its efforts to put power into the hands of their peoples."[24] In the same speech, Hoxha downgraded the possibility of peaceful assumption of power in the capitalist states.

The Chinese Communists have likewise implied that revolutionary war will be necessary in the advanced countries. They cite Lenin's remarks that as a general rule the seizure of power by the proletariat "can happen only by means of a violent revolution," and they have extended that idea into the concept of "uninterrupted revolution" in the course of the transformation of a bourgeois democratic revolution into a socialist revolution.[25] The Chinese contend that: "Violent revolution is a universal law of the proletarian revolution."[26] The actual course of history in the advanced countries cannot easily be reconciled with this thesis. Moreover, the Chinese are focusing on the development of a revolutionary movement in the less advanced countries. The celebrated article in *Red Flag* on the 1960 anniversary of Lenin's birthday, which touched off the open polemics between the Chinese and Russians, said: "The shortening of the period between capitalist economic crises is a new phenomenon. It further signifies that the world capitalist system is drawing nearer and nearer to its inevitable doom." And the article went on to state,

> No matter which way one looks at it, none of the new technology such as atomic energy, rocketry, and the like, has changed the basic character either of the epoch of imperialism or of the proletarian revolution as pointed out by Lenin, contrary to the allegations of modern revisionists. The capitalist-imperialist system absolutely will not crumble of itself. It will be pushed over by the proletarian revolution within the imperialist country concerned, and the national revolution in the colonial and semicolonial countries.[27]

It is probably safe to say, however, that the Chinese Communists have not seriously considered the means for effecting socialist revolution in the advanced countries. Despite Soviet claims to the contrary, the Chinese do not dissent from the theoretical principle held by the Soviet Marxist-Leninists that the question of "peaceful" or "nonpeaceful" transition from capitalism to socialism will vary from case to case, depending on particular circumstances.[28]

The Yugoslav view on the transition to Communist rule in the advanced countries has been clearly given in Kardelj's *Socialism and War*:

> It is quite certain that in highly developed countries there is greater feasibility of a more peaceable path than in less developed countries, where internal contradictions are more powerfully brought out. For this reason it is no accident that in many European countries the working class has adopted a mainly social-democratic outlook.[29]

Kardelj cites both Marx and Engels in support of his thesis of peaceful transition to Communism in the advanced capitalist countries (quoting Marx as mentioning the United States, Great Britain, and Holland, and Engels as mentioning the United States, France, and England).

Luigi Longo of the Italian Communist Party (PCI) has given an interesting example of forthright insistence on the "peaceful" path to the very acquisition of power. At the Conference of Eighty-one Communist Parties in Moscow in late 1961, in the course of Sino-Soviet controversy over the general line of the international Communist movement, Longo said:

> It is possible, in a number of countries, to realise the transition from capitalism to socialism by peaceful means, advancing continuously on the road of development of democracy, without a prior revolutionary

rupture and civil war. . . . The Chinese comrades ask us to indicate what country is advancing along this road. *We reply in all tranquility and firmness that the PCI itself has been moving for some time in this direction* [italics added].[30]

And, as the leader of the Finnish Communist Party wrote in *Pravda*:

There is not a single capitalist country where the Communist Party could accomplish a revolution according to the recipe suggested by the Chinese leaders; that is, confining itself to advancing the slogan of an armed uprising. The transition to socialism can be effected only as a result of the creation of preconditions for it during the day-to-day struggle of Marxist parties against the monopolies, and the unity of all working people in this struggle, including those who do not belong to the working class itself. During this mass struggle, the majority of the people begin to understand the superiority of the socialist order over the capitalist.[31]

The Soviet position on the role of war, and on violent and non-violent revolution, was set forth in clear detail in the Open Letter of July 14, 1963, prompted by the debate with the Chinese Communists. The Central Committee of the CPSU stated:

We would like to ask the Chinese comrades, who suggest building a bright future on the ruins of the old world destroyed by a thermonuclear war, if they have consulted the working class of the countries dominated by imperialism? The working class of the capitalist countries would be sure to tell them: Do we ask you to trigger off a war and destroy our countries while annihilating imperialists? Is it not a fact that the monopolists, the imperialists, are only a comparatively small group while the bulk of the population of the capitalist countries consists of the working class, working peasantry, working intelligentsia? The atomic bomb does not distinguish between the imperialists and working people. It hits big areas, and therefore millions of workers would be destroyed for each monopolist. The working class, the working people, will ask such "revolutionaries": What right do you have to settle for us the questions of our existence and our class struggle? We are also in favor of socialism, but we want to gain it through the class struggle and not by unleashing a world war. . . .

And what is the position of the Chinese comrades on this issue? It is the keynote of all their statements and the letter of the CCP Central Committee of June 14. The Chinese comrades regard the main criterion of revolutionary spirit as the recognition of an armed uprising—always, in everything, and everywhere. Thereby the Chinese comrades actually deny the possibility of using peaceful forms of struggle for the victory of the socialist revolution, whereas Marxism-Leninism teaches that the Communists must master all forms of revolutionary class struggle—both violent and nonviolent. . . .

The question arises: What is the explanation for the incorrect propositions of the CCP leadership on the basic problems of our time? Is it the complete divorce of the Chinese comrades from actual reality; their dogmatic, bookish approach to the problems of war, peace, and the revolution; their lack of understanding of the concrete conditions of the modern epoch? Or is it the fact that behind the rumpus about the "world revolution" raised by the Chinese comrades there are other goals which have nothing in common with revolution?

All this shows the erroneousness and disastrous nature of the course which the CCP leadership tries to impose on the world Communist movement. What the Chinese leaders propose under the guise of a "general line" is nothing but an enumeration of the most central tasks of the working class, made without due consideration for time and for the concrete relation of class forces and without due consideration for the peculiarities of the modern stage of history. The Chinese comrades do not notice or do not wish to notice how the tasks of our movement change in conditions of the present epoch. Reducing the general line to general tasks, which are valid for all stages of transition from capitalism to socialism, they deprive it of its concreteness, purposefulness, and genuine effectiveness. . . .

The socialist revolution takes place as a result of the internal development of class struggle in every country, and its forms and means are determined by the concrete conditions of each given nation. The general regularity lies in the revolutionary overthrow of the power of capital and the establishment of a proletarian dictatorship in this or that form. It is the task of the working class and the Communist parties to make maximum use of available opportunities for the peaceful road to a socialist revolution, not connected with a civil war, and to be at the same time ready for the nonpeaceful method, for the armed suppression of the resistance of the *bourgeoisie.*[32]

It is evident that disparate Soviet, Chinese, Albanian, Yugoslav, and other Communist views differ chiefly in spirit rather than in detailed positions. They are corollaries to views on more active policy questions such as selection of the strategy for extending Communism in the underdeveloped areas, and definition of the role of war in the general transition of the non-Communist world to Communist rule. The Soviet contention that war must be avoided is carried to the point of assigning preservation of peace as the *priority* task of the international Communist movement. The Chinese, in contrast, urge that priority be given to the revolutionary struggle. The capitalists, argue the Chinese, will not really intervene and make war; but if they do, war will be their own doom. The Russians are not satisfied with reasonable assurance of the doom of the capitalists since it means also—as they know—assurance of their own demise.

During 1963 and 1964, a number of Western Communist parties were assailed and a few even split by factional discord. Most of the factionalists adhered to the Chinese line, but some were more revisionist than the Soviet-line parties, and a few were dissident "revolutionary leftists" who disagreed not only with the Russians but also with the Chinese (e.g., by attacking Stalin). In Belgium and in Australia, full-fledged rival Chinese-line parties were formed (as in several other nonadvanced countries such as Brazil and Ceylon); in the United States, Great Britain, France, Italy, and elsewhere, splinter groups within and without weaken the pro-Soviet official parties.[33]

Revolution or "internal war" carries much lower risks than international war. Consequently, the Russians will more readily support revolutionary internal wars in those peripheral situations which seem to hold promise. But revolutionary war waged within the advanced countries would be quite another matter. The Communists do not see circumstances—even in prospect—which would make such actions feasible.

Communist consideration of comprehensive disarmament has presumably taken into account the possibilities of unleashing revolutionary war in many circumstances in which it would be quite out of the question in an armed world. Soviet disarmament proposals and positions have, so far, been intended chiefly for political warfare rather than for serious negotiation. Nonetheless, the Soviet leaders have maintained their stand on general disarmament as a desirable *objective*, even at the expense of further discord with the Chinese Communists—and on an issue which is not unassailable. Although the Russians see serious obstacles and disadvantages to general disarmament, they also would expect (along with other advantages) to see the national liberation movements sweep ahead much more rapidly than would be possible if the imperialists retained their powerful military strength. Ultimately, the Revolution would thus be facilitated in engulfing the economically weakened, neutralized advanced countries. But for the foreseeable future, the Russians do not see disarmament as a practical possibility.

The Soviet leaders also consider another unlikely but not impossible course of events. What if there *should* be a general nuclear war? Apart from frail hopes for Soviet survival and a net military advantage in the Eurasian periphery, the Soviet leaders hope that the capitalist system would be destroyed and that "revolution" in the radioactive debris could create a new socialist society. For the distant English-speaking countries, however, the burden would still have to rest on local popular reaction rather than on projectable Soviet military power. The role of revolutionary war in Communist strategy would be but one of many crucial uncertainties in the post-nuclear world. Overt external war and internal revolutionary war in the West are neither accepted nor rejected as possible future courses, though both are distinctly subordinate in current Soviet thinking to the continuation of the Cold War's peaceful coexistence. Revolution would be preferred to war, and is probably rated as more likely to take place.

In conclusion, the Communists expect but do not clearly foresee the role that revolution may play in the final push against disintegrating capitalism. Their blurred focus on this question leaves undefined their view on the final stages of the world-wide victory of Communism. In time, they may well come to recognize that the reality of the twentieth century bears little resemblance to the notions of Marx, or even of Lenin.

NOTES

1. MILITARY INFLUENCES AND INSTRUMENTS
IN RUSSIAN POLICY, 1860–1965

1. See Michael Florinsky, "The Russian Mobilization of 1914," *Political Science Quarterly*, June, 1927; and S. D. Sazonov, *Fateful Years, 1909–1916* (London, 1928), pp. 195–214.

2. Michael Florinsky, *Russia: A History and An Interpretation* (New York, 1955), II, 1333.

3. Richard Pierce, *Russian Central Asia, 1867–1917* (Berkeley, Calif., 1960), pp. 269–96. See also E. D. Sokol, *The Revolt of 1916 in Soviet Central Asia* (Baltimore, 1953).

4. See Hugh Seton-Watson, *The Decline of Imperial Russia* (London and New York, 1956), p. 346.

5. Count V. Kokovtsov, *Iz moego proshlago (From My Past)* (Paris, 1933), II, 114–46.

6. Mairin Mitchell, *The Maritime History of Russia, 848–1948* (London, 1949), p. 246.

7. Count S. Y. Witte, *Vospominaniya: Tsarstvovanie Nikolaia II (Memoirs: The Rule of Nicholas II)* (Berlin, 1922), I, 143–46; see also the relevant documents published in *Krasnyi arkhiv (Red Archives)*, Vols. 50, 51, 54, and 55.

8. *Istoriya SSSR, Rossiya v XIX veke (History of the U.S.S.R.: Russia in the Nineteenth Century)* (Moscow, 1954), II, 543 ff. See also Seton-Watson, *Decline of Imperial Russia*, pp. 84–89, and Florinsky, *Russia*, II, 982. Pierce, *Russian Central Asia*, p. 23, states that the 1865 seizure of Tashkent by Cherniayev was also against orders.

9. Colonel F. A. Wellesley, *With the Russians in Peace and War* (London, 1905), pp. 19–20.

10. Florinsky, *Russia*, II, 1129, and Seton-Watson, *Decline of Imperial Russia*, p. 89.

11. David Dallin, *The Rise of Russia in Asia* (New Haven, 1949), pp. 32 and 146–48; and Owen Lattimore, *Pivot of Asia: Sinkiang and the Inner Asian Frontiers of China and Russia* (Boston, 1950), pp. 32–44.

12. Dallin, *Rise of Russia in Asia*, pp. 123–43; Peter S. H. Tang, *Russian and Soviet Policy in Manchuria and Outer Mongolia, 1911–1931* (Durham, N.C., 1959), pp. 81–90, 293–340, and 410–12; and Seton-Watson, *Decline of Imperial Russia*, p. 338.

13. Hans von Eckardt, *Russia* (New York, 1932), p. 299. See also the reference to uncited archival materials in Louis Fischer, *The Soviets in World Affairs* (Princeton, N.J., 1951), II, 534.

14. Seton-Watson, *Decline of Imperial Russia*, pp. 198 and 210–13, makes this point well; see also Witte, *Vospominaniya*, I, 37–57, 119–33, and 214–23; Tang, *Russian and Soviet Policy in Manchuria and Outer Mongolia*, pp. 91–104; Frederick McCormick, *The Tragedy of Russia in Pacific Asia* (New York, 1907), I, 17–40; and Andrew Malozemoff, *Russian Far Eastern Policy, 1881–1904* (Berkeley, Calif., 1958), pp. 47–89, 103–37, et passim.

15. Witte, *Vospominaniya*, I, 262.

16. George Vernadsky, *Political and Diplomatic History of Russia* (Boston, 1936), p. 360; and McCormick, *Tragedy of Russia*, p. 15.

17. Seton-Watson, *Decline of Imperial Russia*, p. 209.

18. Dallin, *Rise of Russia in Asia*, pp. 103–11. See also Kokovtsov, *Iz moego proshlago*, I, 358–411.

19. Seton-Watson, *Decline of Imperial Russia*, pp. 327–29.

20. *Ibid.*, pp. 100 and 173; and Florinsky, *Russia*, II, 1131.

21. For further discussion, see Raymond L. Garthoff, "The Stalinist Revision of History: The Case of Brest-Litovsk," *World Politics*, October, 1952, and Chapter 4 of this volume.

22. Fischer, *Soviets in World Affairs*, I, 194, quoted from the original in the archives of the People's Commissariat of War in Moscow.

23. Edward H. Carr, *The Bolshevik Revolution 1917–1923* (New York, 1953), III, 153.

24. *Ibid.*, pp. 165–215. For Lenin's admission, see Clara Zetkin, *Reminiscences of Lenin* (New York, 1934), pp. 18–19; and for Lenin's similar statement to Trotsky, see Chiang Kai-shek, *Soviet Russia in China* (New York, 1957), p. 22.

25. Carr, *The Bolshevik Revolution*, III, 297–303. See also Georg von Rauch, *A History of Soviet Russia* (New York, 1957), p. 122.

26. Kh. Choibalsan, *Kratkii ocherk istorii mongol'skoi narodnoi revoliutsii* (A Brief Outline History of the Mongolian People's Revolution) (Moscow, 1952), pp. 62–74; Carr, *The Bolshevik Revolution*, III, 511–23; and David Dallin, *Soviet Russia and the Far East* (London, 1949), pp. 80–86.

27. Nasrollah S. Fatemi, *Diplomatic History of Persia, 1917–1923* (New York, 1952), pp. 191–243; and Ivar Spector, *The Soviet Union and the Muslim World* (Seattle, 1959), pp. 86–95.

28. Fischer, *Soviets in World Affairs*, I, 390–93.

29. See Colonel I. Kardashov, *Internatsional'nyi dolg vooruzhënnykh sil SSSR* (The International Duty of the Armed Forces of the U.S.S.R.) (Moscow, 1960), pp. 53–59, for a listing of such units.

30. M. N. Tukhachevsky, *Voina klassov* (War of the Classes) (Moscow, 1921), pp. 139–40.

31. See Gustav Hilger and Alfred Meyer, *The Incompatible Allies: A Memoir-History of German-Soviet Relations, 1918–1941* (New York, 1953), pp. 187–208; Carr, *The Bolshevik Revolution*, III, 305–76 and 435–39; Herbert Rosinski, *The Germany Army* (New York, 1940), pp. 193–95; Friedrich von Rabenau, *Seeckt: Aus Seinem Leben, 1918–1936* (Leipzig, 1940), *passim*; Gerald Freund, *Unholy Alliance* (London, 1957), pp. 92–126 and 201–12; Cecil Melville, *The Russian Face of Germany* (London, 1932), *passim*; Erich Wollenberg, *The Red Army* (London, 1940), pp. 232–99; and W. M. Knight-Patterson (pseud. of W. W. Kulski), *Germany from Defeat to Conquest: 1913–1933* (London, 1945), pp. 400–403.

32. Franz Borkenau, *The Communist International* (London, 1938), p. 243; Rauch, *History of Russia*, p. 194; E. H. Carr, *The Interregnum, 1923–1924* (New York, 1954), pp. 201–26; and Walter G. Krivitsky, *In Stalin's Secret Service* (New York, 1940), pp. 40–47.

33. In J. V. Stalin, *Sochineniya* (Collected Works), Vol. 7 (Moscow, 1947), p. 14.

34. Chiang Kai-shek, *Soviet Russia in China*, pp. 11–56; Fischer, *Soviets in World Affairs*, II, 633–77; Dallin, *Rise of Russia*, pp. 210–30. See also Conrad

Brandt, *Stalin's Failure in China: 1924–1927* (Cambridge, Mass., 1958), *passim.*
35. Fischer, *Soviets in World Affairs*, II, 650 and 800–1; Dallin, *Rise of Russia*, pp. 210–30; Chiang Kai-shek, *Soviet Russia in China*, p. 58; and Tang, *Russian and Soviet Policy in Manchuria and Outer Mongolia*, pp. 208–34.
36. Allen Whiting and General Sheng Shih-ts'ai, *Sinkiang: Pawn or Pivot?* (East Lansing, Mich., 1948), pp. 9–91 and 186–267; Lattimore, *Pivot of Asia*, pp. 69–80; Alexander Barmine, *One Who Survived* (New York, 1945), pp. 231–32.
37. Whiting and Sheng, *Sinkiang*, pp. 102–9; Godfrey Lias, *Kazak Exodus* (London, 1956), pp. 101–17; and Chiang Kai-shek, *Soviet Russia in China*, pp. 102–3. Lattimore, *Pivot of Asia*, pp. 77–89, is probably in error in his interpretation of Sheng's position in 1944.
38. Barmine, *One Who Survived*, p. 230.
39. Krivitsky, *In Stalin's Secret Service*, pp. 82–115.
40. See Carl Tinch, "Quasi-War between Japan and the USSR, 1937–1939," *World Politics*, January, 1951, pp. 174–99; Col. S. Shishkin, *Boevye deistviya Krasnoi armii u reki Khalkin-gol v 1939 godu (Combat Operations of the Red Army at Khalkin-gol in 1939)* (Moscow, 1946), esp. pp. 7–57; *Istoriya velikoi otechestvennoi voiny Sovetskogo Soyuza, 1941–1945 gg. (History of the Great Fatherland War of the Soviet Union, 1941–45)* (Moscow, 1960), I, 230–45; and for evidence of Soviet responsibility for provoking the incident at Lake Khasan, see Martin Blumenson, "The Soviet Power Play at Changkufeng," *World Politics*, January, 1960, pp. 249–63.
41. These data on strengths are provided in *O Sovetskoi voennoi nauke (On Soviet Military Science)* (Moscow, 1960), p. 198.
42. The exact date is not known, but this timing is supported by indirect evidence and asserted by Wollenberg, *The Red Army*, p. 237; Rosinski, *The German Army*, p. 195; and Rauch, *History of Russia*, p. 263.
43. See Rauch, *History of Russia*, pp. 287–88, for some details.
44. See the discussion in Raymond L. Garthoff, *Soviet Military Doctrine* (Glencoe, Ill., 1953), pp. 423–38.
45. See Dallin, *Soviet Russia and the Far East*, p. 195.
46. J. V. Stalin, in *Pravda*, February 10, 1946.
47. Walter Kolarz, *The Peoples of the Soviet Far East* (New York, 1954), p. 166; and Tang, *Russian and Soviet Policy in Manchuria and Outer Mongolia*, pp. 423–24.
48. Vladimir Dedijer, *Tito* (New York, 1953), p. 322.
49. Whiting and Sheng, *Sinkiang*, pp. 110–31; and Lias, *Kazak Exodus*, pp. 119–38.
50. Allen Whiting, "Sinkiang and Sino-Soviet Relations," *The China Quarterly*, July-September, 1960, pp. 34 and 36.
51. See O. Edmund Clubb, "The Sino-Soviet Frontier," *Military Review*, July, 1964, pp. 10–11.
52. These figures are rounded from those given by N. S. Khrushchev, *Pravda*, January 15, 1960, and are probably substantially accurate.
53. For authoritative statements of the revised Soviet view, see for example the speeches of Khrushchev, in *Pravda*, January 15, June 22, and October 21, 1960; A. Belyakov and F. Burlatsky, "Lenin's Theory of the Socialist Revolution and the Present Time," *Kommunist*, No. 13, September, 1960; Marshal Rodion Malinovsky, in *Krasnaya zvezda (Red Star)*, January 20, 1960; Major General N. A. Talensky, "Contemporary War, Its Nature and Consequences," *Mezhdu-*

narodnaya zhizn' (*International Affairs*), October, 1960, pp. 31 ff; and A. Butenko, "War and Revolution," *Kommunist*, No. 4, March, 1961, pp. 49 ff.

2. THE MILITARY AS A SOCIOPOLITICAL FORCE IN RUSSIA, 1861–1965

1. The most complete account of these reforms, though not objective in its interpretation, is P. A. Zaionchkovsky, *Voennye reformy 1860–1870 godov v Rossii* (*The Military Reforms of the 1860's and 1870's in Russia*) (Moscow, 1952), which includes a useful bibliographical essay. For a good brief account in English, see Alexander Kornilov, *Modern Russian History* (New York, 1924), pp. 157–62.

2. Cited in Kornilov, *op. cit.*, p. 262.

3. Colonel (now Major General) A. Lagovsky, *Strategiya i ekonomika* (*Strategy and Economics*) (Moscow, 1957), p. 9.

4. Nikolaus Basseches, *The Unknown Army* (New York, 1943), p. 59.

5. Colonel Sventsitsky, cited by Dimitri D. Fedotoff White, *The Growth of the Red Army* (Princeton, N.J., 1944), pp. 43–44.

6. General A. I. Denikin, *Staraya armiya* (*The Old Army*) (Paris, 1929), p. 59.

7. Basseches, *op. cit.*, p. 59.

8. For some background to this measure, see Denikin, *op. cit.*, pp. 147–48.

9. General Nikolai Golovin, *Voennyye usiliya Rossii v mirovoi voine* (*The Russian Military Effort in the World War*) (Paris, 1939), I, 160, provides the figures for casualties—totaling 92,500 by the end of 1916 (including 15,000 held prisoner by the enemy). The estimates of officer active duty and reservist strengths in 1914 are based on the careful study of Col. N. Pyatnitsky, *Krasnaya armiya SSSR* (*The Red Army of the U.S.S.R.*) (Paris, 1932), II, 14.

10. Pyatnitsky, *op. cit.*, p. 14.

11. The official Soviet figures show a total of 314,180 former officers, non-commissioned officers, and rated medical personnel from the pre-Revolutionary army had entered the Red Army by August, 1920; in A. S. Bubnov *et al.* (eds.), *Grazhdanskaya voina* (*The Civil War*) (Moscow, 1928), II, 95. The estimate for the White armies is from Erich Wollenberg, *The Red Army* (London, 1938), p. 73.

12. *Ibid.*, p. 95. The exact figure is 10,339.

13. *Ibid.*, p. 95. This figure (48,409) is for line commissioned officers only.

14. *Ibid.*, pp. 97–98. During 1921, 37,954 officers were dismissed, including 14,390 who had been officers in the White armies at one time.

15. Pyatnitsky, *op. cit.*, p. 116, states that former Imperial officers declined from 76 per cent in 1918 to 10 per cent in 1930. N. Yefimov in *Grazhdanskaya voina*, II (1928), 106, notes that officers with pre-Revolutionary military education declined from 30 per cent in 1923 to 15 per cent in 1926.

16. S. Nikitin-Zubrovsky, in *Voina i revoliutsiya* (*War and Revolution*), September, 1929, pp. 111–14.

17. N. Yefimov, in *Grazhdanskaya voina*, II (1928), 108, cites the official 1924 figure; Wollenberg, *op. cit.*, pp. 72–73, gives the later one.

18. Nikitin-Zubrovsky, *op. cit.*, p. 101.

19. All data above are taken from the official reports cited in *Grazhdanskaya voina*, II (1928), 105–9.

20. These figures were compiled by the author from official data given in the

Soviet Air Force Journal *Vestnik vozdushnogo flota* (*Herald of the Air Fleet*) during the 1920's.

21. See Raymond L. Garthoff, *Soviet Military Doctrine* (Glencoe, Ill., 1953), p. 220.

22. Pyatnitsky, *op. cit.*, I, 21, gives the 1931 and 1933 figures (and other data showing the rise during the 1920's and early 1930's). The 1939 figure was given by Marshal K. Ye. Voroshilov at the 18th Party Congress, *Rech' na XVIII s'yezde VKP (b)* (*Speech to the 18th Congress of the CPSU* [B]) (Moscow, 1939), p. 12. Other official figures for the years 1933–35 are given by Voroshilov, in *Stati i rechi* (*Articles and Speeches*) (Moscow, 1936), pp. 574, 611, *et passim*.

23. Voroshilov, *Rech' na XVIII s'yezde VKP (b)*, p. 32.

24. These illustrations and comments are based primarily on the author's experience in meeting and talking with Soviet officers while traveling in the U.S.S.R. in 1957, 1959, and 1963.

25. This stress upon the need for increased technological preparedness in military men is well reflected in Major General G. I. Pokrovsky's *Science and Technology in Contemporary War* (New York, 1959).

26. Marshal A. Vasilevsky stated in 1952 that 86.4 per cent of officers were members of the Communist Party and Komsomol (*Pravda*, October 10, 1952). Marshal R. Malinovsky said in 1958 that "over 86 per cent" of officers were members of the Party and Komsomol (*Pravda*, February 23, 1958), thus confirming that the figure was still between 86 and 87 per cent. Public Soviet sources in the early and mid-1960's usually say "90 per cent"; for example, Leonid Brezhnev gave the figure of 90 per cent in a speech on July 3, 1965 (*Radio Moscow*, July 3, 1965).

27. The questions of military doctrinal and strategic evolution in the period 1953–62 are examined in detail in Raymond L. Garthoff, *Soviet Strategy in the Nuclear Age* (rev. ed.; New York, 1962), pp. 61–91 and 250–66.

28. Cited by Wollenberg, *op. cit.*, p. 74, and by Colonel James D. Hittle, *The Military Staff* (Harrisburg, Pa., 1949), p. 242.

3. THE MARSHALS AND THE COMMUNIST PARTY, 1945–65

1. See, for example, the long, eulogistic biographical articles on Marshal Zhukov and Chief Marshal of Aviation Novikov, both in *Krasnaya zvezda* (*Red Star*), January 24, 1946.

2. Quoted in *Pravda*, February 10, 1946.

3. See Jan Kowalewski, in Commander M. Saunders (ed.), *The Soviet Navy* (New York, 1958), p. 99.

4. These "theses" were never published, but they were cited in *Sovetskii flot* (*Soviet Fleet*), June 13, 1957.

5. Decree of the Council of Ministers "On the Establishment of a List of Information Constituting a Secret of State, the Divulgence of Which is Punishable by Law," June 8, 1947, in *Izvestiya*, June 10, 1947.

6. For a discussion of the stagnation in Soviet military doctrine, see Raymond L. Garthoff, *Soviet Strategy in the Nuclear Age* (New York, 1962), pp. 61–63.

7. Marshal G. Zhukov was listed as a nominee for the Supreme Soviet elections in March, 1950; he also gave a public address in Warsaw in July, 1951.

8. This decree, never published, is known from references in the Soviet military press, which began at once to publish articles on "one-man command."

9. A complete list of the professional generals and of the "political" and defense-production generals who were elected to the Central Committee in 1939, 1952, and 1956 is provided in an appendix to Raymond L. Garthoff, *The Role of the Military in Recent Soviet Politics* (RAND RM-1638 [Santa Monica, Calif., March 1, 1956]).

10. See *Pravda*, January 13, 1953, for the announcement of the charges.

11. See Raymond L. Garthoff, "The Military in Soviet Politics," *Problems of Communism*, November-December, 1947, pp. 45 ff.

12. See, for example, the secondhand report by former MVD Lieutenant Colonel Yuri Rastvorov, "How Red Titans Fought for Supreme Power," *Life*, November 29, 1954.

13. Colonel I. Nenakhov, in *Voennaya mysl'* (*Military Thought*), September, 1953, p. 6.

14. See editorials in *Krasnaya zvezda*, December 30 and 31, 1954, and the article by Lieutenant Colonel I. Sidel'nikov, in *Krasnaya zvezda*, January 15, 1955.

15. For further discussion of the budget and Soviet comments in budgetary debate in the mid-1950's, see Garthoff, *The Role of the Military in Recent Soviet Politics*, pp. 9–13.

16. N. Bulganin, in *Izvestiya*, February 10, 1955.

17. The "Instructions" have never been published, but the Soviet military press provided substantial extracts and commentaries. See, in particular, *Krasnaya zvezda*, May 12, 1957.

18. See Marshal Zhukov's Leningrad speeches, particularly in *Radio Moscow*, July 16, 1957, and *Krasnaya zvezda*, July 5, 1957.

19. "On Some Questions of Military Science," editorial, in *Voennaya mysl'*, March, 1955, p. 6.

20. The Soviet authorities do not ordinarily announce appointments or transfer of military men, but the military press does mention military-district commanders and some others from time to time—particularly on the occasion of national celebrations, when they usually deliver addresses—so that a diligent attention to the press reveals shifts in commands.

21. See the articles by Colonel General F. Golikov, in *Partinaya zhizn'* (*Party Life*), August, 1958, pp. 15–23, and in *Pravda*, August 29, 1958, and the editorials in *Krasnaya zvezda*, *Sovetskaya aviatsiya* (*Soviet Aviation*), and *Sovetskii flot* (*Soviet Navy*), all of November 5, 1958. See also Marshal V. Sokolovsky and Major General M. Cherednichenko, in *Voenno-istoricheskii zhurnal* (*The Military-Historical Journal*), March, 1965, p. 9.

22. See the articles by Golikov cited immediately above.

4. IDEOLOGY AND THE BALANCE OF POWER

1. Stalin, in answer to a question by Harold King, quoted in *Vneshnyaya politika Sovetskogo Soyuza v period Otechestvennoi voiny* (*The Foreign Policy of the Soviet Union in the Period of the Fatherland War*) (Moscow, 1944), I, 90.

2. "Speech by J. V. Stalin at the Nineteenth Congress of the Communist Party of the Soviet Union," *Novoe vremiya* (*New Times*), October 15, 1952, p. 2.

3. Stalin, "Report to the Plenary Session of the Central Committee of the CPSU (B)" (March 3, 1937), in *Mastering Bolshevism* (New York, 1937), p. 11.

4. Stalin, *History of the CPSU (B)* (New York, 1938), p. 274. See also the reports to the Party Congresses and speeches of Stalin.

5. Stalin, *Bolshevik*, No. 4, February, 1938, *passim*.

6. *Izvestiya* (editorial), January 22, 1929. Italics added.

7. G. A. Deborin, *Pervye mezhdunarodnye akty Sovetskogo gosudarstava i yevo vneshnyaya politika v gody inostrannoi interventsii i grazhdanskoi voiny, 1917–1922 (The First International Acts of the Soviet State and Its Foreign Policy in the Years of the Foreign Intervention and Civil War, 1917–22)* (Moscow, 1947), p. 3.

8. Deborin, *op. cit.*, p. 4.

9. For example, see Stalin's Report to the 17th Party Congress in 1938, in *Leninism: Selected Writings* (New York, 1942), p. 308.

10. A. Zhdanov, *The International Situation* (Moscow, 1947), pp. 7 and 17.

11. Stalin, "Two Camps," *Sochineniya (Collected Works)*, IV, 232.

12. G. M. Malenkov, "Report to the Nineteenth Party Congress on the Work of the Central Committee of the VKP (B)," *Bol'shevik*, No. 19, October, 1952, p. 63.

13. L. P. Beria, "Thirty-Fourth Anniversary of the Great October Socialist Revolution," *Bol'shevik*, No. 21, November, 1951, p. 2. At that time, Beria was of course still "unmasked," and his extollment of the Soviet Union was undoubtedly taken at face value by all good CP members.

14. N. Kosev, "On Revolutionary Vigilance," *Pravda*, February 6, 1953.

15. See Raymond L. Garthoff, "The Stalinist Revision of History: The Case of Brest-Litovsk," *World Politics*, October, 1952, *passim*.

16. Historicus, "Stalin on Revolution," *Foreign Affairs*, January, 1949, p. 209. As Historicus has pointed out, these statements were made to foreigners and were not given wide circulation in the U.S.S.R. The early postwar statements were answers to questions by Alexander Werth (September, 1946), Elliott Roosevelt (December, 1946), Harold Stassen (April, 1947), Henry Wallace (May, 1948), and Kingsbury Smith (January, 1949).

17. Malenkov, in his address on Stalin's seventieth birthday, devoted more attention to this theme than did the other Politburo speakers, although several affirmed peaceful coexistence. G.M. Malenkov, *Bol'shevik*, No. 24, December, 1949, *passim*.

18. G.M. Malenkov, *Bol'shevik*, No. 19, October, 1952, p. 20.

19. *Ibid.*

20. Stalin, "Political Report to the Central Committee, December 18, [1925]," *Sochineniya*, VII, p. 261–62.

21. *Pravda* (editorial), October 18, 1952.

22. *Bol'shevik*, No. 10, May, 1946, p. 77.

23. Stalin, *Bol'shevik*, No. 18, September, 1952, p. 19.

24. Lenin, *Selected Works* (New York, 1943), V, 237 (originally written in April, 1916).

25. Stalin, *History of the CPSU (B)* (New York, 1939), p. 274 (published in 1938).

26. V. Mikheyev, *Bol'shevik*, No. 16, August, 1951, p. 59.

27. Lenin, *Sochineniya* (3rd ed.), XXIV, 122.

28. Stalin, in *Problems of Leninism* (New York, 1934), pp. 66–67 (originally written in 1926).

29. *Pravda* (editorial), September 9, 1952.

30. G. M. Malenkov, *Bol'shevik*, No. 21, November, 1949; V. M. Molotov, *Bol'shevik*, No. 24, December, 1949; A. I. Mikoyan, *Pravda*, March 11, 1950; L. P. Beria, *Bol'shevik*, November, 1951; Malenkov, *Bol'shevik*, No. 19, Octo-

ber, 1952; M. G. Pervukhin, *Pravda*, November 7, 1952. For a restatement shortly after Stalin's death, see A. Nikhonov, in *Kommunist*, No. 7, May, 1953.

31. Frol Kozlov, *Voprosy Ekonomiki*, April, 1952, p. 86.

32. Stalin, *Bol'shevik*, No. 18, September, 1952, pp. 18–19.

33. *Ibid.*, p. 18.

34. *Ibid.*, p. 20.

35. Stalin, *Sochineniya*, VII, 14. (This speech of January 19, 1925, before the Plenum of the Central Committee was first made public in the *Sochineniya*, in 1947.)

36. For a stimulating study, see Marshall Shulman, *Stalin's Foreign Policy Reappraised* (Cambridge, Mass., 1963).

37. Stalin, "On the Right Deviation in the V.K.P.(B.)," *Sochineniya*, XII, 35.

38. Stalin, "Speech at the XIV Congress of the V.K.P.(B.)," *Sochineniya*, VII, 274.

39. Stalin, *History of the CPSU(B)*, *Short Course* (New York, 1939), pp. 78–79. (Russian original checked.)

40. Stalin, *Sochineniya*, XII, 248. The English translation (London, 1930) translated this phrase as "balance of power."

41. Lenin, *Selected Works* (New York, n.d.), VII, 353.

42. Lenin, *Sochineniya (Collected Works)* (2d. ed.; Moscow, 1929), XXII, 265.

43. Lenin, *Selected Works*, VII, 354. See also *ibid.*, X, 104–5.

44. Lenin, "Karl Marx," *Marx-Engels-Marxism* (New York, 1935), p. 29.

45. In *Strategy and Tactics of the Proletarian Revolution* (New York, 1936), p. 65.

46. V. Sorin, *Partiya i oppozitsiya (The Party and the Opposition)* (Moscow, 1925), p. 42. See also pp. 13, 51, 64, and 71.

47. See Lenin, *Sochineniya*, XII, 198 and 265, for examples of adventurism.

48. For a recent discussion, see A. Sevastyanov, " 'Leftism,' An Infantile Disorder of Communism: A Model of Internationalism and Creative Marxism," *Pravda*, May 27, 1964.

49. Bukharin, in *Sedmoi s'yezd Rossiiskoi Kommunisticheskoi Partii (Seventh Congress of the Russian Communist Party)* (Moscow-Leningrad, 1928), pp. 122–123.

50. *Ibid.*, p. 56.

51. M. Leonov, *Moral'nyi faktor v sovremënnykh voinakh (The Morale Factor in Contemporary Wars)* (Moscow, 1946), pp. 105–6.

52. Major General N. Talensky, *Bol'shevik*, No. 10-11, May-June, 1944, p. 14.

53. Vladimir Potëmkin, *Istoriya diplomatii (The History of Diplomacy)* (Moscow, 1945), III, 35, 45, and 48.

54. Stalin, *Leninism*, p. 440.

55. Stalin, *Sochineniya*, VII, 14.

56. Stalin, *Leninism*, pp. 81–82; italics Stalin's.

57. Major General M. Galaktionov, *Strategicheskaya tsel' (The Strategic Objective)* (Moscow, 1944), pp. 128–29.

58. Major General N. Talensky, *Bol'shevik*, No. 3, March, 1946, pp. 28–29.

59. *Obshchaya taktika (General Tactics)* (Moscow, 1940), I, 16.

60. See Clausewitz (*On War*, New York, 1943, p. 14) for a comparative statement that "the objective nature of war makes it a calculation of probabilities."

61. Stalin, *Sochineniya*, V, 166–68.

62. See Nathan Leites, *The Operational Code of the Politburo* (New York, 1951), pp. 66–72.

63. Major General N. A. Talensky, in *Voennaya mysl'* (*Military Thought*), June, 1946, pp. 3–4.

64. *Ibid.*, p. 7.

65. Lenin, *Selected Works*, VII, 358.

66. Lenin, in *Sedmoi s'yezd*, pp. 126 and 129.

67. Stalin, in *Bol'shevik*, No. 3, February, 1947, p. 6.

68. Stalin, *Sochineniya*, VI, 160.

69. Stalin, *History of the CPSU(B)*, pp. 89–96.

70. Stalin, "Two Camps," *Sochineniya*, IV, 232.

71. M. Tanin, *Mezhdunarodnaya politika SSSR, 1917–1924* (*International Politics of the USSR, 1917–24* (Moscow, 1925), p. 5.

72. *Ibid.*, p. 5. The closing ellipsis is an emphasis of Tanin's.

73. Stalin, "Political Report of the Central Committee, 18 December [1925]," *Sochineniya*, VII, 261–62.

74. Stalin, *History of the CPSU(B)*, p. 274.

75. I. M. Lemin, *Bor'ba dvukh napravlenii v mezhdunarodnykh otnosheniakh* (*The Struggle of the Two Tendencies in International Relations*) (Moscow, 1947), p. 12.

76. *Bol'shevik*, No. 11-12, June, 1946, p. 1.

77. Molotov, *Bol'shevik*, No. 24, December, 1949, p. 21; and Mikoyan, *Pravda*, March 11, 1950, p. 4. See also Major General N. A. Talensky, in *Bol'shevik*, No. 11, June, 1951, p. 36: "If the imperialists succeed in unleashing a third war, it will bring the destruction not of individual capitalist states, but of the entire world capitalism."

78. G. Alexandrov (ed.), *Politicheskii slovar'* (*Political Dictionary*) (Moscow, 1940), p. 93.

79. Alfred Vagts, in a stimulating article on "The Balance of Power: Growth of an Idea" (*World Politics*, October, 1948), has contended that the balance of power as something sought, ethically desirable, is peculiar to countries which have experienced the Renaissance, and hence is not shared by successive Russian elites.

80. P. N. Demichev, in *Pravda*, April 23, 1965.

81. N. S. Khrushchev, Speech in Bucharest, TASS, *Radio Moscow*, June 21, 1960. Also in Khrushchev, *On Peaceful Co-existence*, (Moscow, 1961), pp. 246–47.

82. Molotov's letter was not published or, apparently, distributed to the Congress. However, it was disclosed, quoted from, and flayed by the Soviet leaders. The references here cited are given by P. F. Satyukov, in *Izvestiya*, October 27, 1961, and A. I. Mikoyan, in *Izvestiya*, October 22, 1961.

83. O. V. Kuusinen, in *Izvestiya*, October 27, 1961.

5. THE GEOSTRATEGIC ARENA, ECONOMICS, AND TECHNOLOGY

1. Lieutenant General S. Kozlov, *et al.*, *O Sovetskoi voennoi nauke* (*On Soviet Military Science*) (2d ed.; Moscow, 1964), p. 303.

2. G. A. Deborin, "Historical Lessons of the Great Fatherland War," *Voprosy istorii* (*Problems of History*), April, 1965, p. 12. See also Kozlov, *op. cit.*, pp. 304–7.

3. Lieutenant Colonel S. Bartenev, "The Economic Factor and Nuclear War," *Krasnaya zvezda (Red Star)*, July 7, 1964.

4. Kozlov, *op. cit.*, p. 304. See also Colonel G. S. Kravchenko, *Voennaya ekonomika SSSR, 1941–1945 (The War Economy of the U.S.S.R., 1941–1945)* (Moscow, 1963), esp. p. 6; and Major General A. Korniyenko, "The Economic Foundations of the Military Power of States," *Krasnaya zvezda*, September 10, 1965.

5. Colonel General N. Lomov, "Basic Tenets of Soviet Military Doctrine," *Krasnaya zvezda*, January 10, 1964.

6. Colonel A. N. Lagovsky, *Strategiya i ekonomika (Strategy and Economics)*, (Moscow, 1957), p. 194.

7. Colonel General S. Shtemenko, "The Queen of the Battlefield Relinquishes Her Crown," *Nedelya*, January 31–February 6, 1965.

8. Marshal R. Malinovsky, *Bditel'no stoyat' na strazhe mira (Vigilantly Stand Guard Over the Peace)* (Moscow, 1962), p. 26.

9. Marshal V. Sokolovsky and Major General M. Cherednichenko, "The Revolution in Military Affairs, Its Significance and Consequences: Military Art at a New Stage," *Krasnaya zvezda*, August 28, 1964.

10. Colonel V. Larionov, "New Weapons and the Duration of War," *Krasnaya zvezda*, March 18, 1965.

11. Marshal V. Sokolovsky and Major General M. Cherednichenko, "Some Questions on Soviet Military Construction in the Postwar Period," *Voenno-istoricheskii zhurnal (The Military Historical Journal)*, March, 1965, p. 11.

12. N. P. Prokop'ev, *O voine i armii (On War and the Army)* (Moscow, 1965), p. 216.

13. Bartenev, "The Economic Factor and Nuclear War," *Krasnaya zvezda*, July 7, 1964.

14. Colonel (Res.) M. S. Shifman, *Voina i ekonomika (War and Economics)* (Moscow, 1964), p. 198. See also Lieutenant Colonel (Res.) G. Mifteyev, "War and Manpower Resources," *Krasnaya zvezda*, June 4, 1965.

15. Marshal R. Malinovsky, *op. cit.*, p. 25.

16. Colonel General N. A. Lomov, in *Problemy revoliutsii v voennom dele (Problems of the Revolution in Military Affairs)* (Moscow, 1965), p. 46. See also an almost identical statement in Prokop'ev, *op. cit.*, p. 214.

17. This particular quotation is from Major General A. N. Lagovsky, *Rol' ekonomicheskogo faktora v voine (The Role of the Economic Factor in War)* (Moscow, 1959), p. 32. For a more extended discussion of Soviet doctrinal discussions on economic factors in the late 1950's, see Raymond L. Garthoff, *The Soviet Image of Future War* (Washington, D.C., 1959), pp. 23–59, as well as the more recent Soviet works cited in Thomas W. Wolfe, *Soviet Strategy at the Crossroads* (Cambridge, Mass., 1964), pp. 130–52, and in the notes to the present chapter.

18. Marshal R. Malinovsky, *op. cit.*, p. 46. In the same discussion (p. 48), he also stressed the need for heavy military spending, regrettable though the necessity was, so long as general and complete disarmament had not been achieved.

19. N. S. Khrushchev, Interview with H. Shapiro, in *Pravda*, November 19, 1957. See also the analysis by N. Galay, "The Military Significance of the Soviet Economic Reorganization," *Bulletin of the Institute for the Study of the USSR*, June, 1957, pp. 21–29.

20. Marshal R. Malinovsky, "About the Soldier," *Komsomol'skaya pravda (Komsomol Truth)*, June 8, 1965.

21. The two most recent general volumes dealing with this subject are the collective work *Problemy revoliutsii v voennom dele (Problems of the Revolution in Military Affairs)* (Moscow, 1965), and Marshal A. A. Grechko (ed.), *Yadernyi vek i voina (War and the Nuclear Age)* (Moscow, 1964). The most comprehensive single volume, though now dated, remains Major General G. I. Pokrovsky, *Science and Technology in Contemporary War* (New York, 1959) (originally Moscow, 1956). Also deserving special note are two other informative collective volumes: *Sovremennaya voennaya tekhnika (Contemporary Military Technology)* (Moscow, 1957), and *Novoe v voennoi tekhnike (New Developments in Military Technology)* (Moscow, 1958).

6. DETERRENCE, COUNTERDETERRENCE, AND DISARMAMENT

1. Marshal Rodion Malinovsky, *Bditel'no stoyat' na strazhe mira (Vigilantly Stand Guard Over the Peace)* (Moscow, 1962), p. 25.

2. Major General K. Bochkarev and Colonel I. Sidel'nikov, "New Age, New Conclusions—On the Development by the Party of V. I. Lenin's Views on War, Peace, and on Safeguarding the Achievements of Socialism and Communism," *Krasnaya zvezda (Red Star)*, January 21, 1965.

3. Marshal N. Krylov, TASS Interview, *Radio Moscow*, May 6, 1955.

4. For brief but informative reviews of these crises through 1961, see J. M. Mackintosh, *Strategy and Tactics of Soviet Foreign Policy* (London, New York, Toronto, 1962), *passim*.

5. There is no general analysis of the 1961 Berlin crisis, so it is spelled out in this chapter in some detail. A useful article from the standpoint of impact on U.S. military policy is Jack M. Schick, "The Berlin Crisis of 1961 and U.S. Military Strategy," *Orbis*, Winter, 1965, pp. 816–31.

6. For a good general review, see Henry M. Pachter, *Collision Course: The Cuban Missile Crisis and Coexistence* (New York, 1963); and for an additional excellent analysis of Soviet policy calculations, see Arnold L. Horelick, "The Cuban Missile Crisis: An Analysis of Soviet Calculations and Behavior," *World Politics*, April, 1964, pp. 363–89.

7. From the full text of the President's speech, given in Pachter, *op. cit.*, p. 195.

8. See Walter C. Clemens, Jr., "Lenin on Disarmament," *Slavic Review*, September, 1964, pp. 504–25; and by the same author, "The Sino-Soviet Dispute—Dogma and Dialectics on Disarmament," *International Affairs*, April, 1965, pp. 204–22; and "Ideology in Soviet Disarmament Policy," *The Journal of Conflict Resolution*, March, 1964, p. 7–22.

9. Norman Cousins, "Notes on a 1963 Visit With Khrushchev," *Saturday Review*, November 7, 1964, pp. 20–21.

10. Chinese Government Statement, September 1, 1963, as broadcast by *Radio Peking*, August 31, 1963.

11. Marshal Lo Jui-ching, in *Hung Ch'i (Red Flag)*, May, 1965; broadcast by *Radio Peking*, May 10, 1965.

12. M. A. Suslov, "On the CPSU Struggle for the Unity of The International Communist Movement," speech of February 14, 1964, broadcast on *Radio Moscow*, April 3, 1964.

13. Liu Chang-sheng, speech of June 7, 1960, to the World Federation of Trade Unions General Council, in *Peking Review*, June 10, 1960, pp. 10–13.

14. "CPSU Open Letter to the CCP, July 14, 1963," *Pravda*, July 14, 1963; see also Semënov, *Radio Moscow*, April 27, 1964.

15. V. A. Zorin, "The Disarmament Problem and Peking's Maneuvers," *Izvestiya*, June 30, 1964.

16. For the best general volume on Soviet views on disarmament, see Alexander Dallin *et al.*, *The Soviet Union and Disarmament: An Appraisal of Soviet Attitudes and Intentions* (New York, 1965). See also Richard Barnet, "The Soviet Attitude on Disarmament," *Problems of Communism*, May-June, 1961, pp. 32–37; John W. Spanier and Joseph L. Nogee, *The Politics of Disarmament: A Study in Soviet-American Gamesmanship* (New York, 1962), esp. pp. 28–44 and 176–200; and J. M. Mackintosh and Harry T. Willetts, in Louis Henkin (ed.), *Arms Control: Issues for the Public* (New York, 1961), pp. 141–73.

17. Colonel S. Kozlov, "Some Questions of the Theory of Strategy," *Voennaya mysl' (Military Thought)*, November, 1954, p. 23. Italicized in the original.

18. See the discussion and citations in Thomas W. Wolfe, *Trends in Soviet Thinking on Theater Operations, Conventional Operations, and Limited War* (RAND Corporation RM-4305-PR) (Santa Monica, Calif.), December, 1964, pp. 49–58; and his *Soviet Strategy at the Crossroads* (Cambridge, Mass., 1964), pp. 118–29.

19. The best publicly available analysis, and source for most of the data cited here, is J. G. Godaire, "The Claim of the Soviet Military Establishment," in *Dimensions of Soviet Economic Power*, Studies Prepared for the Joint Economic Committee, Congress of the United States, 1962, pp. 33–46; printed as an annex in the *Hearings* of the Committee published under the same title (Washington, 1962).

7. SOVIET MILITARY RELATIONS WITH EASTERN EUROPE, 1943-65

1. The most complete account of the Polish Army established in the Soviet Union is *Wybrane operacje i walki ludowego Wojska Polskiego (Combat Operations of the Polish People's Army)*, edited by General of the Army Stanislaw G. Poplawski (Warsaw, 1957). It is also available in Russian translation, *Boevye deistviya narodnogo voiska pol'skogo, 1943–1945 gg.*, (Moscow, 1961). Another personal memoir is that of a brigade and division commander in the 1944–45 period, Major General V. A. Radzivanovich, *Pod Pol'skom orlom (Under the Polish Eagle)* (Moscow, 1959). For a brief review in English, see Alexander Werth, *Russia at War, 1941–1945* (London and New York, 1964), pp. 635–67; and see Stanislaw Mikolajczyk, *The Rape of Poland*, (New York, 1948), pp. 14–38.

2. *Zycie i Mysl (Life and Thought)*, No. 10, October, 1964.

3. For a surprisingly informative and frank review of this campaign and other developments affecting the Polish Army in the early postwar years, see Ignacy Blum, *Z dziejow Wojska Polskiego w latach 1945–1948 (Annals of the Polish Army in the Years 1945–1948)* (Warsaw, 1960). See also Yaroslav Bilinsky, *The Second Soviet Republic: The Ukraine after World War II*, (New Brunswick, N.J., 1964), pp. 111–18, for a good brief review of UPA resistance to the Polish Government in the postwar period.

4. For a general review of Romanian military developments in 1944–45, see the volume by Colonel I. Cupsa *et al.*, *Contributia Rominiel la Razboiul Anti-*

hitlerist (23 August 1944—9 Mai 1945) (The Rumanian Contribution to the Defeat of the Nazis, 23 August 1944—9 May 1945) (Bucharest, 1958); also available in Russian translation as I. Kupsha *et al., Vklad Rumynii v razgrom fashistskoi Germanii* (Moscow, 1959).

5. For a general account of the origins of the postwar Romanian officer corps, see Ithiel de Sola Pool, *et al., Satellite Generals: A Study of Military Elites in the Soviet Sphere* (Stanford, Calif., 1955), pp. 82–95. This account draws on that study for a number of developments in the period from 1944 to 1953.

6. Reports unofficially coming to the writer's attention from reliable sources during travel in Eastern Europe.

7. The main source for developments in 1944–45, as well as the wartime partisan underground, is Lieutenant General Sh. Atanasov *et al., Kratka istoriia na Otechestvenata voina (A Short History of the Fatherland War)* (Sofia, 1958); see especially pp. 72–81.

8. See the accounts "Pro-Soviet Group in Sofia Stronger," *The New York Times,* April 18, 1965; and "Sofia Describes Plot: Liberals Involved," *The New York Times,* April 21, 1965; confirmed by *Radio Sofia,* April 22, 1965. After a trial in June, 1965, General Anev was sentenced to eleven years in prison, and five other officers received terms of five to fifteen years. See David Binder, "Bulgarians Find 9 Guilty of Plot," *The New York Times,* June 20, 1965.

9. See Pool, *op. cit.,* pp. 96–122, for an account of developments in the Hungarian armed forces from 1944 to 1953. See also A. I. Puškaš, "The Antifascist Forces of Hungary in the Struggle for the Liberation of the Country (September, 1944 to April, 1945)," *Voprosy istorii (Problems of History),* No. 3, March, 1965, pp. 59–71.

10. This development, and much of the information in this discussion, was recounted by General Béla Kiraly, in "Hungary's Army Under the Soviets," *East Europe,* March, 1958, pp. 3–14.

11. Pool, *op. cit.,* p. 120.

12. General Béla Kiraly, "Hungary's Army: Its Part in the Revolt," *East Europe,* June, 1958, pp. 10 ff.

13. Particularly useful is the volume of collected articles, mostly from the Czech military-historical journal *Gistorie a voenstvi (Military History),* published in Russian translation under the editorship of Colonel S. I. Grachev, Soviet Army, as *Roshdenie Chekhoslovatskoi narodnoi armii (Birth of the Czechoslovak People's Army)* (Moscow, 1959).

14. See Pool, *op. cit.,* pp. 28–54, drawn upon in this chapter for additional details on developments in the leadership of the Czechoslovak armed forces from 1943 to 1953.

15. See *The Soviet-Yugoslav Dispute: Text of the Published Correspondence* (London and New York, 1948), especially pp. 12, 19–20, and 31–32.

16. *Ibid.,* p. 51; CPSU Letter of May 4, 1948, to the CPY, from the text later released by the Soviet Government.

17. See H. Peter Krosby, "The Communist Bid for Power in Finland in 1948," *Political Science Quarterly,* June, 1960, pp. 229–43, and James Billington, "Finland," in Cyril E. Black and Thomas P. Thornton (eds.), *Communism and Revolution* (Princeton, N.J., 1964), pp. 124–30.

18. In Yugoslavia, for example, by 1963 a total of 105,000 officers had graduated from the fifty-four military schools since the end of the war. Cited by Colonel General Ivan Gosnjak, *Tito—Strategist of the Revolution and Founder of the People's Army* (Belgrade, 1963), p. 85.

19. For other accounts, see Thomas W. Wolfe, *Soviet Strategy at the Crossroads* (Cambridge, Mass., 1964), pp. 210–15; and Richard F. Staar, "The East European Alliance System," *The United States Naval Institute Proceedings*, September, 1964, pp. 28–39.

20. Marshal V. D. Sokolovsky, *et al.*, *Voennaya strategiya (Military Strategy)* (2d ed.; Moscow, 1963), p. 475.

8. THE MILITARY FACTOR IN THE SOVIET DECISIONS ON POLAND AND HUNGARY IN OCTOBER, 1956

1. These figures on voting were provided by a member of the Central Committee who participated in the election.

2. *Radio Warsaw*, November 9, 1956.

3. *Radio Warsaw*, November 13, 1956.

4. This revelation was made over *Radio Budapest* on October 31, 1956, in a declaration of the Revolutionary Committee of University Youth.

5. For security reasons, the official who revealed these details was not identified by name. See Leslie Balogh Bain, "Witness Tells How Soviet Dictated to Budapest Reds," Washington *Evening Star*, October 31, 1956.

6. This crucial fact was revealed by Major General Maleter in a broadcast interview on *Radio Budapest*, November 2, in response to press inquiries as to what had occurred in the secret meetings of the Hungarian and Soviet leaders.

7. See Tibor Meray, *Thirteen Days That Shook the Kremlin* (New York, 1959), pp. 144–71 and 197–204. According to Meray, Mikoyan accepted Tildy's intentions to withdraw from the Warsaw Pact and declare neutrality, as well as to withdraw Soviet troops. See also the *Report of the Special Committee on the Problem of Hungary*, U.N. General Assembly, Eleventh Session, Supplement No. 18 (A/3592), New York, 1957, esp. pp. 41–48 and 54–57.

8. As quoted on *Radio Moscow*, July 21, 1956.

9. This was confirmed by Tildy in a press conference broadcast on *Radio Budapest*, November 3, 1956.

10. *Ibid.*

11. *Ibid.*; also reported in news broadcasts of that day which indicated that the discussions would continue that night.

12. Nagy in a broadcast message on *Radio Budapest* the morning of November 4. The tactic of "arrest by invitation to negotiation" is a standard Communist tool. In the aftermath of the Revolution (on December 11, 1956), the chairman of the Budapest Central Workers Council, Sandor Racz, and his deputy were arrested after accepting an invitation to confer with Kádár in the Parliament building. (See E. Marton, Associated Press correspondent in Budapest, Washington *Evening Star*, December 13, 1956, and John McCormac, *The New York Times*, December 14, 1956.) A similar and notorious instance of the postwar era took place in March, 1945, when the sixteen leaders of the Polish Underground Army were arrested and taken to the Lubyanka Prison in Moscow after responding to an invitation in Marshal Zhukov's name to enter talks "in an atmosphere of mutual understanding and confidence." See Z. Stypulkowski, *Invitation to Moscow* (London, 1951), p. 211.

13. Elie Abel, "Hungarian Chief Seeks Nagy's Aid," *The New York Times*, November 12, 1956.

14. Editorial, *Jen-min Jih-pao (People's Daily)* and *Hung Ch'i (Red Flag)*, September 6, 1963.
15. *Ibid.*

9. SINO-SOVIET MILITARY RELATIONS, 1945-65

1. For example, Stalin informed Yugoslav Party Leaders that he had advised the Chinese Communists to enter a coalition government. See Vladimir Dedijer, *Tito* (New York, 1953), p. 322.
2. These data are taken largely from Lieutenant Colonel Robert Rigg, *Red China's Fighting Hordes* (Harrisburg, Pa., 1952), pp. 100, 248, 251, 277, and 297. See also Max Beloff, *Soviet Policy in the Far East, 1944–1951* (New York, 1953), pp. 20–64; F. F. Liu, A *Military History of Modern China, 1924–1949* (Princeton, N.J., 1956), pp. 227–29; and General L. M. Chassin, *La conquète de la Chine par Mao Tse-tung* (Paris, 1952), *passim.*
3. Rigg, *op. cit.*, p. 255.
4. *Ibid.*, p. 276.
5. See Harold C. Hinton, "Communist China's Military Posture," *Current History*, September, 1962, pp. 150–51.
6. The full texts of the treaty and associated agreements are given as an appendix to Beloff, *op. cit.*, pp. 260–67.
7. This estimated figure is given by Rigg, *op. cit.*, p. 302.
8. Rigg (*op. cit.*, p. 321) notes reports that the Russians unofficially provided training to some Chinese Communist airmen in the U.S.S.R. in 1947–49. If true, this is the one exception to nonassistance from 1946 to 1950.
9. Allen S. Whiting, *China Crosses the Yalu* (New York, 1960), pp. iv–v *et passim.*
10. *Ibid.*, p. 135.
11. Rigg, *op. cit.*, pp. 323–24.
12. The piston light bombers were used in combat but once; a flight of ten sent down the North Korean coast was intercepted by U.S. jet fighters and nine were destroyed.
13. Rigg, "Red Army in Retreat," *Current History*, January, 1957, p. 3.
14. Allen S. Whiting, " 'Contradictions' in the Moscow-Peking Axis," *Journal of Politics*, February, 1958, pp. 127–61.
15. Rigg, *Current History*, January, 1957, p. 3.
16. *Hsinhua*, June 18, 1957. See Greg MacGregor, "Peiping General Criticizes Soviet on Seized Plants," *The New York Times*, June 24, 1957.
17. See the text in Beloff, *op. cit.*, pp. 265–66.
18. George A. Modelski, *Atomic Energy in the Communist Bloc* (Melbourne, 1959), pp. 181–95.
19. Rigg, *Current History*, January, 1957, p. 5.
20. *Ibid.*, p. 3.
21. See Edward Crankshaw, "Sino-Soviet Rift Held Very Deep," *Washington Post*, February 12, 1961.
22. Marshal Yeh Chien-ying, NCNA (New China News Agency release), Peking, July 27, 1955.
23. See the detailed account of the 1954–57 debate in Alice L. Hsieh, *Communist China's Strategy in the Nuclear Era* (New York, 1962), pp. 15–75.
24. *Ibid.*, pp. 72–75.

25. See *Hsinhua*, August 15, 1963, and September 1, 1963, and *Hung Ch'i* (*Red Flag*) and *Jen-min Jih-pao* (*People's Daily*), September 6, 1963.

26. See Hsieh, *Communist China's Strategy*, pp. 76–109, and Hsieh, "China, Russia and the Bomb," *The New Leader*, October 17, 1960.

27. *Ibid.* See also Donald S. Zagoria, *The Sino-Soviet Conflict, 1956–1961* (Princeton, N.J., 1962), pp. 169–71.

28. *Hung Ch'i* and *Jen-min Jih-pao*, September 6, 1965.

29. Cited in *China Quarterly*, April-June, 1964, p. 238.

30. *Radio Moscow*, July 10, 1964.

31. Hsieh, *Communist China's Strategy*, pp. 109–10.

32. *Ibid.*, pp. 106–8.

33. *Ibid.*, p. 112. See also Zagoria, *op. cit.*, p. 192.

34. Hsieh, *Communist China's Strategy*, pp. 114 and 116. For discussion of the conference, see also Zagoria, *op. cit.*, pp. 189–94.

35. Hsieh, *Communist China's Strategy*, p. 116.

36. Zagoria, *op. cit.*, p. 193.

37. Yu Chao li, in *Hung Ch'i*, August 16, 1958. See also *Liberation Army Daily*, October 24, 1958, and *Jen-min Jih-pao*, November 12, 1958.

38. *Hung Ch'i*, October 16, 1958.

39. See A. Kashin, "Chinese Military Doctrine," *Bulletin of the Institute for the Study of the USSR*, Munich, November, 1960, pp. 39–44.

40. See John R. Thomas, "Soviet Behavior in the Quemoy Crisis of 1958," *Orbis*, Spring, 1962, pp. 38–64; Hsieh, *Communist China's Strategy*, pp. 119–36.

41. A. M. Rosenthal, "Warsaw Reports Soviet-China Pact," *The New York Times*, August 7, 1958, and "Soviet Atom Arms To Go To Peiping, Warsaw Learns," *The New York Times*, August 18, 1962.

42. See Hsieh, *Communist China's Strategy*, pp. 103–09 and 155–61.

43. Editorial, *Jen-min Jih-pao*, February 4, 1959.

44. Hsieh, *Communist China's Strategy*, p. 164.

45. David A. Charles, "The Dismissal of Marshal P'eng Teh-huai," *The China Quarterly*, October-December, 1961, pp. 63 ff.

46. *Ibid.*, pp. 64–65 and 74–75.

47. See Ronald Farquhar, "China Posts Go To 18 Rightists," *Washington Post*, April 18, 1959.

48. See the Institute for Strategic Studies, *The Military Balance: 1964–65* (London, 1964), pp. 8–10, and *The Communist Bloc and the Western Alliances: The Military Balance, 1962–1963* (London, 1962), p. 8, and the same serial for 1963–64 (1963), pp. 9–10.

49. See Clare Hollingsworth, "China Soon to be Nuclear Power," *Manchester Guardian Weekly*, October 1, 1961; *China News* (Taiwan), July 10, 1962; Richard Frykland, "Chinese Reds Believed Building MIG Fighters," Washington *Evening Star*, December 31, 1964; and Seymour Topping, "New Jet Fighters Detected in China," *The New York Times*, December 30, 1964. See also references cited in Note 48.

50. See references cited in Note 49, and "Missile Submarine in Red China's Navy," *The New York Times*, November 14, 1965.

51. See Zagoria, *op cit.*, pp. 335–36.

52. Marshal R. Malinovsky, TASS, January 24, 1962, Italics added.

53. Editorial, *Pravda*, January 7, 1963.

54. *Pravda*, September 21 and 22, 1963.

55. Li Fu-Ch'un, *Hung Ch'i*, August 16, 1960.

56. Chen Yi, *NCNA*, January 5, 1962.

57. See *Kyodo*, Tokyo, October 28, 1963 (evening edition), and "Peking Foresees A Delay of Years on Atomic Bomb," *The New York Times*, October 29, 1963.

58. *Jen-min Jih-pao*, November 19, 1963.

59. *Kung Tso T'ung Hsün (Work Correspondence)*, Peking, February 1, 1961.

60. Victor Zorza, *The Guardian*, London, October 9, 1964.

10. WAR, PEACE, AND REVOLUTION IN SOVIET POLICY

1. A. Belyakov and F. Burlatsky, "Lenin's Theory of the Socialist Revolution and the Present Time," *Kommunist*, No. 13, September, 1960, pp. 15–16. See also A. Butenko, "War and Revolution," *Kommunist*, No. 4, March, 1961, pp. 49–60; and Major General N. A. Talensky, "Contemporary War, Its Nature and Consequences," *Mezhdunarodnaya zhizn' (International Affairs)*, October, 1960, pp. 31 ff.

2. M. Suslov, Report to the CPSU CC Plenum on February 14, 1964, "On the CPSU Struggle for Cohesion of the International Communist Movement," *Radio Moscow*, April 3, 1964. See also the Soviet Government statement of September 20, 1963, *Radio Moscow*, September 20, 1963; G. P. Shakhnazarov, "War, Peace and Revolution," *Radio Moscow*, June 10, 1964; and Keremitsky, *Radio Moscow*, October 12, 1963.

3. Lu Chih-ch'ao, "Examination of the Question of War Must Not Run Counter to the Marxist-Leninist Viewpoint of Class Struggle," *Hung Ch'i (Red Flag)*, August 15, 1963.

4. "Statement by the Chinese Government: A Comment on the Soviet Government Statement of August 21," NCNA, *Radio Peking*, September 1, 1963.

5. "For the General Line of the World Communist Movement, Against Left Opportunism, Nationalism, and Adventurism," editorial, *Kommunist*, No. 14, September, 1963, p. 16.

6. Soviet Government statement, TASS, *Radio Moscow*, September 20, 1963.

7. "Apologists of Neo-colonialism," *Hung Ch'i (Red Flag)* and *Jen-min Jih-pao (People's Daily)*, October 22, 1963.

8. *Radio Moscow*, September 20, 1963.

9. *Ibid.*

10. *Ibid.*

11. M. D. Kammari, "Theory, Politics, and Ideology: On the Relation Between War and the Revolution," *Krasnaya zvezda*, August 6, 1965.

12. M. Suslov, Speech of February 14, 1964, *Radio Moscow*, April 3, 1964.

13. *Ibid.*

14. Soviet Government statement, *Radio Moscow*, September 20, 1963.

15. "Foreign Policy and the Contemporary World," editorial, *Kommunist*, No. 3, February, 1965, p. 12.

16. M. E. Airapetyan and V. V. Sukhodeyev, *Sotsialisticheskaya vneshnyaya politika (Socialist Foreign Policy)* (Moscow, 1964), p. 54.

17. G. P. Shakhnazarov, "War, Peace and Revolution," *Radio Moscow*, June 10, 1964.

18. For example, see the especially colorful diatribe in "Unmask the Dangerous Maneuvers of the N. Khrushchev Group with Regard to the Alleged Strug-

gle Against the Personality Cult," *Zeri i Popullit (Voice of the People)*, Tirana, broadcast on *Radio Tirana*, June 14, 1964.

19. Major General K. Bochkarev and Colonel I. Sidel'nikov, "New Age, New Conclusions—On the Development by the Party of V. I. Lenin's Ideas on War, Peace, and on Safeguarding the Achievements of Socialism and Communism," *Krasnaya zvezda (Red Star)*, January 21, 1965. See also "Socialist Foreign Policy and Social Progress," *Kommunist*, No. 12 (August, 1965), p. 4, for an authoritative statement from the Brezhnev period.

20. Suslov, *op. cit.*; see also the Soviet Government statement, *op. cit.*, September 20, 1963. For authoritative statements from the Brezhnev period, see the editorial articles "The Noble Aims of Soviet Foreign Policy," *Pravda*, August 8, 1965, and "The National Liberation Movement and Social Progress," *Kommunist*, No. 13 (September, 1965), *passim*.

21. *Kommunist*, No. 14, September, 1963, p. 13.

22. See *XXII s'yezd Kommunisticheskoi partii Sovetskogo Soiuza, 17–31 oktyabrya 1961 goda, stenografRicheskii otchet (XXII Congress of the Communist Party of the Soviet Union, October 17–31, 1961, Stenographic Record)* (Moscow, 1962), III, 231–73.

23. Soviet Government statement, *Radio Moscow*, September 20, 1963.

24. See, for example, Yu. Frantsev, "Confused Reasonings of the Peking Theoreticians," *Izvestiya*, October 11, 1963.

25. Suslov, *op. cit.* See also D. Tomashevsky, "Lenin and Socialist Foreign Policy," *International Affairs*, April, 1965, p. 9.

26. P. Fedoseyev, "Materialist Understanding of History and the 'Theory of Violence,'" *Kommunist*, No. 7, May, 1964, pp. 51–66.

27. *Ibid.*, p. 62. See also M. D. Kammari, *Krasnaya zvezda*, August 6, 1965.

28. "Marxism-Leninism—Foundation of the Unity of the Communist Movement," *Kommunist*, No. 15, October, 1963, p. 33.

29. *XXII s'yezd*, p. 256.

30. *Kommunist*, No. 14, September, 1963, p. 27.

31. *Ibid.*

32. "Peaceful Coexistence—Two Diametrically Opposed Policies: Comment on the Open Letter of the Central Committee of the CPSU (VI)," Editorial Boards of *Hung Ch'i (Red Flag)* and *Jen-min Jih-pao (People's Daily)*, December 12, 1963; broadcast by *Radio Peking*, December 11, 1963. The Chinese have made clear that the post-Khrushchev Soviet leaders are considered guilty of the same views; e.g., NCNA, *Radio Peking*, March 1, 1965, and May 3, 1965.

33. *Hung Ch'i and Jen-min Jih-pao*, October 22, 1963.

34. *Hung Ch'i and Jen-min Jih-pao*, December 12, 1963. Again, this was written to apply to Khrushchev, but now applies to his successors. For example, see Lin Piao, *Hung Ch'i*, September 3, 1965.

35. *Radio Tirana*, June 14, 1964.

36. "N. Khrushchev Has Openly Unfurled the Banner of Division and Treason," *Zeri i Popullit*, October 4, 1963.

37. "Leninism, Victorious Banner of the Revolution, and the Struggle Against Imperialism and Revisionism," *Zeri i Popullit*, broadcast by *Radio Tirana*, April 22, 1965.

38. P. N. Demichev, "Leninism—Scientific Foundation for the Policy of the Party," *Pravda*, April 23, 1965.

39. "The Great Victory of Leninism," editorial, *Hung Ch'i*, April, 1965; broadcast by *Radio Peking*, May 3, 1965. See also Lin Piao, *op. cit.*

40. Marshal Lo Jui-ching, in *Hung Ch'i*, May, 1965, broadcast by *Radio Peking*, May 10, 1965. See also "The Historical Experience of the War Against Fascism," *Jen-min Jih-pao*, May 9, 1965, for a similar statement.

41. Fan Hsiu-chu, "Struggle Between the Two Lines over the Question of Dealing with US Imperialism, *Ta Kung Pao (The Great Utopia)*, July 26, 1965. See also Lin Piao, "Long Live the Victory of the People's War," *Hung Ch'i* and *Jen-min Jih-pao*, September 3, 1965.

11. INTERNAL REVOLUTIONARY WARFARE
IN COMMUNIST STRATEGY

1. See Cyril E. Black and Thomas P. Thornton (eds.), *Communism and Revolution* (Princeton, N.J., 1964), Chapters 4–8, for analyses of a number of these cases.

2. Translation in *Army*, March, 1961, p. 24.

3. Mao Tse-tung, *Strategic Problems of China's Revolutionary War* (written in December, 1936) (Peking, 1954), pp. 3–4; see also pp. 2, 5, 18, and 31.

4. N. S. Khrushchev, speech of January 6, 1961, in *Kommunist*, No. 1, January, 1961, p. 19.

5. "Apologists for Neocolonialism," *Hung Ch'i (Red Flag)* and *Jen-min Jih-pao (People's Daily)*, October 22, 1963. Fourth in a series of major and authoritative Chinese Party replies to the Open Letter of the CPSU of July 14, 1963.

6. "Peaceful Coexistence—Two Diametrically Opposed Policies," *Hung Ch'i* and *Jen-min Jih-pao*, December 12, 1963. Sixth in the series above noted.

7. *Hung Ch'i*, October 22, 1963.

8. N. S. Khrushchev, "Questions and Answers . . .", *Izvestiya*, December 21, 1963. See also the editorial, "For the Unity and Solidarity of the International Communist Movement," *Pravda*, December 6, 1963.

9. "For the Unity and Solidarity of the International Communist Movement," editorial, *Pravda*, December 6, 1963.

10. "Proletarian Internationalism—The Banner of the Working People of All Countries and Continents," editorial, *Kommunist*, No. 7, May, 1964, p. 45.

11. G. Starushenko, "The National Liberation Movement and the Struggle for Peace," *International Affairs*, October, 1963, p. 4.

12. M. Suslov, "On the CPSU Struggle for Unity of the International Communist Movement," Central Committee Plenum Speech of February 14, 1964, full text broadcast by *Radio Moscow*, April 3, 1964.

13. *Ibid.* See also M. Suslov, Speech to the 17th Congress of the French Communist Party, *Radio Moscow*, May 15, 1964.

14. "Proletarian Internationalism—The Banner of the Working People of All Countries and Continents," editorial, *Kommunist*, No. 7, May, 1964, p. 34.

15. Suslov, *Radio Moscow*, April 3, 1964.

16. "The General Line of the International Communist Movement and the Splitting Platform of the Chinese Leadership," editorial, *Kommunist*, No. 14, September, 1963, p. 9. See also *Kommunist*, No. 7, May, 1964, pp. 34–35.

17. "Marxism-Leninism, the Foundation of the Unity of the Communist Movement," editorial, *Kommunist*, No. 15, October, 1963, p. 30.

18. Suslov, *Radio Moscow*, April 3, 1964.

19. See the excellent discussion by Tang Tsou and Morton H. Halperin, "Mao Tse-tung's Revolutionary Strategy and Peking's International Behavior," *The American Political Science Review*, March, 1965, pp. 80–99.

20. Lin Piao, "Long Live the Victory of the People's War," *Hung Ch'i* and *Jen-min Jih-pao*, September 3, 1965; NCNA, *Radio Peking*, September 2, 1965.

21. Mao Tse-tung, "On the Rectification of Incorrect Ideas in the Party" (December, 1929), *Selected Works* (New York, 1954), I, 106.

22. Mao Tse-tung, "Problems of War and Strategy" (November 6, 1938), *Selected Works*, II, 272.

23. General Vo Nguyên Giap, *People's War, People's Army* (Hanoi, 1961), p. 48 *et passim*.

24. Mao Tse-tung, "Guerrilla Warfare" (1937), quoted by Brigadier General Samuel B. Griffith, USMC (Ret.), in *Mao Tse-tung on Guerrilla Warfare* (New York, 1961), p. 43.

25. Mao Tse-tung, *Strategic Problems of the Anti-Japanese Guerrilla War* (May, 1938) (Peking, 1954), p. 6.

26. Quoted by Lieutenant Colonel Robert Rigg, in *Red China's Fighting Forces* (Harrisburg, Pa., 1952), p. 226.

27. See, in particular, Mao Tse-tung, "On the Protracted War" (June, 1938), in *Selected Works*, II, 157–243.

28. In Griffith, *op. cit.*, p. 41.

29. Mao Tse-tung, "On the Protracted War," *Selected Works*, II, 224.

30. Che Guevara, in *Army*, March, 1961, p. 24.

12. THE REVOLUTION AND THE WEST

1. See Franz Borkenau, *European Communism* (New York, 1953), pp. 441–555. See also Mario Einaudi, Jean-Marie Domenach, and Aldo Garosci, *Communism in Western Europe* (Ithaca, N.Y., 1951); Hugh Seton-Watson, *From Lenin to Khrushchev* (2d ed.; New York, 1960), pp. 218–25, 291–300, and 385–92; Angelo Rossi, *A Communist Party in Action* (New Haven, 1949); Hadley Cantril and David Rodnick, *On Understanding the French Left* (Princeton, N.J., 1956); Charles A. Micaud, *Communism and the French Left* (New York, 1963); and Henry Pelling, *The British Communist Party* (London, 1958). The situation in Iceland is discussed in Donald E. Neuchterlein, *Iceland: Reluctant Ally* (Ithaca, N.Y., 1961), and M. S. Olmsted, "Communism in Iceland," *Foreign Affairs*, January, 1958, pp. 340–47. For Japan, see Rodger Swearingen and Paul F. Langer, *Red Flag in Japan: International Communism in Action, 1919–1951* (Cambridge, Mass., 1952).

2. The estimated Communist strengths here cited are compiled from the U.S. Department of State publication *World Strength of the Communist Party Organizations* (Intelligence Report) (Washington, 1965), *passim*. For earlier figures, including the 1946 estimate, see *Communism's Postwar Decade*, Supplement to the *New Leader*, New York, December 19, 1955, pp. S6–S7.

3. "Theses on Imperialist 'Integration' in Western Europe (The Common Market)," TASS, *Radio Moscow*, August 27, 1962, and other press and radio accounts of the Conference. For a more recent optimistic Soviet discussion, see the editorial article "The Revolutionary Vanguard of the Working Class," *Pravda*, October 13, 1965.

4. V. S. Semënov, "Growth of the Class Struggle in the Capitalist Countries," in *Velikaya khartiga kommunisticheskikh i rabochikh partii* (*Magna Carta of the Communist and Workers' Parties*) (Moscow, 1961), pp. 209–72. See also S. Vygodsky, "A Factor Deepening the General Crisis of Capitalism," *Mezhduna-*

Notes 259

rodnaya zhizn' (*International Affairs*), April, 1962, pp. 38–45; A. A. Arzumanyan (ed.), *Rabochoe dvizhenie v kapitalisticheskikh stranakh, 1951–1961* (*The Workers' Movement in the Capitalist Countries, 1951–61*) (Moscow, 1961), *passim;* and A. A. Arzumanyan and A. M. Rumyantsev (eds.), *Problemy sovremennogo kapitalizma i rabochii klass* (*Problems of Contemporary Capitalism and the Working Class*) (Prague, 1963), *passim*, presenting speeches given at a conference of August-September, 1962.

5. Ts. A. Stepanyan, "The Twentieth Century—Century of the Victory of Communism," *Velikaya khartiga*, pp. 24–79, esp. pp. 47–49.

6. For discussions of the CPUSA, there is an excellent trilogy: Theodore Draper, *The Roots of American Communism* (New York, 1957); Draper, *American Communism and Soviet Russia* (New York, 1960); and David Shannon, *The Decline of American Communism* (New York, 1959). For a general bibliographical guide, see Robert Delaney, *The Literature of Communism in America* (Washington, D.C., 1962), and see Daniel Aron, *Writers on the Left: Episodes in American Literary Communism* (New York, 1961).

7. Peter Kihss, "1,500 From F.B.I. Said to Inform on U.S. Reds," *The New York Times*, October 18, 1962.

8. Among the many volumes analyzing the methods and techniques of the Communist conspiracy in the advanced countries, see Gabriel Almond, *The Appeals of Communism* (Princeton, N.J., 1954); Raymond Aron, *The Opium of the Intellectuals* (London, 1957); Philip Selznick, *The Organizational Weapon* (New York, 1952 and 1960); Evon M. Kirkpatrick, *Target: The World* (New York, 1956); Kirkpatrick, *Year of Crisis* (New York, 1957); Robert Strausz-Hupé, *et al, Protracted Conflict* (New York, 1959); and William R. Kintner and Joseph Z. Kornfeder, *The New Frontiers of War* (Chicago, 1962).

9. For an authoritative Soviet statement, see N. S. Khrushchev, "For New Victories of the World Communist Movement," *Kommunist*, No. 1, January, 1961, pp. 3–37.

10. A. Belyakov and F. Burlatsky, "Lenin's Theory of the Socialist Revolution and the Present Time," *Kommunist*, No. 13, September, 1960, pp. 15–16.

11. See Chapters 4 and 10, above; see also A. Butenko, "War and the Revolution," *Kommunist*, No. 2, February, 1961, pp. 49–60.

12. N. S. Khrushchev, *Radio Moscow*, March 16, 1962.

13. *Fundamentals of Marxism-Leninism*, Moscow, 1959, pp. 528–29. For a more recent restatement, see the editorial article in *Kommunist*, No. 15, October, 1963, *passim*.

14. J. Armstrong, " 'Global Poker' versus Grand Strategy," *World Marxist Review*, June, 1962, p. 61.

15. Editorial, "On the Threshold of 1960," *World Marxist Review*, January, 1960, p. 6.

16. A. Sovetov, "Leninist Foreign Policy and International Relations," *International Affairs*, No. 4, April, 1960, p. 9.

17. G. Starushenko, "Peaceful Coexistence and the Revolution," *Kommunist*, No. 2, January, 1962, p. 86.

18. N. S. Khrushchev, Interview with Gardner Cowles, broadcast TASS account, *Radio Moscow*, April 25, 1962.

19. "The Marxist-Leninist Viewpoint on the Paths of Transition from Capitalism to Socialism in Various Countries," in Mandarin to China, *Radio Moscow*, March 27, 1962. Also, Vladimirova, "Marxism-Leninism," in Albanian, *Radio Moscow*, August 30, 1962.

20. "Program of the CPSU," *Pravda*, November 2, 1961.

21. "The Twenty-second Congress of the CPSU and the Nature of the Present Era and Paths for Advancement of Society," *Radio Moscow*, May 10, 1962; and Vladimirova, "Marxism-Leninism," *Radio Moscow*, August 30, 1962.

22. Mehmet Shehu, Speech to the People's Assembly, *Zeri i Popullit (Voice of the People)*, broadcast by *Radio Tirana*, July 16, 1962.

23. Gogo Nushi, Election Speech, *Radio Tirana*, May 25, 1962.

24. Enver Hoxha, Election Speech, *Radio Tirana*, May 30, 1962.

25. Lu Ting-i, "Get United Under the Banner of Lenin," *Radio Peking*, April 22, 1960.

26. "The Proletarian Revolution and Khrushchev's Revisionism: Comment on the Open Letter Issued by the Central Committee of the CPSU," *Jen-min Jih-pao (People's Daily)* and *Hung Ch'i (Red Flag)*, March 31, 1964, as broadcast by *Radio Peking*, March 30, 1964.

27. *Red Flag* article on the ninetieth anniversary of the birth of Lenin, broadcast on *Radio Peking*, April 20, 1960.

28. For example, see the article cited in Note 26, above, broadcast by *Radio Peking*, March 30, 1964.

29. Edvard Kardelj, *Socialism and War* (London, 1961), p. 86.

30. Luigi Longo, *Interventi della delegazione del PCI alla conferenza di Mosca degli 81 partiti communisti ed operai (Remarks of the PCI Delegation to the Moscow Conference of Eighty-one Communist Parties)* (Rome, 1962), p. 40. Cited in *Survey*, London, June, 1962, p. 109.

31. V. Pessi, "On the Splitting Activities of the CCP Leaders in the International Communist Movement," *Pravda*, July 18, 1964.

32. *Pravda*, July 14, 1963. See also especially "Marxism-Leninism, Basis of the Unity of the Communist Movement," *Kommunist*, No. 15, October, 1963, *passim*; and Erkki Tuominen, "The Socialist Revolution and the Bourgeois State," *Problemy mira i sotsializma (Problems of Peace and Socialism)*, Prague, June, 1964, *passim*.

33. For a good resumé, see Kevin Devlin, "Boring from Within," *Problems of Communism*, March-April, 1964, pp. 27–39.

Bibliographical Note

The extensive chapter notes provide a general guide to useful sources. This Note is designed to highlight ten major studies of particular importance.

BLACK, CYRIL E., and THOMAS P. THORNTON (eds.). *Communism and Revolution*. Princeton, N.J.: Princeton University Press, 1964. 476 pp. A very useful study of Communist views and actions with respect to the role of revolution.

DALLIN, ALEXANDER, ET AL. *The Soviet Union and Disarmament: An Appraisal of Soviet Attitudes and Intentions*. New York: Frederick A. Praeger, 1965. 299 pp.

DINERSTEIN, HERBERT S. *War and the Soviet Union: Nuclear Weapons and the Revolution in Soviet Military Thinking*. Rev. ed. New York: Frederick A. Praeger, 1962. 288 pp. An interpretation of differing strategic conceptions as they may have been related to political conflicts in the 1953–55 period.

ERICKSON, JOHN. *The Soviet High Command: A Military-Political History, 1918–1941*. New York: St Martin's Press; London: Macmillan and Company, 1962. 889 pp. An excellent, thorough study of the Soviet military institution and of Soviet military-political relations.

—— (ed.). *Nuclear Strategy: A World Dilemma*. New York: Frederick A. Praeger, 1966. A useful symposium on the impact of recent military developments on Soviet military and foreign policy.

FEDOTOFF-WHITE, DIMITRI D. *The Growth of the Red Army*. Princeton, N.J.: Princeton University Press, 1944. 486 pp. A very good study of the development of the Soviet armed forces from 1918 to 1940.

GARTHOFF, RAYMOND L. *Soviet Military Doctrine*. Glencoe, Ill.: Free Press, 1953. 587 pp. A comprehensive study of Soviet military thought and doctrine up to 1953.

——. *Soviet Strategy in the Nuclear Age*. Rev. ed. New York: Frederick A. Praeger, 1962. 301 pp. A thorough analysis of developments in Soviet military doctrine and strategic thought from 1953 to 1962.

SOKOLOVSKY, MARSHAL VASILY D. (ed.). *Military Strategy: Soviet Doctrine and Concepts*. Translation. With an Introduction by Raymond L. Garthoff. New York: Frederick A. Praeger, 1963. 395 pp. The single most significant Soviet work in this field, published in the U.S.S.R. in 1962.

WOLFE, THOMAS W. *Soviet Strategy at the Crossroads*. Cambridge, Mass.: Harvard University Press, 1964. 362 pp. An excellent analysis of developments in Soviet military doctrine and strategic thought from 1962 through 1964.

Index

Communist world revolution, 10, 11, 13, 24, 65, 66, 75, 112, 126, 127, 192, 196, 199, 202, 204, 206, 220–37
Congo, 202, 219, 222
Conscription, 5, 135, 145
Constantinople, 9; *see also* Istanbul
Council of Ministers, 44
Council of Mutual Economic Assistance (CEMA), 153
Counterdeterrence, 60, 61, 110, 112, 130; *see also* Deterrence
Crimea, 46
Crimean War, 4, 29
Cuba, 25, 114, 120, 121, 122, 186, 198, 209, 214n, 216, 223; missile crisis (1962), 94, 114, 120–23, 125, 186, 198
Cyrankiewicz, Jozef, 156, 158, 160
Czarist policy, 3–9, 27, 30
Czechoslovak Legion in Russia (1918–19), 144
Czechoslovakia: pre-1945, 19, 20, 76, 118, 133; wartime Government-in-Exile, 143, 144; post-1945, 134–38, 143–44, 148, 149, 150, 151, 152, 208, 231
Czinege, General Lajos, 143

De Gaulle, Charles, 223
Demichev, Pëtr N., 94, 205
Denikin, General A. I., 31
Deterrence, 3, 26, 60, 61, 110–12, 128, 129, 130; mutual, 3, 111, 126, 128, 191, 209; stabilized, 126
Dinnyes, Lajos, 141
Disarmament, 5, 6, 13, 14, 25, 26, 59, 74, 123, 124–28, 183, 236
"Doctors' Plot," 44, 47
Dubna, 178
Durnovo, P., 8

Duszynski, General Zygmunt, 137, 138
Dzhungaria, Sinkiang, 7, 8
Dzhurov, General Dobri, 140

East Germany, *see* Germany: German Democratic Republic
"East Turkestan Republic," 17, 21, 22
Eastern Europe, 13, 14, 19, 20, 69, 70, 76, 93, 100, 118, 128, 133–54, 155–72, 178, 184, 193
Economic development, 58, 60, 61
Egypt, *see* United Arab Republic
Eighth Route Army (Chinese), 174
Eisenhower, Dwight D., 111
Engels, Friedrich, 233
Enzeli, Iran, 12
Escalation of hostilities, 108, 197, 198–99, 227
Estonia, 10, 11

Far East, 3, 7, 8, 9, 27, 46, 60, 76, 183, 187, 188
Farkas, General Mihaly, 141, 142, 163
Federal Republic of Germany, *see under* Germany
Feng Yu-hsiang, General, 15
Finland, 10, 11, 14, 21, 26, 28, 36, 84, 149, 208, 234
"First echelon," *see* Warsaw Pact
Fokin, Admiral Vitaly A., 56
France: pre-1945, 5, 11, 28, 69, 85; post-1945, 76, 101n, 113, 116, 118, 208, 221, 223, 225, 232, 233
Free Germany Committee (1943–45), 145
French Communist Party, 223, 231, 236
Frunze, Mikhail V., 34

Hungary: pre-1945, 11, 20, 26, 133, 140; post-1945, 134, 141–43, 159

ICBM (Intercontinental Ballistic Missile), 108, 117, 120, 122, 123, 124, 180; *see also* Missiles
Ignatyev, Count A. A., 36
IL-28 (Soviet-built jet light bomber), 122, 176, 177, 185
Ili, Sinkiang, 7, 21, 22
Iliev, General P., 140
Illy, General G., 141
"Imperialism," *see* Capitalism
India, 183, 186
Indochina, 76, 209; *see also* Laos, Viet-Nam
Indonesia, 25, 186, 208, 213, 223
Inevitability of war, 24, 69, 74, 193
Ingr, General S., 143
Inner Mongolia, 20
Institute for World Economics and International Relations (Moscow), 224
Intelligence services: Soviet, 17, 52, 146, 207; Western, 67
Internal war, 193, 198, 202, 207–37; *see also* Guerrilla warfare
International Brigade, 17
Interservice rivalry, 50
Iran, 21, 76, 134; *see also* Persia
Iraq, 113, 214n
IRBM (Intermediate Range Ballistic Missile), 122
Istanbul, 118; *see also* Constantinople
Italian Communist Party, 148, 223, 231, 233–34, 236
Italy, 17, 21, 100, 101n, 208, 221, 223, 225
Ivanov, General Blagoi, 140
Izvolsky, A. P., 4

Japan, 8, 9, 15, 16, 17, 21, 28, 69, 100, 101n, 174, 175, 223, 231, 232
Jaruzelski, General Wojciech, 138
Jedrychowski, Stefan, 158
Jet aircraft, 106, 107, 116, 121, 122, 137, 150, 151, 176, 178, 185, 186
Johnson, Lyndon B., 116
Jordan, 113
Joswiak-Witold, Franciszek, 161
"Just wars," 197

Kádár, János, 162, 164, 167, 169, 170, 171
Kaganovich, Lazar M., 52, 157
Kamenev, S. S., 34
Karakhan, L. M., 15
Kardelj, Edvard, 233
Kars, Turkey, 21
Kashgaria, Sinkiang, 8
Katyn Forest massacre (1940), 134
Kazakhs, 16, 21, 22
Kazakhstan, 6
Kazakov, General M. I., 49
Kemal Ataturk, 12
Kennedy, John F., 115, 116, 117, 120, 121
Kerensky, Aleksandr F., 33
Kethly, Anna, 167
Khalkin-Gol (Nomonhan), Mongolia, 17
Khasan, Lake, 17
Khiva, 6
Khrulev, General Andrei V., 43
Khrushchev, Nikita S., 46, 48, 49, 50, 51, 52, 53, 54, 56, 57, 62, 95, 96, 97, 103, 104, 106, 113, 114, 115, 116, 119, 120, 121, 123, 124, 125, 155, 157, 163, 171, 173, 177, 183, 184, 187, 188,

Tildy, Zoltan, 165, 167
Timoshenko, Marshal Semën K., 40
Titarenko, S., 185, 186
Tito, Marshal, 20, 95, 140, 146, 147, 156, 163
Tombor, General Jenö, 141
Transcaucasus, 11, 113
Trotsky, Leon, 11, 12, 16, 83, 95, 199, 202
Truman, Harry S., 19
Truman Doctrine, 94
Tu-2 (Soviet-model piston bomber), 176
Tu-4 (Soviet piston bomber, copy of U.S. B-29), 176
Tu-16 (Soviet-model jet medium bomber), 185, 186
Tudor Vladimirescu Division (Romania), 138
Tukachevsky, Marshal Mikhail N., 13, 34, 35, 39
Turkey, 9, 10, 12, 21, 113, 118, 121, 122
Turkish Straits, 9, 21, 129
Tuva (Tannu Tuva), 7, 8, 9, 10, 12, 15, 20
"Two camps," 22, 70, 73, 75, 89, 90

Uborevich, I. P., 34
Ukraine, 10, 11, 46, 48, 59, 136
Ukrainian Insurgent Army, 136
United Arab Republic (U.A.R.), 25, 113, 137, 168, 213, 214n
United Nations, 21, 26, 74, 125, 168
United States, 5, 19, 21, 22, 71, 90, 104, 107, 110, 111, 112, 113, 114, 115, 117, 118, 119, 120, 121, 122, 124, 125, 176, 183, 184, 187, 191, 196, 211, 221,

231, 232, 233; Air Force, 115–19; Army, 115–19; Marines, 113, 117; Navy, 116, 118, 121, 122; Department of State, 188
Urals, 9
Uranium, 98, 99, 178
Uriankhai, *see* Tuva
Urumchi, Sinkiang, 16, 17, 21, 22
Ussuri River, 7

Valona Bay, Albania, 147
Vasilevsky, Marshal Aleksandr M., 37, 43, 44, 46, 47, 49, 51, 55
Vatsetis, I. I., 34
Velchev, General Damyan, 140
Veres, Peter, 141
Versailles, Treaty of (1919), 86
Vershinin, Chief Air Marshal Konstantin A., 43, 44, 56
Vienna, 19, 21, 115, 164
Viet-Công, 114, 211, 217
Viet-Nam: North, 114, 208, 209, 211, 216; South, 208–9, 217
Vo Nguyên Giap, General, 216, 217
Voronov, Chief Marshal of Artillery N. N., 46, 55
Vörös, General János, 141
Voroshilov, Marshal Klimenty Ye., 34, 37, 54

War production, 98–99, 102–8, 129; in China, 177, 178, 180–81, 184–85, 187; in Eastern Europe, 150–51
Warsaw, 19, 155, 157, 158, 160, 161, 183
Warsaw Pact, 26, 55, 116, 117, 118, 120, 139, 145, 147, 148, 149–52, 153, 154, 167, 168, 170, 171, 178, 179; "first echelon," 152